MASTER OF THE MISSISSIPPI

THE STORY OF HENRY SHREVE
Who Taught a River to Fetch and Carry for a Nation

'Encampment of the Travellers' and the vignette of Cave-in-Rock on the title page are reproduced from Charles Bodmer's hand-colored drawings for Prince Maximilian von Wied Neuwied's TRAVELS IN NORTH AMERICA, 1843.

BY FLORENCE L. DORSEY

Master
of the Mississippi

HENRY SHREVE
and the Conquest of the Mississippi

Published by
LITERARY CLASSICS, INC. · NEW YORK
1941
The Riverside Press Cambridge
HOUGHTON MIFFLIN COMPANY · BOSTON
Distributors

The Riverside Press
CAMBRIDGE · MASSACHUSETTS
PRINTED IN THE U.S.A.

REMOTE STORAGE

To the memory of my father

HENRY SHREVE DORSEY

Foreword

THIS book is compiled from letters written by Henry Miller Shreve, journals kept by his father and brother, letters by members of the Shreve family, records and descriptions by early adventurers into the Mississippi, Ohio, and Red River countries, and from histories of various parts and phases of the Mississippi Valley. Data furnished by Emma Carter Edwards, great-granddaughter of Henry Shreve, and by her husband, Colonel Nelson G. Edwards, were of especial value. The work done by J. Fair Hardin, of the Shreveport Bar Association, in searching out old court records, which are published for the first time in his *Outline of Shreveport and Caddo Parish History*, has added substantially to Shreve history. Grateful acknowledgment is made to the authors and publishers of works listed in the bibliography and notes accompanying this biography. Generous aid in securing copies of certain reports and letters in government files at Washington, D.C., was given by the Honorable Sol Bloom, of the House of Representatives of the United States; former Secretary of War Harry Hines Woodring; Major-General J. L. Schley, Chief of Engineers of the War Department; Captain P. A. Feringa, of the Corps of Engineers, Assistant Chief of River and Harbor Section of the War Department; and Mr. P. M. Hamer, Chief of the Division of Reference, National Archives. Unfailing assistance was rendered by many members of the staff of the New York Public Library.

F. L. D.

Illustrations

ERRATUM

On the picture opposite page 74 and in the List of Illustrations:

FOR 'Jolly Flatboatmen'.......Reproduced with the permission of the St. Louis Mercantile Library Association

READ 'Raftsmen Playing Cards'....Reproduced with the permission of the City Art Museum, St. Louis

CHAPTER

One

I T WAS a broad valley — a native tribe from its eastern
rim of the Alleghanies might spend a generation migrating through it before sighting the Rockies that walled
it on the west. Hardy *coureurs des bois*, starting across it
at the first spring thaw, would see the snows vanish,
freshets cover the lowlands and trickle to stream beds, the
streams dry up, the prairie parch and bitter winds drive
snow across it while they traversed two thirds of its width.
A man could go for days on the plains and see no shadow
but his own. The sunlight was pale golden, or it blazed
like a furnace. The prairie wind was soft, or it was a tor-
nado that plucked up forest trees and laid them down like
straws. The rivers carried a boat along briskly or beat it
ruthlessly to pieces; they dried up and left it stranded, or
plunged out of their banks in a flood that drowned the
earth for miles. Men told widely different things of the
Valley, but all men talked of it.

The Valley was not a ravine or bowl. It was a vast plain
slightly tilted between two mountain rims. The flatness
of its area of a million and a quarter square miles was
amazing. Ages, tirelessly forming a continent, had laid

down mass after mass of lava, raising a rugged structure above the globe's tepid waters. Convulsions sucked the ocean into the lowlands; coral deposited its limestone, through aeons of time, thousands of feet deep. Cataclysms drained the seas away, but the ocean poured back in from the north, the west, the south, laid floor upon floor of limestone and subsided. Volcanoes belched, the eastern mountains emerged slowly. Giant reptiles overran the uneasy earth crust. The western mountains warped up and broke into jagged teeth, and into the Valley downwarp the ocean rushed past the new ridges, striking down great fern forests.

Through thousands of years the ocean ebbed out, **great** forests rising behind it. Then the land grew arid; its sluggish amphibian monsters crowded into the vanishing pools and perished. In one of the tilting continent changes, an immense stream was left to roar down the Valley to the southwest, where it emptied into the western ocean. Millenniums later, the center of the Valley sank low, drawing the primeval great river from its southwestern course into a shorter southward line to meet a gulf that reached far up into the continent. The monsters disappeared, mammals inhabited the plains; trees became firm wood; flowers, once invariably green, now were colored. Then came the tragedy of the Great Ice Age. Ceaseless snow fell and froze, building ice thousands of feet deep. Glacial drifts tore the Great River wider and gouged basins in the solid rock. After hundreds of centuries the ice receded far north and the brimming basin lakes fed the Great River, glutting it. It stormed through its wide bed between cliffs, carrying masses of glacial débris which it emptied into the gulf, building land that pushed the gulf steadily southward. At last the large lakes, having found an outlet to the eastern ocean, withdrew, and the Great River, weary but still powerful, too lean to fill the bed it had torn in its lusty youth, flowed crystal clear through its northern gorges, wound against one ancient cliff-side and then the other, accepted a muddy torrent which the Indians centuries later named Pekitanouis and the white men, Missouri, and near where it had anciently poured into the north-reaching gulf, the Ohio tumbled over a worn coral reef to meet it.[1]

In the Great Valley, Indian civilizations had flourished, hunters ranged, and when the white men came, trappers wandered and soldiers fought the battles of faraway nations. From the newly independent United States had come land-hungry men after the British had yielded ownership of the eastern half of the Valley. Following the trail Daniel Boone had blazed, settlers moved in from the south through the Cumberland Gap, from Virginia across the Great Kanawha, from the Central States to Pittsburgh and the Ohio, from New England and New York along the Great Lakes. The free provisions of the Northwest Ordinance were extended to the entire territory from Canada to the Gulf. By 1802 three western states had been added to the new nation.

The highways of this western territory were the rivers, along which the settlers came to chop out their farms in the wilderness. Many of these early emigrants were unpaid Revolutionary War veterans. The new and still shaky national government had no money with which to pay them, but there was the Great Valley, a fertile virgin land stretching from the Alleghany ridges westward, parcels of which immense area could be turned over to the veterans in lieu of back pay. All that these men had to do was to get themselves and their belongings across a thousand miles or more of savage country, build shelters, ward off Indians, and, with what few tools they had, gouge a living or a fortune from the soil. An appalling prospect, but not without allure; for adventurers brought back to the East almost incredible tales of the Valley's natural wealth. It was a land of sunlight, wild fruit, and inexhaustible game, into which Providence had stretched a convenient road, the Ohio River.

No sooner would these emigrants set up their cabins in the wilderness than the trading boats would hunt them out. River traffic became a flatboat flotilla transporting the bulky produce of the farms — the grain, bacon, hemp, lumber, tobacco — that could have reached its eastern market across the mountains by horseback and wagon only at prohibitive cost. The Monongahela, the Allegheny, the Ohio, the Cumberland, the Tennessee, the Mississippi, carried the flow of goods to New Orleans, to be loaded on ships bound for the east-coast ports.

Until 1800 this delta city was under the lax control of the faltering Spanish Government, but when Napoleon covertly demanded its cession to France and threatened restraint on the natural outlet for the Valley, loud protest rose from the western farmers. A near crisis came two years later, with an order to close the port and the rumor that Napoleon, momentarily at peace in Europe, intended to conquer an American empire. Goods piled up on the New Orleans docks and western riflemen began organizing to stop the French.

President Jefferson, with faith in the diplomatic solution, instructed the United States Minister to France, Robert Livingston, to purchase the small but important district of New Orleans. James Monroe was sent over to hasten the deal. And Jefferson wrote to his friend, Pierre Samuel du Pont de Nemours, a French political economist and statesman, saying that if France held New Orleans, it would seal a union of the United States and Britain against her — the letter to be shown to Napoleon.

Perhaps it did its work. Napoleon had conceived a grand conquest of the United States, using New Orleans as his military base. But his expedition to Santo Domingo had been a failure, he needed money, and now came this threat of American-British coalition. He changed his scheme: America in possession of New Orleans would create a maritime menace to Great Britain, his most hated enemy. He would make the sale of the New Orleans region — of the whole of Louisiana.

The American negotiators were aghast. They had no use for all that wilderness. But Napoleon would sell all or nothing. Hesitantly the American envoys accepted the huge area to gain the Mississippi outlet, agreeing to pay for it the staggering sum of fifteen million dollars. Jefferson took the outcome in his calm stride, but the American people were vehement in their disapproval. This trackless waste that had been loaded off upon them was larger than the whole former Union, which was itself so immense that it could never be settled. No one knew how little this land, for which a ruinous amount had been paid, might be worth.[2]

To quell the doubts of the nation, Jefferson sent his kinsman, sensitive, melancholy, twenty-eight-year-old Meriwether Lewis, and confident, red-haired, thirty-four-year-old William Clark to explore some of the purchase. Starting from the French village of St. Louis, they paddled up to the head of the Missouri River, climbed the Rockies, and went on to the Pacific. They returned with a sensational report of immense fertile plains, navigable rivers, lofty mountains, and deep gorges. It was a magnificent country, unbelievably beautiful. Indeed, one of their party, young John Colter, had been so thrilled with the Shining Mountains that he had not come back with the others. John Colter said that after such scenes as these, he 'would be lonesome in St. Louis.' [3]

The adventurous Zebulon Montgomery Pike, twenty-six-year-old government engineer, polished, commanding, carrying in his pocket a small book of purported Thibetan philosophy, had headed an expedition to explore the Mississippi to its source. The trip was full of labor and danger, but exhilarating. Pike had seen the Upper River with the eyes of a military engineer and the heart of a poet. It was said that a light shone in his plain face whenever he spoke of the stream's beauty, once the muddy inpour of the Missouri was passed. Islands dotted it, limestone cliffs towered above it a hundred to eight hundred feet, miles of rapids foamed in it, the Falls of St. Anthony were flung down over a triple reef. [4]

To the fan-shaped empire of the Mississippi, another young adventurer, Henry Shreve, was to devote the best of his life.

Israel Shreve, Henry's father, had been one of the early settlers in the Valley. Until the Revolutionary War broke out, Israel had lived in a farm settlement of Friends in Burlington County, New Jersey. [5] He had watched the colonists make their meager preparations to fight for 'a redress of wrongs.' They were short of arms, ammunition, and clothing, but most of all they were short of men. One day Israel shocked the Quaker neighborhood by riding off to war, with his thirteen-year-old son John.[6] When he returned years later, he found his farm denuded by enemy troops, his cattle driven away, his house burned, his family sheltered by relatives. His name was stricken from the roll of Friends because he could not repent of his unpeaceful ways.[7] On July 7, 1788, with his wife, six of his nine children, and all his possessions in three canvas-covered wagons, he had set out to cross the sixty-mile-wide barrier of the Alleghanies and make a new home. It rained incessantly. The caravan plodded over muddy roads, forded swollen streams, toiled up mountain trails stony enough 'to dash all to pieces.' Ridge succeeded ridge day after day. On the first of August the party reached its destination, a new white hewn-log house in Westover County, Pennsylvania, lent to Shreve until he could find a farm to rent.[8]

Israel Shreve left his family in the white log house and joined Colonel George Morgan's expedition to Upper Louisiana, as chief surveyor of New Madrid, a city which Morgan planned as the capital of a Utopian colony. In a few months Israel returned from this ill-fated venture, unpaid and poorer than ever.[9] He looked about for ground to rent for himself and his four sons, and happened upon 'Washington Bottoms,' land that young George Washington had selected from the wilderness years ago and later divided into five farms. He applied, through the President's agent, for a lease.[10] Washington cherished a deep friendship for Israel Shreve. This tall stout colonel of the Second Regiment of New Jersey had spent the winter at Valley Forge, fought at Quebec, at the torrid battle of Monmouth Courthouse, had been wounded at Brandywine; he had rallied mutinous troops back into line and demanded a pardon for them. Washington wrote his agent to lease the 'Bottoms' to Shreve on the colonel's own terms. The terms agreed upon were sixty pounds sterling a year. Later, Israel Shreve bought the land on lenient payments. He lived contentedly in this haven for ten years, and died there,[11] on December 14, 1799, on the same night that his general, Washington, died.

Henry, the fifth child of Israel Shreve's second wife, Mary Cokely, was born on October 21, 1785, at 'Mount Pleasant,' the old Shreve homestead on Rancocas Creek, New Jersey.[12] 'Mount Pleasant' was the home of Caleb, Israel Shreve's brother, who had given refuge to Mary Shreve and her children when their house was burned. Henry was not quite three years old when his parents moved to Pennsylvania. As a boy he had played along the banks of the Youghiogheny and watched the swarms of craft that went by when the spring or autumn freshets quickened the current: trading boats loaded with every sort of farm produce, and the boats of emigrants, with families, tools, livestock, and fowls crowded together, all types of boats bound downstream to the Ohio on a long one-way journey to the West. Israel Shreve, perplexed that so many men sailed past this prosperous countryside, ignoring it, had written to his brother in New Jersey, 'It seems as if people are crazy to get afloat on the Ohio . . . and set out for they know not where.' [13]

Henry Shreve was fascinated with the river and its travelers: the Indian canoes darting along; the white man's *pirogue*, made by splitting a log, hollowing and trimming down the halves and splicing them together with a flat wide timber to form a broad bottom; the keelboats, long, narrow, pointed at both ends, a small cabin midway of the deck; barges, long, wide, pointed only at the bow, the large cabin leaving but a margin of deck; the keelless flatboats, the bottoms built like a floor and fenced to carry horses, cattle, and poultry. These flatboats were dubbed 'Kentucky arks,' or, more generally 'broadhorns,' from the sweeps which extended far out into the stream. Many of the boats had sails, but used them warily on the crooked rivers.

The boats went downstream gaily, slightly aided by oar or setting-pole, but those that returned with cargo made a laborious trip. It was a punishing business to pole, row, and tow loaded craft up the swift inland rivers. The flatboats never came back; they were cheaply thrown together, meant to be discarded at the last port down.

Flatboat crews walked back through swamp and forest, often from New Orleans. Henry had seen them arriving in Brownsville, their faces haggard, eyes haunted. Even at that, perhaps they had the best of the keelboat or barge hands who worried their laden vessels upstream, pushing and tugging, trudging mosquito-ridden shores with a *cordelle*, or tow-rope, over their shoulders. Indians and panthers lurked in the canebrakes they passed, and the poisonous moccasin lay in the swamp reeds.[14] Two thousand miles of toil and danger to bring a petty cargo of sugar, coffee, indigo, or cotton.

Exhausting trials were soon forgotten in a waterfront tavern. From there, fragments of the flatboatmen's adventures would drift even to the sedate Quaker farms — tales of breasting the uproarious Mississippi, of the jungle-like swamps and somber forests, of trade and riches, savages and river pirates. More and more amazing were the stories that travelers brought back. Most of the tales began, 'In Louisiana,' and swept on to the most astounding climaxes. Louisiana was on all men's tongues.

There were, too, the more stolid accounts of several Brownsville merchants who had made the trip West. Henry Shreve's oldest brother, John, sailed down the Ohio and Mississippi once with a cargo of flour for the West Indies, and returned with his own graphic description of the wilderness. Twenty-one-year-old Henry Shreve early knew why men left their good, prosaic farms and sailed off into adventure on anything that would float. In the summer of 1807, he began building his first boat on the Monongahela at Brownsville, Pennsylvania.

It was a keelboat of thirty-five tons burden, with a movable mast, a rudder, and a small cabin amidships.[15] He had been planning it for a long time as he went about his tasks on the home farm several miles east of Brownsville. Now he turned definitely from the comfortable Quaker homestead and took to the rivers.

When the last seam of his boat was caulked and the paint dried, he hired a crew of ten men from the Brownsville waterfront. They were French and half-breeds, seasoned boat-hands. In October, 1807, he headed out on the drab Monongahela, bound for the remote Mississippi port, St. Louis.

Henry is described as being five feet eleven inches tall, so slight as to appear no more than seventeen years old, yet extremely athletic and strong.[16] In a world gone reckless and wearing the new long pantaloons against which ministers of every faith railed, Shreve, like all Quakers, kept conservatively to knee breeches. These and a broad hat added to the youthful boat captain's boyishness. His eyes were sometimes dreamy, at others, intent and pene-trating. His determination, though quiet, never relaxed. His crew appears to have accepted him as their *patron*, or master, without question.

A swing of the boat brought it straight downstream. On the right Brownsville basked in the autumn sun, its houses sketching a double frieze along the natural bluff terraces. Behind the town, on Redstone Creek, rose forest trees of enormous size out of the soil that covered a city built by a race so long vanished that even the Indians had no legends about it. Brownsville was a prosperous town, with a brewery, a ropewalk, a paper mill, and considerable boat-building. The terrace population, with its four Friends' meeting-houses, was reserved and decorous. Below it the waterfront was offhand and roistering, its taverns and gaming-houses kept lively by arriving crews.[17]

Henry Shreve hurried the boat along to make the most of the daylight. Very little night sailing was done on the inland rivers, for they were beset with drift-timber and shoals. At dark the boat was moored below a point of land where the current was mild. The crew cooked its supper ashore at a roaring fire. Small game and a great side of salt pork were roasted; prodigious amounts of hominy, pota-toes, and meal cakes were boiled or baked. The men piled their platters again and again, dousing the first courses with bear's oil, and the last with molasses. They ate ener-getically, made a thorough job of it, demanded their whiskey ration, and brought out the playing cards for the inevitable game of *vingt-et-un*, called *vingt-un* along the rivers. They played absorbedly. There were cries of tri-umph or chagrin, confused babble, a blustering challenge, and presently the ground about the fire was trampled in a mêlée of fights. It was the boat-hands' orthodox way of ending a day. They not only enjoyed it utterly, but to them it was necessary to find out early who was the champion and might wear a feather in his cap for all the world to see. When the wrangle was finished for the evening, the men got their blankets and rolled up to sleep on deck or ashore.[18]

By dawn they were up. Some hunted the day's supply of game, others cooked. They ate breakfast hastily and got the boat on its way. It neared the important little town of Pittsburgh. The banks were higher; bronzed hills rose on the right. Suddenly the stream widened, the current whipped against the boat side; the Allegheny River had wound out of the hills to meet the Monongahela and flow on with it as one stream — the Ohio.

All the world, indeed, wanted to get afloat on the Ohio. Nosed to the Pittsburgh shore were river craft of every kind waiting to go downstream. With the first sign of high water they would pull loose and drift toward the Mississippi. After his boat had been rowed into a berth at the crowded bank, Henry Shreve set off up Market Street to buy his cargo for St. Louis. He was sailing his own boat and he would carry his own goods.[19]

He found Pittsburgh bleak and dingy, its houses breathing out the black smoke of the 'fossil' coal that cropped from the hills and was sold from door to door for five cents a bushel.[20] The market offered a bewildering array of products: blown and plate glass from local factories, locks and clocks, foundry castings of every kind, tools, furniture, woolen and cotton cloth from the town's weaving mills, china, tin, rope, and Seneca oil, which oozed from the rock and coal fissures in the hills and was in popular demand as a liniment. Shreve bought what he wanted, had his miscellaneous cargo loaded in his keelboat, backed out of the throng of craft, and was off, not waiting for a freshet.

The river was a third of a mile wide below Pittsburgh, the water greenish and the current leisurely. Father Marquette, the frail, gentle priest-explorer, had called this stream the Ouabache; his companion, Joliet, had called it La Rivière de la Divine; the French generally termed it La Belle Rivière; the Indians had long ago named it Ohio, or 'beautiful stream.'

Against the green water and browning foliage of the high forest-grown shores showed the plaid flannel shirts and bright head-kerchiefs of the boat-hands who poled indolently or lolled forward, singing to a lazily thrummed guitar. Nothing could look more worthless than a boat-man in his idle hours. At times one roused to halloo men ashore or to yell taunts at a 'broadhorn' crew poling a flat penlike craft from a bank to head it downstream, or to gibe 'flatters' with having to walk back home from their lowest port.

But a keelboat crew, too, might have to walk a good part of the way back, and with a *cordelle* over their shoulders when there was no wind to fill a sail and the poles made slow time. It was cheaper and easier for a trader to use a flatboat — there were a great many cargoes floating downstream. The need was to get goods from the South and West. Henry Shreve resolved from the very first that he would be primarily an up-river man.

Pennsylvania was well behind him now. The hills of Ohio rose on the right and the hills of Virginia on the left — West Virginia had not yet been carved out. One morning the boat-hands pointed out Charlestown on the Virginia shore to their *patron*. It had a two-story pillory and stocks in front of the stone courthouse that faced the river — there were not many towns that could punish two culprits at once! A crowd stood about the pillory, a favorite loafing place in every river town. The county court was likely in session, for whenever court was held anywhere along the rivers, men came to the 'gathering' from far up and down, even though they had no legal business, to hear news, talk politics, to buy or sell, gamble, drink, or fight.

A few hours' run, and Wheeling lay ahead on a high cliff against rugged hills. The crew put up glib arguments to stop here, but the newest *patron* on the rivers knew better — boat-hands being what they were. For Wheeling was a notoriously gay port, with its horse-races, cockfights, gaming-places, and plentiful other diversions. Citizens of the more sober Ohio towns contrived errands there to bask in the free-and-easy atmosphere. It was not altogether urgent business that crowded the twice-a-week stagecoach from Philadelphia.

Steering became a tense job, absorbing the *patron's* whole attention. Forest trees that stood on the high banks threw their reflections far out on the water, leaving only a strip of the river's width light. It was important to keep in this strip, for, mingling with the reflections were trees that had fallen from the washed banks and had been pushed by the current well out into the stream; their heavy roots had buried themselves in the river bed, their tops waving above the surface. A partly submerged tree with roots firmly embedded was known as a 'planter'; one that was loosely set, and its top nodding downstream with the drive of the water, was a 'sawyer.' Boat-owners knew them generally as 'snags'; the French boat-hands called them *chicots*, the teeth of the rivers. The stretching boughs could rip the stoutest vessel apart.[21] '*Chicot, chicot!*' the men would call back and forth as they held their metal-tipped setting-poles ready to jab at the menacing driftwood if the boat came too near it.

A few days later, Shreve reached Marietta, Ohio, at the mouth of the Muskingum, a serious old town, settled by New Englanders, a good place to put in for fresh supplies of salt pork and tobacco. Here, as at Brownsville, an earth-covered prehistoric city reared behind the town, overgrown with trees whose rings showed them to be more than nine hundred years old.

A *patron* stepping ashore was greeted on every side, 'What's the news?' At this time the specific query was: 'What is the latest about Aaron Burr? Has he gone to England? What do people East think of Chief Justice Marshall's letting him go on a technicality last month?' Could Burr really have been up to treason? It seemed impossible. For handsome, elegant Aaron Burr had charmed the people of Marietta when he had stopped here on his way West two years ago. He had been Vice-President of the nation, and but for a single vote would have been President instead of Jefferson. He was a grandson of Jonathan Edwards, the noted Congregational minister, the son of the president of the college at Princeton, and had not lost his popularity in the West by his distressing duel with Alexander Hamilton in 1804.

Shreve was not glib at passing on hearsay. He had little news to bring ashore except simple facts: the river stage, the wind's direction, his destination. He was less astonished than many others at Burr's mad enterprises. His father had known Burr well, had admired his courage at Quebec, had wintered at Valley Forge with him, had fought beside him at Monmouth Courthouse, but had recognized that he was a brilliant, restless, troublesome man, soundly disliked by Washington, hated by the soldiers.

And Burr's aide, Blennerhassett? Poor Blennerhassett! He had lived about nine miles down the river from Marietta in his island retreat, a proud, scholarly Irishman, with a lovely young wife and two little sons. He had fled South just before last Christmas, disgraced. His island had been seized by creditors and rented out, his furniture sold.

Shreve made his few purchases and set out again. Some time later he steered past the north side of a long island, close to its shore. This was Blennerhassett's Island, the most beautiful retreat in the western world. The sun slanted past the landing and its massive double gate, gilding a tree-bowered walk that passed a long landscaped garden to the white mansion. Semicircular porticoes ran from the front corners to independent wings. One of these wings had been fitted up as a chemical laboratory, the papers had reported, for Blennerhassett was a scientist. He was a linguist, too, familiar with many languages. It was said he could repeat the greater part of the *Iliad* in Greek. Here in this garden-surrounded palace, the only one in the Mississippi Valley, the young Irishman had entertained many intellectuals. On a summer evening two years ago Aaron Burr had drawn his boat up to the island. Never had Harman Blennerhassett received a more delightful guest. He and his wife were carried away with Burr's manner and broad grasp of world affairs. Burr's proposal to establish a colony on Washita River in Louisiana sounded innocent enough; his bold plan to march an expedition against the Spanish in Texas, to take over that country and, perhaps, all of Mexico, savored of the magnificent. Whether Blennerhassett ever suspected that Burr also planned to take some of the American territories along the Mississippi and add them to the empire over which he would possibly rule was not clear, but Blennerhassett pledged his aid and in a year had spent his fortune building and fitting out boats for the venture. Then President Jefferson had issued a proclamation against it. Blennerhassett was ruined.[22]

Burr's hunger for power could not have seemed strange to Henry Shreve; there was much of it in himself. It had made him adept at games, stronger, faster than his companions; it had urged him to build a large boat and attempt an unusually hard voyage; it was later to drive him into pioneer fields and to undertake the nearly impossible. But it would never lead him to such aggression as Burr's; there was so much in the Valley that needed peaceful conquering.

The banks had grown rough and hilly, the bright foliage and white branches of the sycamores vivid against the brown oaks. Flocks of birds on the way south chattered in the trees; occasional deer swam across the stream. Shreve marveled that, when any man could have a boat, so many stayed ashore. He floated on past Gallipolis on the right. The French there had had a sorry time, the boatmen said. They had been lured from France by a bogus land broker and sold this ground; then, after their houses were built and farms planted, they found that the land had never been the broker's to sell and their titles were worthless. Some tried to repurchase their places, others had drifted away.

No one, the men clacked in their half-French jargon, could talk to the *patron* long. He was always studying the river or pecking at charts. But then somebody had to think of such things. There he went now, in his dull clothes, walking as lightly as an Indian, his eyes intent on the Chatterawah River as it rolled into the Ohio from the south — Big Sandy, some called that stream. It was not much to look at, but it was the end of Virginia.

And the beginning of Kentucky, land of tales and bloody battles. The first white men who came to the Kentucky region had been amazed to find it uninhabited by Indians. Beautiful, inviting, abounding in game, its very richness kept the Indians from living in it; to settle here was to court massacre from other tribes who desired it. After centuries of conflict, the Indians on both sides of the Ohio had agreed that all their tribes might hunt here, but none should settle on this ground.[23]

When the European empires had touched their affairs, the Indians believed that in their hands lay the balance of power in the French and British struggle in the New World. The Lenape, or Delaware, Indians in Pennsylvania, cheated out of much of their land by a son of William Penn, nursed a deep resentment against the English. With their kinsmen, the Shawanese, they joined the French. The fall of Quebec to the British in September, 1759, broke French power in America, though the war dragged on. Then the Pennsylvania Quakers prevailed on their governor to send Christian Post, a Moravian missionary, to persuade the Indians to lay down their arms. A plain, simple man, the envoy carried a pipe of peace and a message of regret to the Delawares for the wrong done them. 'I cald dam all togader,' he wrote back, 'and told dam wat we bous had agreed on wan we saw one anoder last, and wat you are sorre for.' When the pipe of peace was passed around, no one declined it. With their Indian allies gone, the French soon gave up their useless struggle.[24]

As a result, the drift of the British settlers into the Valley quickened, greatly alarming the Indians. The French had filtered into the Valley casually, taken their places beside the aboriginals with neighborly mildness, toiled or worshiped with them and intermarried with them; but the British were dynamic, aloof, imperious. Where the Briton settled, the Indian vanished. Still, in spite of the seeping of whites into the mid-Valley, the Indians still peopled it. French and English statesmen signed treaties about it far across the ocean, but it was the red man's land.

Pontiac, intelligent chief of the Ottawas, saw with desperate vision that, if it was to remain the homeland of the Indians, they must make a stand for it. He had prayed, fasted, laid out campaigns, and pleaded with other chiefs to join him against the greedy whites. But though the British posts fell, co-operation was too half-hearted, and in two years the whites had regained control. The way was clear for the tall, gaunt, blond men to overrun the wilderness. The British bought Kentucky, part of Tennessee and of the Ohio watershed from the discouraged red men for 10,430 pounds sterling, or two hundred boatloads of goods. Indians who resented the sale treaty held sullen councils and made ferocious attacks on the white invaders, but their cherished hunting ground slipped away from them.

Kentucky's settlers were vivid contrasts to the softer white populations east, north, and south. Its backwoodsmen were the hardiest, its statesmen the shrewdest, its boat-hands the toughest, its urban gentlemen the most elegant, its riflemen world-renowned marksmen, its women proverbial for their beauty and fashion. Kentuckians made the poorest boats and best firearms, raised the finest horses, drank the choicest liquors, used the most colorful invective, went everywhere, saw everything, formed their own opinions. The word Kentucky, pattering on all sides as an adjective, meant the best and the worst — it was always a superlative. Kentucky was midway the length of the Valley, its position was pivotal; it would, Shreve believed, become a key-point in American commerce.

About four hundred and eighty miles from Pittsburgh, Shreve came to the first hint of the South, a growth of scraggly cane on the low banks of Licking River where it flowed in from the left. Across the Ohio from it, on a fine high double bank, sat a neat, prosperous town once named Losantiville, but now called Cincinnati. It, too, had been built on the site of a prehistoric city whose pyramids and walls supported trees nearly a thousand years old. The Indians, revering this site as the tomb of their ancestors, had sworn that, before they would yield it to the white men, the Ohio would run with blood. But for reckless Anthony Wayne and his slight, mild-looking twenty-year-old aide, William Henry Harrison, who had quit medical school to become a soldier, the Indian threat might have been carried out. Now Harrison was a weathered veteran of thirty-four and had been for six years the governor of all the Indiana Territory, including the Illinois country.

Below Cincinnati a half-day's run was Big Bone Lick Creek, where the huge bones of unbelievable animals had been found, with horns as long as a canoe, teeth so large that a man could hardly lift one in his hand. The mastodons had come here to a salt lick, become mired in the wet trampled ground about it, and perished. Great beasts like them still roamed the West, the boat-hands insisted — the Indians said so. But if one did not believe, why should they care? They would drive the boat along when the wind died, set the poles in the river bed where it was shallow enough, throw the weight of their bodies against them, singing as they worked.

The river was rising. Boats of every type seemed to spring out of each landing Shreve passed, to swarm along with him. A sharpness had come into the air. Wild geese winged south in long triangles; the islands were noisy with duck, pelican, and crane; clouds of passenger pigeons tailed out of the northeast. Shreve figured that in another day he would pass over the Falls of the Ohio.

Just upstream from the Falls, on a lofty bank commanding a fine view of the river and foaming rapids, sat Louisville with its hundred and twenty houses. Because of the difficulty of getting boats over the Falls except at high water, even if guided by the special local pilots, cargoes often had to be unloaded here, carried by land around the Falls, and stowed on another boat. It made the port a busy place of storage and exchange.

Louisville was the county town and had long been a port of entry for foreign goods. Most of the houses on its mile-long street that ran parallel to the river were large and of brick. Many people moved about in the street. The waterfront was lively. A clanging set up in the town, deeper and shriller clangs joining in — it was noon, and the bells on top of the taverns were calling men from the groups about the market and courthouse to dinner — men in homespun, woodsmen in leather suits and coonskin

caps, traders from up and down the rivers. Negroes
hostlered horses, pushed barrows, drove plantation carts.
Rifles, belt-knives, and harness buckles caught the sunlight.

Not far beyond the town, the Ohio began churning over
ledges of a limestone reef. When the water was high, boat-
hands insisted upon going over the Falls without a town
pilot; they had voluble scorn of a special pilot when they
did not greatly need him. By watching the eddies, Shreve
could pick out the low places in the ledge. With much pro-
fanity and shouting, the crew guided the craft easily over
the reef and past stranded vessels that were being pounded
to pieces in the angry water. The keelboat still rocked,
with the ledge well behind it, for there was a drop of more
than twenty feet in the river bed in the next two miles.

The high tree-lined shores formed a canyon that opened
distantly ahead of the boat and closed distantly behind it,
day after day. Then, on the right the prairie came into
view, flat, treeless, a gray-yellow sea of coarse grass with
a gauze of dead seed stalks rising above it. The prairie
vanished, at times, behind a hill or a clump of shore trees.
Each time it came back into view it was more incredible.
Stretching away forever, it was like the meditation at a
Friends' service, serene, with no intent, no goal.

The Wabash River came in from the north, flooding its
low banks. Mallard and teal covered acres of standing
overflow, moving in and out the reeds and willows. The
prairie became charred earth where the Indians had burned
the grass off in their autumn round-up of game that fled
ahead of the flames. From the south the blue Cumberland
flowed. Almost beside it lay the Tennessee, known as the
Cherokee River because the villages of the Cherokee In-

dians were scattered along it. There had been talk, Shreve recalled, of opening a channel through Muscle Shoals, a series of islands and bars a hundred miles or so up the Tennessee.[25]

The west wind was raw. Shreve kept his lookout in a loose greatcoat; the boat-hands pulled their *capots* (capes with *capuchon*, or hood), made of Mackinaw blankets, around them as they bent over their card games. The boat neared the Grand Chain of Rocks, a broken stone ledge that reached in great fragments across the stream — another graveyard of luckless boats. After this there would be only a few miles of the Ohio. At sunup Shreve, from the cabin top, searched for a glimpse of the distant Mississippi; but an autumn mist lay like a deep snow on the earth. When the mist melted, there was the Mississippi lying ahead, chalky-gray and turbulent.

The men grasped their oars to help turn the boat around a long willow-grown point of land that separated the two rivers. Shreve bore on the tiller, but the Ohio current carried them on westward. The plunging Mississippi forced the boat back, the down-rush caught it, beat against its side, driving it downstream. The men bent to the oars, straining backs, yelling warnings, swearing fervently. At last the boat was righted and pulled to the low east bank.

Now all but two of the men deserted the oars, ran forward on the land side, grasped branches of low-hanging willows and walked briskly toward the stern. Here they ran around the water side of the deck to the bow, clutched the willows again and made down the land side to the stern. By this ancient device of 'bushwhacking,' the craft moved laboriously ahead. At times an oblique surge of water raced against the boat, threatening to beach it on the flat shore. The 'bushwhacking' had to be abandoned and the boat rowed out into the stream. Some of the men held poles ready to jab their iron points at the logs piled along the sandbars and islands if the current pushed the boat too near them.

In spite of the danger, fighting with the headlong stream was exhilarating. All the stories that Shreve had ever heard of the blustering Mississippi had not quite prepared him for this. He would have to give battle for every mile of gain against the racing water.

When a clear sweep of river lay ahead, free of planted or piled timbers, the sail was set. Beyond the low east bank spread the level Illinois country, which at various times had been a part of the province of Quebec, and a county of Virginia, but was now a district of Indiana. The dry prairie grass bowed in white waves as the wind passed over it. On the left, the Missouri country of Upper Louisiana showed a bold high bank topped with oak and hickory, walnut and maple, and the lofty sycamore stretching its bare white branches.

But there were not many moments when Shreve could relax and watch the scene drift by. In the most innocent-looking piece of river a hill of swirling water would appear, drawing the boat toward it, all hands staving to keep it from spinning into the center of the 'boil.' No human effort could work it upstream out of one of these swirls. It would have to escape downstream, then fight far around past the upheaval. After a struggle with one of these river demons, the men were exhausted and the boat had to be tied up to shore while they rested.[26]

Late on the first day up the Mississippi, the startling

rocks of Grand Tower loomed ahead in the dusk, several shafts of stone rearing abruptly out of the water to the height of a hundred feet. Grand Tower had once been a promontory jutting from the Missouri cliffs. The river, in age-long attack, had cut it from the shore. A strong eddy whipped past this stone castle, lashing at the boat.

A few miles above here a band of river pirates were known to use a cavern in the Illinois bluffs, Devil's Oven, as a hideout. All up and down the rivers, any convenient cave was likely to harbor one of these murderous bands of marauders and their loot. The taverns from New Orleans to Philadelphia rang with legends of them, none too sensational to be true. A *patron* had to be on the alert for any sign of their scouting skiffs, all the while he watched constantly for driftwood, minded the tiller, and at times took the oar from an exhausted man.

Day after day the drab river wound ahead, broad and awesome, but marred by half-submerged trees that seemed to wade out from every caving bank or island head. A 'sawyer,' always swayed by the current, sometimes bowed below the surface, out of sight. At any minute it might rise, tangling or overturning a boat that happened to be in its way. Enormous and deeply embedded 'planters' stretched their stout limbs under water, threatening to rake unwary craft.

Many of the embedded sycamores were five to twelve feet in diameter. It was said that Judge Tucker, of Upper Louisiana, a half-brother of John Randolph, had cut a cross-section from a hollow sycamore and put a roof on it, to make a comfortable cabin which he used for a law office.[27] The sycamores, living, were kings of the forest; dead, they dominated the river from their graves.

On the third day, Shreve passed the village of Cape Girardeau on the high west bank. The men babbled about it and subsided. It was not an old settlement, having been established only fourteen years before by the colorful Don Louis Lorimier, about whom many an anecdote had trickled back to the Monongahela. Despite his Spanish title, Don Louis was a French nobleman from Canada, tall, straight, blue-eyed, and strikingly handsome. His long fair hair was worn in a queue and fastened by ribbons with which he whipped along his saddle horse. He was a superb horseman and could hunt with the Indians, galloping as long and fast as they did. He was excessively fond of display and his generosity was proverbial. To the red men he was a magnificent, showy white god sent down among them. He had married a beautiful half-French Indian princess, Charlotte Bougerville, and was made commander of Cape Girardeau by the Spanish governor of Louisiana. He ruled like a kindly lord. A group of Germans had settled here among the French and looked askance at easygoing ways. The newcomers had made the town different, the men reported to the *patron*; then brushed the matter aside. If the Germans wanted to make their lives dull by not gaming or fighting, who cared? Four days more would bring the boat to Ste. Genevieve. It was truly French; it would be a good place to stop off.

But Shreve was not minded to stop along the way now, except perhaps at Kaskaskia, and that would be no treat to boat-hands. It was a sorry port, they held, off the Meche-sebe River and up a poor little stream several miles. It had too much law, too many judges; the British-Americans had done that. No sooner did they take over a good town than they began to brand everything as wicked.

When Kaskaskia was all French, it was the greatest town
in the Valley: now it was spoiled. But Ste. Genevieve —
oh, well! The oars found the rhythm of a song:

> ˙Derriere chêz nous il y a un etang,
>   Ye, ye ment.
> Trois canards s'en vont baignans,
> Tous du lông de la rivière,
> Legèrement, ma bergère;
>   Legèrement, ye ment.' *

Kaskaskia, the oldest white settlement in the Mississippi
Valley, had once been the largest Indian village in the middle country, the home of the Kaskaskia tribe of the Illini
nation. Joliet and Marquette, on their exploring trip down
the Mississippi in 1673, turned up the Illinois River to
visit it. On a prairie bank opposite a tower of rock on the
other shore, they found a scattering of large communal
huts, some roomy enough to accommodate twelve families. Father Marquette, with his will of a conqueror and
heart of a child, was delighted with the fine-looking, intelligent Kaskaskia Indians and, in 1675, seven years before
Philadelphia was laid out, he founded a mission among
them. Sieur de La Salle had come to Kaskaskia on his way
to explore the Lower Mississippi and had built a fort on
the rock tower across from it. In 1700, to save these
peace-loving Indians from further attacks by tribes to the
north, the French fathers removed them south on the

---

* This song was recorded by John Bradbury in *Travels in the Interior of
America*, published in London in 1812. Bradbury gave this translation:
> 'Behind our house there is a pond,
>   Fal la de ra.
> There came three ducks to swim thereon,
> All along the river clear,
> Lightly, my shepherdess dear;
>   Lightly, fal de ra.'

Kaskaskia River. Eighteen years later, Kaskaskia had been made, for a while, the capital of a territory reaching to the Rocky Mountains. Now it was the capital of Indiana Territory.[28]

Shreve did not stop at Kaskaskia. Time was precious. He wanted to get his trading done at St. Louis and pull back up the Ohio before ice should block it. He was having difficulty making two or three miles an hour in this staving current, the heaviest on the whole river. No wonder so few traders ever tried the stiff run upstream from the Ohio!

On a December day, after nearly six weeks of sailing, Shreve sighted St. Louis.[29] From a distance the village looked like a cluster of white boulders on its high tree-fringed shore. As the boat drew nearer, the bank appeared to grow higher, a limestone bluff rising in two terraces forty feet above the water. On the broad lower terrace sat widely spaced wooden houses, whitewashed and gleaming in the sun, and pretentious mansions of stone enclosed by masonry walls. In a semicircle on the upper terrace, behind the town, were weathered fort towers. Above the whole reared a massive, irregular Indian mound.[30]

Below the bluff a sandbar began midway of the town's length and extended north for some distance. Flatboats, *pirogues*, canoes, and a few keelboats were tied up at this beach. Two roads, gouged into the cliff by crowbar and hammer, led from the sandbar up to the town; ox-carts rattled up and down these rough, steep ways. Shreve nosed his boat to the beach and made it fast. The excited boat-hands did last things hastily, demanded their pay, and climbed stony Rue Bonhomme (later Market Street) to the nearest tavern.

Along the sandbar, beside cargoes loading or unloading, were other boat captains, swarthy boat-hands, and water-front roustabouts. French merchants from the town bar-gained and bought, keeping an elegant, leisurely air; blacks ran to and fro, doing their bidding. Indians squat-ted in motionless groups, friendly but watchful. Voices rose in different French dictions — the French of New Or-leans, of the Upper Louisiana villages, of Canada, of Paris. Here and there an English phrase stood out. The younger St. Louis merchants affected long pantaloons and high beaver hats; the older ones wore breeches and tricornes, with an occasional braided pigtail tucked up under a work-aday comb. Young and old clutched the inevitable snuff-box. The tall youth in Quaker gray and broadbrim was an unusual type of visitor here, but surprise was kept polite. He had come direct from Pittsburgh, so he was not quizzed for news. It made little difference to St. Louis what hap-pened off there. The cargo was another matter; goods from the East did not often enough make their way to this port.

Shreve displayed samples of his wares, offering no com-ment on them. The St. Louisians made careful bids. Shreve accepted or rejected the bids briefly. The mer-chants glanced at him. He was cool for a boy and firm. Their trading grew more intent. At last the whole cargo was sold, the payments to be 'packs' of furs.

There was very little money in this part of the country except what seeped in from boatmen's pay — Mexican silver dollars, worth about fifty cents each, cut into four 'bits' with a chisel. Fur and tobacco were the common currency, principally fur. Each type of pelt had a definite value. One pound of deerskin equaled one *livre* (about eighteen cents here), one pound of otter pelt equaled so many pounds of deerskin, and so on.

Shreve's bargains were not written down. A St. Louis merchant was proud that his word was as good as his signature. After the deals were made, blacks, who hovered near their masters, were dispatched to the warehouses up in the town. Presently a train of high-wheeled carts, the oxen hitched one before the other, creaked down Rue Bonhomme. The drivers walked beside the oxen with long whips in lieu of reins and kept up a chorus of 'Chuck ci, marche deau!' A small army of slaves followed the carts to the keelboat. The loaded carts made way beside the boat for empty ones, groaned up the rough road, and, in a while, rattled down again. At last the hold was empty.

With his new fortune in pack-promises tucked away in his mind, Shreve trudged after the last of the carts up Rue Bonhomme to the village. He looked curiously about him. This was different from any other town he had visited. The whitewashed wooden houses were built of logs set upright in the earth, not laid cribwise. The roofs extended in wide overhangs that sheltered the balconies which invariably flanked the house on two or more sides. Hand-split broad shingles, hung to the rafters with large wooden pegs, clattered in the wind. The stone houses were gray and massive, each with a full block of ground inside the yard wall.

The handsomest of the mansions was that of the elder Auguste Chouteau, the present patriarch of the village. It fronted on Rue Principale, called, in the days of the monarchy, Rue Royale (later to be Main Street). This place was a veritable fortress. Its solid masonry was two and a half feet thick; the heavy stone wall around the grounds was pierced every ten feet with musket holes.

Back of the palatial home ran the Rue de l'Eglise, on which stood a small wooden church, the only church in the village. A block farther inland lay the last street, the Rue des Granges, or Street of Stables. Beyond it was open ground, dotted by the semicircle of dilapidated Spanish forts, and from there stretched the Common Field. All French settlements along the middle river practiced community farming. There was nothing strenuous in this public farming, for in the spring the ground was plowed, often with a crooked tree root, planted, and the crop then blithely left to Nature until harvest time. Common river gossip was that St. Louis was even less energetic about its farming than other French towns, and was nicknamed 'Pain Court,' or 'Short-of-Bread.'

In the distance gleamed a beautiful sheet of water covering nearly a hundred acres, Chouteau's Pond, a pleasure resort for the town people. Its high grassy banks were lined with trees, and from it a stream of water tumbled through a picturesque gorge to turn Mr. Chouteau's mill.

The crooked, narrow streets of the village teemed with men. There were overland adventurers, *coureurs des bois*, in buckskin suits and fur caps, flintlock muskets in their hands; boatmen, or *voyageurs*; ordinary townsmen known as *habitants*, dressed much as the boatmen were, in a *capot* made of a Mackinaw blanket, invariably white, with *capuchon* attached, cotton or leather trousers held up by a varicolored worsted belt from which hung a knife and tobacco pouch, a gay kerchief winding the head, deerskin moccasins on the feet. There were spruce military men from the

American garrison which had been placed over the village when it passed from French rule four years ago; Anglo-Saxon or Scotch-Irish woodsmen from Kentucky who had wandered up through the Missouri country carrying their inevitable fine rifles; negroes bearing burdens, loading or unloading carts; blacks bringing casks of water on carts or sledges from where it gushed out of the cliffs above the river; Indians stalking solemnly as through a dream. There were women of the *habitants* dressed in full cotton skirts, shawl-like mantles, with head-kerchiefs tied over the eelskin that bound their hair. Fashionable ladies of the gentry, their handsome cloaks pushed aside from short-waisted empire gowns, broad hats set back to show the ringlets on their foreheads, rode past in carriages driven by negro slaves. They peeped over large muffs at the tall young man in sober gray. He was dressed almost as simply as a *habitant*, yet he had an air of youthful authority.

Everywhere were French houses, French dress, French ways. St. Louisians did not feel American. It had been a shock to them when the very ground under their feet was turned over to America by Napoleon only twenty days after it escaped from ten years of Spanish domination. They had still been celebrating its return to France when the word came that they had been sold out to another alien rule. Now they felt like exiles. A St. Louisian's hand would shake on his snuffbox when he mentioned it. Once the King of France had embodied all possible idea of national splendor, and even in these unfortunate days of no king, French authority was like the voice of God.

St. Louis was born French, its citizens hastened to tell a stranger. It was in the Pyrenees that Pierre de Laclède

Ligueste first thought of it: he used to gaze over the world from his mountain home and dream of founding a great and beautiful city in far-off Louisiana. He had come to New Orleans, and then, with a party of followers, up here, choosing this site from the whole wilderness. When the village was only fourteen years old, Pierre Laclede, as he was usually called, died on his way up from New Orleans. Auguste Chouteau, who had been his fifteen-year-old aide when the venture was begun, carried on the plan to develop a great city here between the mouths of the east-reaching Ohio and the northwest-stretching Missouri.

Shreve could see that its site was well chosen, but before this could become a great city there would have to be a better way to reach it than by rowing up the Mississippi.

Among the houses on the side streets were stores, taverns, and billiard halls. To a Quaker it was strange for a town to boast a dozen billiard rooms and only one small church. Not but what Shreve's men had tried to improve his viewpoint: The *Bon Dieu* had created men for happiness, had He not? they often argued. Well, then it was their duty to play, dance, laugh, enjoy. Sounds of lustily performed duty floated out now from the taverns on the winter air.

Most astonishing to Shreve were the warehouses where he went to select his furs. He had had to ask the way to these, for no shop or store was degraded by a business sign. Pelts were stacked high on every side of a fur store and heaped in hills about the floor, hung from rafters and bulging from adjoining sheds. They had been brought from near and far by *coureurs des bois* well known to the local merchants. St. Louis had its own trappers, one heard again and again in tones suddenly grown hard. No one could come to St. Louis and control its fur market.

Shreve did not know that, a year ago, a stout, square man of forty, with aggressive forehead, straight long hair, deep-set acquisitive eyes, and heavy German accent, had come from New York to locate one of his lieutenants and establish a branch of his fur business in St. Louis. The French merchants had closed a wall of blankness against him. His ways were not their ways. John Jacob Astor had set his thick neck and stubborn chin and gone around past them, farther and farther west. His trappers paddled up every stream, his pelts leaked into this closed French market from every point. Some day, he had resolved, it would find him its master.

Shreve was not only inexpert at selecting furs; he knew almost nothing about them. But it was easy for a novice to trade in St. Louis unless he grew crafty, whereupon, though the same French courtesy might prevail, it was suddenly as empty as the sky.

Dusk had fallen when the business of rounding up pelts was finished and Shreve started back to the sandbar. Since there was as yet no inn here, it was customary for St. Louis merchants to offer lodging to a reputable trader. But the invitations were rarely accepted; a *patron* felt less anxious about his boat if he slept on it. Shreve was particularly cautious. His boat was new and costly, and it was like a partner to him. They had faced destruction together a dozen times in the past weeks. He would sleep aboard.

The evening music had begun in all quarters of the town, and in another hour or so there would be dancing in every mansion, cabin and tavern. The glow of leaping wood fires on window panes made the streets look bleak. Shreve turned down Rue Bonhomme to the waterfront. Halfway across the river, Bloody Island, the dueling ground, lay barren and sinister, and beyond it, the black woods of the Illinois shore. From the guarded craft along the beach came the scrape of fiddles and thump of feet, gabbling over card games, and cheers for a fist fight. In a while these noises died and there was only the swish of water and friendly bumping of boats.

In the morning the loyal members of Shreve's crew, especially loyal because their entire pay was spent, drifted back to him. Those who had been luckier at dice, billiards, or *vingt-un* lingered ashore and their places had to be filled from penniless and stranded boat-hands who haunted the sandbar. The boat was examined, caulking patched, supplies bought, and cargo stowed.

When Shreve pulled out of St. Louis on the gray, blustering river, the isolated village hardly knew that he had come and gone. Some day this Quaker youth's penetrating mind and almost superhuman effort were to sweep the Valley into a new era and this remote trading-post to a place of power, but Shreve, watching the cluster of white houses fade into the limestone cliff, had no vision of this. He was a fledgling *patron*, and he had all he could do to keep his craft from being driven against the embedded driftwood that thrust up through the water.

The men were silent, their poles alert to help the rudder. It was again a mystery to them why they left the warmth and gaiety of the shore taverns for these lonely water stretches. There was plenty of work ashore, safe work in a few daylight hours, then music, candlelight, games, dancing, and a decent bed. Out here it was labor from dawn to

dark, every minute beset by danger. After that, a hasty
supper and black night, with the yelp of wolf and cry of
panther. They slept exhausted, they slept cold, and the
current jerked at the boat to tear it loose and hurl it
against bar or snag. Why had they sailed again, why had
they sailed?

Their oars swung, their bodies swayed. The river — it
caught at the heart, it wrung the soul. The river — it
drew men back, it held them to it. A song began fitfully
and settled to a contented drone:

> 'Le fils du roi s'en va chassant,
> 　Ye, ye ment.
> Avec son grand fusil d'argent,
> Tous du lông de la rivière.
> Legèrement, ma bergère;
> 　Legèrement, ye ment.'*

The *patron* felt the pull of the great river on him, too; it
plunged along as though exulting in its power, careless of
whether it blessed or destroyed. It made a man strong to
feel the surge of it under his feet. A man ought to be
strong, but not ruthless. He could do what the river could
not; he could control his strength with still greater strength
so that it served more than his own hunger for power.

By the second morning Shreve sighted the Ste. Genevieve landing on the Upper Louisiana shore. The quaint
town, inland a piece, had a reputation of sucking up boat
crews whether they had money or not. There was no mer-
rier place on the rivers. One dancing party followed an-

---

* 'The prince to chase them he did run,
　Fal la de ra.
And he had his great silver gun,
　All along the river clear.
Lightly, my shepherdess dear;
　Lightly, fal de ra.'

other, the taverns and billiard rooms never closed, the *vingt-un* tables were crowded from dark to sunup. And Sunday in Ste. Genevieve — there was a proper Sunday! If the church bell rang, as it often did when the *prêtre* was so minded, there was a Mass and everyone hurried to it just as he was. But it lasted no more than a half-hour or so, and after that the whole town was free to play as it would. On Sunday night there was always the grand ball of the gentry, with a new king and court to rule over each one. A boatman without even a silver bit in his pocket could look in the windows.[31]

Shreve gave no order to stop, though the boats lingered past the landing. A stream of carts with high solid wheels — not the modern spoke-wheels seen in St. Louis — came and went. A few of the carts carried wood or stone; more of them brought lead to the waiting boats, for this was the outlet of the Upper Louisiana lead mines in the wilds of the Missouri country. Loads of sugar, coffee, cotton prints, and trinkets from arriving cargoes were trundled back to the town. Jewelry was in great demand here; everyone made everyone else a present of it at the Sunday night grand balls. The Ste. Genevieve merchants, haggling with the *patrons* beside the moored boats, were dressed as the carters and boat-hands, in heavy cotton trousers, plaid shirts, *capots*, and moccasins. They were weathered and brown. One had to look again to distinguish them from the Illinois Peoria Indians who had taken refuge here from enemy tribes and stood about, wrapped in their blankets, waiting.

No one, not even the Indians themselves, knew what they were waiting for, what hopes they had, or fears. They had grown stupefied as their land slipped from them.

They were waiting, perhaps, for this unreality of white
men and white ways to pass, for felled forests to stand
again, for the buffalo to return. The buffalo had lived
peaceably near the Indian tribes for centuries, although
the red man hunted them, ate their flesh, and made wig-
wams of their hides. But they fled forever the approach of
the European, as if they sensed what the deer and swan
and prairie hen did not — that utter extermination
stalked in his path.

The old Spanish fort near Ste. Genevieve was in ruins.
The boat-hands gloated over that. Less than five years
ago this was Spain, and then for nearly three blessed weeks
it was France again; now, unhappily, it was America.
Well, the good miracles of God fell as they would — in a
while it might be France once more. Meanwhile, no one
wickedly wore a sour face, but danced and laughed even
under this wretched rule. The *patron* was American — of
course, he could not help that.

The days were short for sailing, the evenings long for the
boat-hands to play and drink and fight. Shreve hurried
the boat along when he could, and spent hours studying
his charts by candlelight, going over notes he had made.
Beyond the many penciled items, a few general facts stood
out: the country was vast, its resources abundant, its
settlements widely separated; the main travel and trade
routes were the rivers; these streams reached into the
farthest regions and were navigable for most of their
lengths, but their currents sorely hampered upstream
going, and their piled and planted driftwood menaced
craft on every side.

It puzzled Shreve that these handicaps were accepted
with such inertia. Men had spent centuries of effort hunt-

ing a fast, short route to tap the riches of India and Cathay; early Spaniards had searched fanatically for a strait through this great unwanted continent that had loomed as a barrier across the west sea passage to the Orient; the French had dreamed that the Mississippi might empty into Mar Vermejo (Red Sea), as the Gulf of California had been named by *conquistadors*, who believed it to be just a stone's throw from China. Joliet and Marquette had dashed this illusion by floating down the Great River as far as the mouth of the Arkansas without finding any hint that it might empty into the western ocean. La Salle had decided that the Ohio might flow into the western sea almost at the door of China and had led an expedition down it; but his men had deserted him at the Falls of the Ohio and all Canada had laughed at his attempt, dubbing his home site above Montreal 'La Chine.' Henry Hudson had vanished nearly two hundred years ago while hunting a northwest passage to the Orient. And here, right at hand, was a land far richer than India or China, and no one bothered to find a quicker, better way to reach or handle its wealth.

A short trade route, a fast trade route, was Henry Shreve's dream. The inland rivers were a remarkable system of natural roads branching into a land of unmeasured riches, but they were not good roads and there were no fast conveyances for them.

The third day down from St. Louis he saw on the west shore several mills worked by log water wheels, the logs cut in spirals and laid in the river parallel to the bank. One end of the log was held in place by cables, the other was connected with the mill's gearing. The current turned the spirals fitfully. The *patron* was interested in every humdrum thing like that, but the men thought more of ports. They were coming in sight of Cape Girardeau again, perched on a white bluff. Dull as the boatmen admitted it to be, thrifty, part-German and all, it was the last real village for a long time. It was hard to pass.[32]

Nearly two days later, Shreve reached the Ohio. The men staved with oar and pole to head into it as the Mississippi current dragged at the boat to bear it past. The Ohio islands and shore woods, so clamorous a few weeks ago with pelicans, parroquets, wild geese, and jays, were silent now. There were days of rowing, poling, of stretching the sail and furling it. Shreve did not have men enough to *cordelle* the loaded boat. Hasty meals and leaden sleep, but still time for singing and shouting, for a stolen dice game, the passed bottle.

This was not so heavy a pull as that up the Mississippi, but wearily long. Men grew irritable over their card games; fights were likely to be savage. A question about the rivers tossed by the captain into a wrangle might cool it off — boat-hands never tired of educating their *patrons*. If a knife flashed suddenly in an argument, a roared order set every man to work. Shreve was quick of foot and strong. He was considerate, but no man dared disobey him.

The trip from Pittsburgh to St. Louis had taken forty days; the return voyage took even longer. It was early spring when Shreve edged his boat up to the crowded Pittsburgh shore and made known along Market Street that he had a cargo of furs, such as the sample pelts he carried.

The merchants gathered to dicker with him. They remembered him as hardly more than a boy, but a boy with a stubborn will. They looked critically at the pelts. They were not in a hurry for furs, they said. The roads were bad for getting them to Philadelphia. Their offers were miserable.

Such a reception at the end of his first trading trip, from which he had hoped so much, was a disappointment to Shreve. Across his mind flashed some of the hard moments of his long voyage: the lunging Mississippi hurling the boat headlong at a timber-piled bar, the desperate jabbing of the poles, the labored breathing of the men, the bitter wind, aching hands, an abrupt glance into a chasm of death, a surge of relief, nausea. And before one's heart quit hurting against his chest, an onslaught of floating logs, a trough that sucked the boat into a swirling 'boil.' Frosted feet and the breath like a dagger in the side — and now these suave gentlemen who had sat snugly at home would pay a trifle for all that! Shreve turned away. The merchants were not worried. The youngster had a big cargo of furs on his hands, he would be back in a while, begging to have them taken at any price.

He did not come back. It was the townsmen who got anxious, but the furs were beyond their grasp. Shreve had put them on wagons for Philadelphia. It didn't matter to him that western furs had always been laid down in Pittsburgh to be handled by middlemen. It would be done differently this time. Warnings of snow-piled mountain roads and swollen streams did not deter him. The wagons were loaded and sent.

Thus was established the first direct fur trade between the distant French village of St. Louis and the important port of Philadelphia.[33] There was much talk of it along the waterfronts. Henry Shreve profited handsomely from his sale of furs. Soon he was out on the Ohio again, bound for St. Louis and another cargo.

CHAPTER

Two

FOR three years Henry Shreve floated his boat down the Ohio, drove it up the Mississippi to St. Louis, and brought it back laden with furs for Philadelphia.[1] He did well enough at it, but it became monotonous. He wanted to cover new roads. He had, moreover, fallen in love with auburn-haired Mary Blair of Brownsville, and a man who aspired to marry Adam Blair's daughter would have to amount to something. Shreve determined to expand his trade and planned a new venture.

He set out again for Pittsburgh, where he bought an assorted cargo with great care to trade in the remote Indian lead mines in northern Illinois. 'Prior to that time the British had monopolized the traffic of the Upper Mississippi,'[2] but if Canadians could reach down to the Indian lead country, Shreve saw no reason that it should not be tapped from the south.

March winds were whipping the Ohio as he turned into it. He paused briefly at St. Louis, and on May 2, 1810, he sailed from there toward the north.[3] His crew of twelve had agreed to this trip, which would reach well outside of civilization, where Indians were said to be troublesome.

and the river itself beset with falls and rapids. The roar of the Missouri, belching its flood and drift-timbers, was frightening enough. The savage inpour drove the craft toward the Illinois shore.

With that torrent well behind, the boat moved along in a clear, mild stream. Oars could dip in rhythm, and the sail go up. On the right, presently, limestone bluffs reared two hundred feet, their summits level with the Illinois prairie. The reflection of the white cliffs and their fringe of pale green trees pierced the water, giving it a false depth. On the west spread the Missouri meadow. Wild duck raised a hubbub in the sloughs that cut this lowland; raccoons fished and washed their catch with worried care. Ruffed grouse, called pheasants in the middle country, peered from hiding-places. White sandhill cranes showed like a scatter of sheep in the distance.

The bluffs persisted on the east. Far up on the face of the limestone, some distance upstream from the village of Alton, appeared two dragon beasts painted by the Illini-weks. The monsters had faces somewhat like bearded men, deer antlers, scale-covered bodies, eagle wings, and dragon tails. Marquette had described them as so skill-fully drawn that 'Good painters in France would find it hard to do as well.' The red, green, and black pigment was fading, but it would outlive the dwindling Illinois tribe.

According to Indian legend, a monster, believed to be a giant bird, lived many thousand seasons before the white men came, while the mammoth still roamed the prairies. One that had its haunt near here would swoop down and carry off a deer in its talons. Once, however, it bore off a warrior to a neighboring cliff and devoured him, and, after that, would eat only human flesh, depopulating whole villages. At last a great chief, inspired by Manitou, gathered a band of braves, hunted down the monster, and shot volleys of poisoned arrows into it. There were many romantic variations of this legend, but the Illinois Indians stoutly maintained that such a winged reptile had actually once existed.[4]

The cliffs on the east bank vanished and appeared as by magic on the west — the river had meandered across its ancient bed to push against its other wall. Occasional Indians, darting along in their canoes, left off spearing fish to stare at the keelboat. A white man's boat from downstream was an uncommon sight. The trade of the Upper River Indians was with the British and French who came up the St. Lawrence, through the Great Lakes, and down the Ouisconsin to the Mississippi. The fish-spearing Indians along here were the Osaki, or 'people of the outlet' — called by the French, Sac — who had been driven from their old home at the mouth of the Ottawa River by the savage Iroquois. They had united with the Wagosh, or Fox, tribe and taken possession of most of the territory once occupied by the peaceful Illinois nation.

At night Shreve brought his boat into a cove or slough. At sunrise hunting had to be done to supply game;[5] then the voyage was resumed. The Upper Mississippi was a revelation to Shreve in spite of all he had heard of it. It wound, sparkling and clear, between steep hills that opened at intervals to show better the prairie that stretched flat from their tops. The hills were not true hills; they were the slope-sides of cuts made by glaciers or storming waters deep into the limestone foundation of the flat country. The prairie was a carpet of young grass and early flowers, dandelions, strawberry and other plants that blossomed close to the ground. Along the rivulets wild plums and crabapples were rose and white with bloom. The voyage savored of a holiday until the churning Des Moines rapids began tossing the boat.

Because the water was too low, the loaded craft could not be poled safely over the successive ledges of stone that crossed the river bed. The crew had to go overboard and tug with cables and bars. When the boat had been pulled into the boiling trough, it was paddled to the next reef. There were eleven miles of these rapids, alternate ledges and troughs; then a quiet stream lay ahead. Though the men were tired, there was the never-failing panacea, the customary round of whiskey after a straining piece of work. Complaints changed to boasts — not many *voyageurs* ever sailed the Upper River! It would be something to tell about in the taverns across the whole country. Nor would it dwindle in the telling.

For a while it was easy going, the sail up and gleaming in the spring sunlight. Rock River poured in from the right, and a short pull above it, an island of stone rose abruptly forty feet out of the water. Rock Island was one of only three or four islands in the Mississippi that were of the same stone formation as their banks. The top of the rock was capped by Fort Armstrong. For three miles the boat skirted the narrow island of stone and then began a tussle with the Rock River rapids.

These reefs were a singular formation, the ledges reaching out first from one shore and then the other, lapping well past each other in midstream.[6] Shreve wound the boat in and out the reefs, the water slapping its sides. Several ridges stretched entirely across the river. The wading and tugging began again, the air full of cries and

curses. There were eighteen miles of these upper rapids.
and then quiet water again.

The hills rose higher on either side. Green islands split
the stream into channels. An occasional Indian seen along
here was usually of the Fox tribe, dressed only in breech-
cloth and leggings, his upper body brightly painted and
his red-dyed horsehair headdress flicking in the breeze.
The Fox were warlike, alert, and, above all, avaricious.

Shreve kept near the east shore, and one day he turned
up the Galena, or Fever, River until he came in sight of an
Indian village. After fourteen days of sailing, poling, hunting food, and wading rapids, he had reached the lead mines
of the Sac and Fox Indians.[7]

At first the Indians were inhospitable. This boat of
Shreve's was unlike the white men's boats they were accustomed to seeing — *pirogues*, or Mackinaw boats with flat
bottoms and sides, pointed prow and square stern, or even
canoes. Shreve displayed his miscellaneous wares: likely
spades, hoes, chisels, crowbars, iron pots, tinware, ladles,
nails, rope, and sheet tin. Still the Indians held themselves aloof. These goods were worthy but not glamorous.
White men from the north brought gewgaws, rum and
whiskey.

There was little trading the first few days. A boat without liquor for sale was almost an affront. Shreve, undis-
couraged, made himself a guest of the Indians, fished,
hunted, and played games with them. One day in a foot-
race he came out ahead of their best runners.[8] They chal-
lenged him again and again. He won every race. The Indians were amazed. He was as fleet as Keokuk, as quick
of hand and eye. Had he met Keokuk along the river?
He was a Sac, eighteen harvests old, not a chief's son, yet

a leader. The sun favored him, the water was as his own blanket about him, the air lifted his feet from the ground. Thus also was the young white boatman — truly a white Indian.

A feast was prepared. Hoarded wild rice was brought out and added to the lean spring fare of game and fish; salt was swept up with turkey wings from the meager deposit left in the gullies by the last heavy rains. When the celebration was over, lead, which Shreve had found so scarce before, appeared from hiding-places. It was in the form of flat, irregular cakes.

The Indians had their own method of mining. They lifted the top soil off with hoes made of animal shoulder blades, then loosened the ore and hauled it out in baskets. Now they went at it with new tools, sledged the ore back to the village, and threw it on roaring fires. When the fires died down, the lead cakes were picked out of the ashes. It was customary for traders to fashion molds, melt the lead again in pots, and cast it in a convenient shape for stowage.[9]

The Indians mined, built fires and smelted until Shreve's boat had all it could carry. He built a flatboat and bought a Mackinaw boat that had come down from the Lake country, and loaded them. At last all his lead was stowed — sixty tons of it.[10]

With no upstream struggle, men could be spared from the keelboat to handle the other two. Shreve launched his triple cargo on a voyage down fifteen hundred miles of winding, surging river to New Orleans. It was a perilous trip even for men who knew the Lower River. But Shreve decided that it would be easier to float these heavy loads down the unfamiliar stream and ship them to an east-coast market by sea than to push and pull them up the Ohio. Besides, it was a new adventure.

Shreve took leave of his Indian friends on July first [11] and soon headed his boats into the Mississippi, though it seemed to him a pity to turn back south without seeing the river above here. Zebulon Pike had written that it offered 'a prospect so variegated and romantic that a man may scarcely expect to enjoy such a one but twice or thrice in the course of his life.' [12] The hills on the west at Prairie La Crosse were like 'distant clouds'; Lake Pepin, a sudden widening of the river for twenty-seven miles, had limestone cliff walls that rose four hundred feet, the water appearing black against them; the Falls of St. Anthony tossed up a mist of spray as they plunged down their stone terraces. But Shreve's business lay in the opposite direction. He was an adventurer, but not an idle one.

An easy run brought the lead boats to Rock River rapids, where the men picked a zigzag way between the reefs when they could. At times they waded, finding a channel with their exploring feet, and pulled the craft over ledges and shoals. The July daylight was long, the water tepid. It was not too bad, the boatmen shrugged. Their cursing meant nothing — a man was likely to swear when he did not sing or pray.

There was a long stretch of singing river before they came to another reach of cursing river at the lower rapids. In the clear air the hills had a sharp outline. The prairie grass was knee-high; larkspur and marigold, wild rose and prairie turnip, raised their faces above it. By autumn only the sunflower, smartweed, and such long-stalked flowers would be able to see over it.

When the heavy current of the incoming Missouri

caught the boats and hurried them along, Shreve had a foretaste of the long, dangerous trip ahead of him. He had to watch whirls and driftwood, shout warnings and orders. But 'his little flotilla reached St. Louis in twelve days — the commencement of the American trade on the Upper Mississippi.' [13]

It was midday when Shreve tied up at the St. Louis beach. No carts were rattling down steep Rue Bonhomme. Darkies lolled in the scant shade of boat prows. A few *patrons* waited under improvised deck awnings. Shreve climbed the deserted roadway and made for the new white log inn.[14] At this time of day the town merchants would be found backed to the huge cold fireplace of the inn's main hall, which served also as a dining-room. Traders from the lower ports, Kentuckians and the few Easterners, occupied places of less honor. Shreve sat where he could see and hear the most.

The commonest talk among the British-Americans was of the sorry plight of American overseas shipping. While England and France had been warring on each other, the neutral United States had darted in and acquired trade they had once enjoyed. Both had struck back at the audacious new merchant marine, and across it at each other. British orders in council declared an arbitrary blockade in the English Channel, forbidding neutral vessels to enter a French port without first paying a tax in an English port. Napoleon had come back with a paper blockade of all British ports and a decree confiscating every ship that submitted to the English tax and 'right of search.' Congress had put on a final adverse touch by prohibiting all vessels, American or foreign, from leaving the ports of the United States. American tempers had blown up at this prohibition, and it had been hastily replaced in the past year by the slightly less unpopular Non-Intercourse Act which forbade all trade with England and France.

Although Americans liked to boast that they had enough trade up and down their own streams, the whole Valley felt the stagnation at the New Orleans sea outlet. Loungers in the white log inn passed out blame with a free hand to England, to President Madison, and to Jefferson before him. But not to France — not in St. Louis. It would give trading a chill.

Shreve was keenly interested in all this, until politics was edged aside by a more sensational item: John Colter, who had gone West with Lewis and Clark and stayed behind, had finally got back to Missouri in May. Hardships must have unsettled his reason, for he insisted that he had discovered a region such as no white man had ever seen before. Fleeing from a band of Blackfeet Indians, he had come upon a canyon that defied all description, he claimed, its rugged sides a riot of colors. A river plunged down hundreds of feet to rush along its bottom. There were unbelievable yellow-stone formations, hot springs boiling out of the earth, geysers of water shooting high in the air — scenery so terrible or sublime that it had dumfounded him. He kept babbling his nightmare fancies, trying pathetically to get someone to believe him, poor fellow! (It was to be sixty years before John Colter's tale of the Yellowstone region — 'Colter's Hell,' as skeptics called it — was corroborated.)[15]

One thing that Colter had related was credible: there were beavers by the thousands in the Far-West streams. St. Louis gentlemen had little interest in American politics, but beavers — that was another matter. It brought them to life. A wealth of beavers! Had John Jacob Astor laid claim to them?

Only a month before John Jacob Astor had formed the Pacific Fur Company and planned to establish a fur-trading post on the west coast. There he would draw all the best pelts, and with the fleet of ships he proposed building, he would carry furs direct to China, an avid market. Until now St. Louis had been the fur center of the world. But Astor would change it all. He must rule. He was like that! Hands clutching jeweled snuffboxes gestured in despair. Astor — Astor — the name stood out like knobs in the sonorous French.

Then another topic caught the attention of the St. Louis gentlemen: Shreve, answering the usual questions put to a trader, had disclosed that he was not buying a cargo here. He had filled three boats with lead on the Galena River.

Lead from Fever River? That had always gone north before, someone protested. But things were changing — the Americans had dared set up an English school in St. Louis, as if the two French tutors had not always taught what was needed. Still, there were some good changes. A ferry had been established, a pair of *pirogues* with a plank on top of them. St. Louis had been raised from a village to a town last year. It was prospering; already the town treasurer had reported receipts of $529 and expenditures of $399.[16] As a port it had a great future, if Astor could be stopped. Lead from Galena — that was something to consider.

Shreve did not stay long in port. His boats were soon out on the river, swept along at a rate sometimes so perilous that they had to be held back with the oars. The current between St. Louis and the Ohio raced at four miles an hour, twice the speed of the Upper River. From the Missouri to the Balize, the Mississippi was a 'wild, furious, whirling stream.' [17]

Well below the mouth of the Ohio, New Madrid sat aloft on a horseshoe bend. This was the town that Israel Shreve and his associates had surveyed for Colonel Morgan, using a type of surveying so superior to that employed by the United States Government that James Madison, hearing of it, had written to President Washington about it. Later, Congress adopted the method in surveying all new territory.

Morgan, like other men before him, had dreamed of setting up an ideal colony in the wilderness. Its capital was to be the most beautiful city on the continent. The streets were to be sixty feet wide, with a fifteen-foot walk on either side. A park and highway were to border the river for miles; a tree-lined drive was to encircle the natural lake that had been selected as the center of the city. All mistakes that had been made in other colonies were to be corrected here. Morgan foresaw that the undisciplined habits of the settlers might, in time, exhaust the natural wealth of the country. Animals had been slaughtered in criminal prodigality, deer killed and only their hams taken — a wastefulness not practiced by the Indians; trees had been recklessly felled until every settlement was bare and unattractive. Such wanton destruction could not be tolerated in this Utopia. The rivers and landings at New Madrid were pronounced forever free. Churches of every creed would be fostered. There need be no taxes — men were to give spontaneously for the welfare of the community.

Morgan's expedition had set out in midwinter on the Ohio. Besides Israel Shreve, the party included Colonel Christopher Hays, Captain Hawling, David Rankin, John Hinkson, and many others. General Benjamin Harrison, of Kentucky, and his two sons joined the colony later. On Saint Valentine's Day in 1789, Morgan and his followers reached the appointed site and went zealously to work. But suddenly the whole idealistic scheme was brought to an end by Spanish interference.

The New Madrid site was in Upper Louisiana. Though James I of England had granted the colony of Virginia this ground and all other land in a four-hundred-mile strip from the east coast to the Pacific — wherever that legendary ocean might be — and later, to clinch the matter, Governor Spotswood of Virginia had gone, with a select company and 'an abundant variety of liquors,' to the summit of Blue Ridge, where he claimed the strip in the name of King George, drank the King's health copiously, and fired a volley, Spain still held the territory and ruled it through Governor Miro at New Orleans. Morgan had permission from the Spanish Minister in Washington to plant his colony at New Madrid, obviously with the consent of Governor Miro. But Miro was plotting secretly with the traitorous commander of the United States Army, smooth-talking General James Wilkinson, to dismember the Union. Wilkinson, who, like Burr, dreamed of setting up his own empire, had led Miro to believe that Kentucky and other areas of the West would be turned over to Spain. Morgan's American settlement on the Mississippi was a menace to the plotters because its citizens would see and hear too much. Wilkinson had Miro shut down on it. The colony's land was confiscated; Spanish troops were set over it; Morgan and his supporters scattered.[18]

Spanish New Madrid lived on and, in spite of backsets, prospered for a while. But now it was poor and shabby. The houses did not gleam with whitewash, the chapel was dilapidated. Local military officers had all they could do to look important in their cockades, faded plaid shirts, and any sort of trousers. The town felt neglected, never ceasing to regret the change from Spanish to American rule.

Below New Madrid the shores were low and of soapy-looking clay. Back of a fringe of willows rose the cotton-woods; beyond these, towered the sycamores. Long, narrow islands, one hundred and forty of them from St. Louis to New Orleans, inhabited only by birds, made green, clamorous lines on the opaque water. Drift-logs stacked at the heads of the islands. From the silt-filled crevices between the timbers grew willows and spindling shrubs. Fallen trees sprawled from crumbling banks into the stream.

At the bends, the steep, concave shores where the river bit into the land, the trees of large growth were undermined. Opposite each bend a point of low bank formed from which the water receded into the growing bite, the stream eating into one shore and deserting the other, changing its bed gradually so that now only a few hundred miles of the Lower River ran where the early French explorers had sailed.

These timber-filled bends and projecting points often left a cramped passage along snag-flanked islands. At Devil's Race-Ground, two days below New Madrid, the boats had to be inched through the snags, the half-naked men jabbing at the débris with the spiked poles. Halfway down Tennessee Territory, at Plum Point, Shreve found the channel even worse. Enormous trees reared in the passage, gutted wrecks of craft helped to choke it.[19] Only by the grace of Destiny could a boat creep through undamaged. The nation's main road was in a wretched state.

Shreve led his boats cautiously down the winding river under the glaring July sun; at dark he tied them up at a sheltered bank. Nights were sultry. Frogs and insects kept up a medley. The shore forest was in deep gloom even when the river was white with moonlight. Tired as the *patron* was at the end of a day, he had to stand watch or sleep with his hand on his rifle, for panthers prowled the woods, and hostile Indians often attacked sleeping crews. It was usually in the dead of night that the severe electrical storms, so common on the Mississippi, lashed furiously down the river. Lightning slit the dark, the wind drove the boats against the shore, and through the din of thunder sounded the crash of trees toppling from the banks of the nearest bend.

Now and then a flotilla of flatboats, traveling together for safety or company, would catch up with Shreve's fleet. There was a mingling of shouts, bellows, squeals, and barks. Men visited from boat to boat, bragging, gaming, and fighting. A swarm of craft made for crowding at the narrow channels; the crew got too little sleep. Shreve would let his lead fleet fall behind.

Six hundred miles from St. Louis, Shreve's boats filed past the Arkansas River where De Soto first came upon the Mississippi. Earlier explorers had called the great river Espiritu Santo (Holy Spirit); De Soto named it Rio Grande. The French boat-hands still used the Indian name, Meche-sebe. In an unmarked grave there on the

Arkansas shore, Pierre de Laclède Ligueste, founder of St. Louis, was buried, having died of fever on his way back from New Orleans thirty-two years before. His city had not yet fulfilled his hopes. The driving current of the Mississippi and the half-submerged dead forests — not John Jacob Astor — had kept the world from its door.

As the lead boats floated southward, the late July days were stifling. Miles of dense cane grew a short distance back from the low banks, its stalks so close together that a bird could hardly fly under the green roof of narrow leaves. Bear and panther could break a path in the cane, and Indians crept in and out these trails. Gnarled swamp cypresses, gray long moss hung from the branches, stood among the water-edge reeds, raising hollow roots, or 'knees,' in wide clusters about their trunks. Streamers of moss had caught from tree to tree, spreading a drab canopy. Heaped against the shores or rearing in the channel were dead drift-trees, overgrown with weeds and vines. Dully the alligators rose beside the driftwood, to view the boats and sink.

Nine hundred miles below the little town of St. Louis, Shreve reached the large town of Natchez, in the Territory of Mississippi, carved three years ago, along with Alabama and Georgia, out of the immense Territory of Georgia. Georgia had been developed as an English colony, but Natchez was predominantly French.[20] The town lay along the crest of a bluff that rose two hundred feet above a low, narrow bank which furnished a waterfront. This low bank was kept lively by dice games, giddily dressed women, and performing Indians. Many boats lined the bank. The river was only a mile wide here, but a hundred feet deep. Below Natchez the current was slower, so that it was no great task to bring cargoes up the three hundred miles from New Orleans. Trade between the two ports was brisk.

Shreve climbed the road to the town. He found Natchez prosperous but simple. No show here of luxury or formality, as in St. Louis, though the atmosphere was gay and light. French, Spanish, British-Americans, and negroes mingled in the streets. Men were not too serious over their trading to turn from it at any moment for a game of chance or a flirtation. The women, piquant but plainly dressed, were as care-free as moths. Few boat-hands were to be seen; the waterfront diversions caught most of them the minute they stepped ashore.

Carts loaded with fruit, crated fowl, or early cotton wound in from the plantations. Choctaw and Muskogee Indians strolled about, playing musical instruments made of cane, and hoping for gifts of rum or tobacco. The Natchez Indians, with a culture much like that of the Aztecs, once lived about here. Eighty years ago, maddened by a white man's treachery, they had attacked the town, and in the war that followed, this proud, sun-worshiping tribe was nearly exterminated.

When Shreve set out again with his boats, he found that, although the Mississippi was quieter below Natchez,[21] sand shoals and driftwood still bedeviled navigation. The slow going irked him. He felt vaguely that something should be done to make river travel faster. It was not easy for him to accept anything as inevitable.

Two days' floating brought the lead boats past the north boundary of the Spanish province of West Florida. Only the width of the Territory of Orleans, or Lower Louisiana, separated West Florida from the large Spanish province of Texas. Below this the river made one of its wide détours, a circle of fifty miles that returned to within six miles of where it started. The Mississippi was living up to its reputation of being the crookedest long river in the world.[22]

Shreve kept a curious lookout for Rivière Rouge, or Red River, for he had heard that it was blocked by a mat of ancient driftwood for more than a hundred miles. This barrier, called the Great Raft, was so solid in places that a man could ride across it on horseback.[23] Except for the Raft, Red River of the South would be navigable for a thousand miles, a highway for a valuable Mexican trade. But when he reached the stream, Shreve found it open as far as he could see, though its brick-colored water crept along sluggishly. The Raft, it seemed, did not begin for several days' paddling upstream.

Below Red River a succession of large sugar plantations, swarming with negro slaves, lined the shores. Sugar-cane had been introduced from Europe into Santo Domingo two years after Columbus discovered the western world. It soon spread to the continent, being grown mainly for the manufacture of rum and molasses. Only fourteen years before, in 1796, Etienne Boré,[24] who had left Kaskaskia when it became too American, and settled in New Orleans, had discovered a process for granulating sugar. The new granulated sugar proved immensely popular and began to replace the maple sugar of the North. Sugar-cane was improved and a golden industry had sprung up.

Two hundred miles below Natchez, Shreve's fleet passed Baton Rouge, a Spanish military post on the West Florida shore.[25] The town had been founded by the French, and named for a bark-stripped tree on whose red wood the In-

dians had painted a fish and a bear to indicate the boundary between two tribes. It was a town of a hundred poor
cabins on a street that lay between the river and a hill.
But the Spanish had established good forts and an arsenal
here, the very ones that Aaron Burr had promised his
American adherents he would seize for them as a supply
base for their attack on Mexico. (He had told his Spanish
conspirators quite a different story.)

South of Baton Rouge were occasional isolated settlements of Acadians who had drifted here when they were
driven out of Nova Scotia by the British in 1755. The
Acadians' houses were thatched with palmetto leaves and
set high on stumps for coolness. Underneath them, pigs
and chickens disputed the best dust wallows. Long moss,
pulled from the trees, lay drying on shed roofs. Later it
would be whipped into shreds and sold for filling mattresses.
The Acadian women, robust and sweet-faced, stripped to
the waist, barefooted and with only a petticoat about
them, worked in the corn or tobacco fields. From their
tobacco the Acadians manufactured *perique*, famous for
its excellent flavor. No one but Acadians knew how
perique was made; they guarded the secret jealously,
handing it down in families from one generation to another.[26]

The Mississippi was narrower here than it was above the
mouth of the Missouri and was well over a hundred feet
deep. Shreve, drawing to the end of his long voyage, had
to control his restless crew with a stern hand. When they
sighted New Orleans down the brassy river, they shouted
hilariously and sang and winded the horn.

New Orleans lay on the edge of a low, narrow waist of
ground between the Mississippi and thirty-five-mile-long

Lake Pontchartrain. On the whole continent there was
not another site that equaled this for a trade center. To
the north stretched the Mississippi for fifteen hundred
miles; the Missouri reached from the Mississippi twenty-
five hundred miles into the west and northwest; the Ohio
and its branches pierced a thousand miles into the northeast; the Arkansas and Red Rivers tapped the far southwest; Lake Pontchartrain flung a strand of bayous and
smaller lakes deep into the Indians' wilderness; and three
Mississippi delta arms led to the Gulf and the seas of the
world.

La Salle had selected this very place a century and a
quarter earlier for a colony he proposed to establish for his
king, Louis XIV. With four ships bearing men and supplies he sailed from France, in 1684, toward the mouth of
the Mississippi. But his navigators passed the Mississippi
without finding it. The expedition was stranded on the
Texas coast. Two years later, La Salle and a small party
set out afoot in search of the Meche-sebe (which he had
named Rivière Colbert). Hardships and La Salle's rigid
discipline made the men mutinous and quarrelsome.
When he interfered in a petty wrangle that began between
some of the men over a buffalo marrow-bone, one of them
shot him.[27]

In 1717, a Scotch gambler and economic theorist, John
Law, who had managed to become the financial director of
France under the child-king, Louis XV, decided that distant Louisiana was ripe for exploit. Peering shrewdly from
under the curls of his blond wig, he went about organizing
the *Compagnie d'Occident*, backing it with the *Banque
Générale*, which he controlled. In order to lure emigrants
to his projected New World colony, he advertised that

Louisiana's streams glinted with gold and some of its wild-
flowers produced diamonds from the moisture in their cups.
Gold and diamonds said to have been picked up in Louisiana were displayed in shop windows. Having created himself Duke of Arkansas, Law ordered Sieur de Bienville,
Governor of Louisiana, to search the Lower Mississippi
country for the most advantageous site for a capital.[28] It
is not surprising that Bienville chose the same place that
La Salle had selected, a site commanding the waterways
of half a continent, yet open to the sea. Here a few rows of
cabins were put up for the adventurers who flocked to
Law's ships and the poor souls transported against their
wishes. Fantastic stories about the prosperity of this
colony were published by Law in the French newspapers.
Men all over France speculated in stock of the *Compagnie*,
pushing the price of a share to 20,000 *livres*. Mobs fought
in the streets of Paris to get near the *Banque* before a new
stock issue was snapped up. Then in 1720, the bubble col-
lapsed. The *Compagnie* was bankrupt. France was impov-
erished. At New Orleans a handful of disillusioned settlers, preyed upon by fever and homesickness, clung to
their strip of ground in a wilderness of water. Inevitably
boats on the rivers west of the Alleghanies floated their
cargoes to New Orleans. The disheartened village in the
Far South came to be one of the most important ports in
the world, with a population of seventeen thousand.

Vessels of all kinds outlined the crescent bank — boats
from the inland waters along the upper half of town,
ships from the seven seas along the lower part. The waterfront droned with leisurely activity, cargoes loading and
unloading. White men ordered the negroes slouching
along in rhythm as they carried their burdens ashore or
aboard.

Shreve left his fleet with his restless men and set off
down the bank to the ocean ships. He walked around
groups of half-naked brown Portuguese in shrill argument. Blond Dutch and Swedes, West Indies Frenchmen,
urbane Kentuckians, a few unmistakable Easterners, and
elegant New Orleans merchants bargained in a medley of
tongues. Piles of stuff moved past him on high-wheeled
carts toward stores and warehouses, while barrows of
goods trundled by to loading craft. Sacks of coffee, waiting on the beach, propped against rum barrels; cans of
tallow and bear's oil near partly opened bales of silk; lumber, fruit, indigo, hides, ore, sugar, wine, cotton, china,
French shoes, and New England linen were moved to and
fro.

Shreve found a ship bound for Philadelphia and had his
cargo paddled to it. He would go aboard himself the
morning after loading was completed. Trips to the Gulf
were not begun late in the day, for it was hard to pick
the way down a delta arm after dark.

Having promised his boats to one of the junk dealers
who haunted the waterfront, he turned to the town. Between the beach and the town was the Levee, an earthen
embankment that ran for miles along the river. The sun
dropped low and the usual evening promenaders began to
saunter along the top of the Levee. Young gentlemen,
French belles, *grandes dames*, priests, roués, beautiful
quadroons and octoroons mingled democratically as they
enjoyed the river breeze. In the shadows of the orange
trees lurked the mothers of the dark beauties, ready to
seal 'engagements' of their daughters to white lovers.
Such affairs were arranged decorously. These dusky ladies
of love were rigidly respectable — that is, faithful to one

lover as long as the contract of a month or a year was in force. Fickleness would outlaw one from her caste. To the young Quaker it was novel to see such easy comradery of gallant, lady, libertine, and *fille de joie*.

New Orleans [29] looked different from other French towns on the Mississippi. The houses, set on high pillars, were of wood or brick plastered with white mortar. They were surrounded by galleries and decorated with a profusion of ornamental woodwork. Fig and orange trees that showed above the walls were not tall enough to shade the houses. The streets, unpaved, were separated from the footpaths or board walks by drainage ditches. Demoiselles, closely chaperoned, talked from their balconies to admirers in the street below. Ladies of the gentry set forth in small one-horse carriages for the customary evening drive. They were attended by female slaves, but handled the reins themselves. These New Orleans women were pale, dark-eyed, their smooth hair covered with draped lace veils.

Up the narrow streets from the river rolled the high-wheeled carts. Their squeaks were a shrill bedlam above all other sounds. New Orleans was used to this noise and did nothing about it. Under the late Spanish rule, when the delta had been infested with smugglers and pirates, carts were ordered to squeak so they could not be used in smuggling. Even now Jean Lafitte, once a town blacksmith, and his brother, Pierre, had a large band of pirates on the Gulf west of the delta, setting the whole country agog with their exploits.

Shreve turned to the Market, a large picturesque building with high-pillared arcades, crowded in this first cool hour after a torrid day. Peddlers, most of them Catalans, were filling their packs for journeys inland. Nuns from the Ursuline convent bargained placidly at the food stalls; tanned sailors pushed about, gabbling in alien jargons. American soldiers, boat-hands, aloof Spaniards from the vanished régime, French *habitants*, and negroes bought and sold.

Shreve sauntered on past the billiard rooms so typical of French towns. At this twilight hour there was more church-going than gaming, for a steady stream of worshipers turned in at a near-by chapel as the bells rang out the Angelus. The churches were all Catholic and French. The Americans, as Valley Frenchmen distinguished the settlers of British blood from themselves, had no churches. When the Atlantic coast settlers drifted into the mid-Valley, the imported honeybee winged ahead of them and the buffalo fled before them, but the church lagged well behind. The French had put up their places of worship as inevitably as they built shelters for their families. The British, although of pious stock, did one thing at a time when they came West — they would conquer the wilderness first and then burnish up their souls when they had time to spare.

Lights came on in the town. The carts had vanished to give place to the carriages. At night New Orleans was more like a European capital than a New World port.

A few days later Shreve and his lead cargo passed down the Balize delta arm and out to sea. The dull waters of the river reached far out into the blue Gulf after the ship. The pirates of Barataria did not molest the craft, never dreaming what a wealth of potential bullets lay in its hold.

To a *patron*, used to the hazardous trips on the inland

rivers, this was a mild voyage. Even squalls off Cape Hatteras were tame compared to the fierce storms that raged down the Mississippi. There might be dangerous hours at sea, but there was seldom a safe hour on the Valley streams.

It was autumn when the little ship put in at Philadelphia. Shreve found a ready market for lead and cleared eleven thousand dollars on his sale.[30] He had had an adventurous journey up and down the Mississippi, an ocean voyage, and had built up the capital he needed. More than that, he had opened to Americans the Upper Mississippi trade, heretofore monopolized by the British.[31] The young Quaker *patron*, who had established the direct fur business between St. Louis and Philadelphia, had now instituted a lead traffic from the remote Galena River to New Orleans.

When Shreve had outfitted himself in Philadelphia, with worldly, un-Quakerish clothes, he went by stage to Brownsville. Here he set earnestly about two things: the building of a new boat and the courting of a wife.

CHAPTER
Three

AS HE floated his cargoes of lead down the Mississippi, Henry Shreve had planned the kind of boat he would build when he reached home. It would be a handsome barge with nearly three times the capacity of his keelboat. In the evenings, while his men played or wrangled in the light of a campfire, Shreve had dreamed of the woman he wanted to marry — pretty nineteen-year-old Mary Blair.

Perhaps the Blairs, although Quakers, like the Shreves, would be aloof. Adam Blair never forgot that his family history reached back for centuries in Scotland and Ulster.[1] Mary was proud and spirited. She was fastidious. Her gray dresses and white neckerchiefs were quietly rich. Shreve thought of himself simply as a river man, one of an enigmatic class of Valley adventurers, but he had made up his mind to win Mary Blair.

Word passed around Brownsville that young Henry Shreve was back. He had not been lost on the dangerous streams, as had been feared but had instead been on the Upper Mississippi, far north of St. Louis, helping himself to some of the trade heretofore monopolized by the British.

Adam Blair thought well of this venture. He had always approved of the Shreves, descended as they were from Sir William Shreve, of the Isle of Wight, whose wife was from the powerful Fairfax family in England. There was the blood of two Holland merchant princes in their veins, too.[2] All this carried weight with Adam Blair. A young man with such a background would likely be practical and courageous. When Henry Shreve called at the substantial Blair home, he found a ready welcome.

Mary sat the width of the broad fireplace from him, properly demure. Her feet were decorously close together, hands clasped in her lap. The candlelight burnished her auburn hair. Shreve, in spite of his sophisticated long-skirted coat, brocaded waistcoat, and pantaloons, had the bronzed, muscular look of an outdoor man and the peculiar grace of an adventurous one. His hair, shorter than the Quaker round cut, was sunburned and unruly. He never talked long about anything but the rivers. Mary watched him intently as he told of the plunging Mississippi, its wilderness shores and widely separated ports. It was not altogether the candleglow that warmed her eyes.

Shreve's courtship was earnest and persistent, even though the building of a new boat occupied half his mind. On the last day of February, 1811, he and Mary Blair were married.

Late in the spring, Henry Shreve sailed from Browns-ville in his new boat, ninety-five tons burden,[3] bound for New Orleans, not for Galena. This barge was too heavy to pull over the rapids, and by then the St. Louis men would have swarmed to the Galena trade. There had been some talk of Mary's going with him, but that had been abandoned. Nicholas Roosevelt, of New York, had taken his bride to New Orleans the year before on a flatboat and returned by sea. But Shreve would have to bring his barge back up the rivers; it would take months to do it, even with an upstream crew of forty men. Mary was to give birth to a child late in November — there would be little more than time for Shreve to make the trip and get back before then.

The sailing day was a proud one and a sad one. When the men paddled the barge to midstream, the sail, though not needed, was run up — it made a pretty sight, rounding in the breeze. Shreve's friends stood on the shore to see him off, the wind whipping the women's full skirts and the broad hats waved by the men. But there was Mary, her face white against her red hair. It would be six months before Shreve saw her again, if ever. When a man started a long trip on the Mississippi, there was one chance in three that he would not come back.

Even before the town faded, Shreve had to give his whole attention to steering. His elation over the new barge, one of the river's largest boats, was tempered by his awareness that these journeys kept a man too long away from his family; they cost too much toil. Yet he could not imagine any other way of life for himself except plying the water-roads, though the torturing labor it took to bring a loaded boat up the rivers grew more appalling to him each time he witnessed it. There ought to be a better way to bring cargoes upstream than by racking men's bodies.

There were, of course, a few steam vessels on the eastern waterways, but those streams were quiet and safe compared to the inland rivers. Nicholas Roosevelt had made soundings last year of the Ohio and Mississippi and was collaborating now with Robert Fulton on a steamboat for the Mississippi.[4] If this steamboat could run upstream against the powerful Mississippi current, the hardships of western travel and transportation would soon be over.

Shreve had long been interested in the problem of steam navigation and had read every account of its development that he could find. For more than a century men had tried to invent steamships. Their experiments had brought down upon them ridicule and persecution, for never had there come out of the human mind a more fantastic notion than that boats could be navigated by fire. Men had always moved about on the water by means of oars, poles, or sails, insisted the all-wise public, and thus they always would move on the water. A few determined inventors, nevertheless, had succeeded in propelling vessels by fire, and the most outraged head-waggers could not foresee where it would end.

Most fanatical of the steamboat experimenters in America had been John Fitch, a weak-framed, ill-nourished fellow who trudged from door to door, cleaning and mending clocks. He had earned a scant living at his trade, slept along roadsides, and nursed his dreams of steam-driven boats. Henry Shreve's father, Israel Shreve, had watched John Fitch's struggles sympathetically. Fitch had spent the cold winter at Valley Forge repairing firearms. He was mild and simple, insignificant in appearance, timid of speech, but profoundly original.

Fitch had been fascinated with accounts of the steam engine that Thomas Newcomen, a blacksmith of Dartmouth, England, had invented, and John Smeaton, of Leeds, had improved. James Watt, repairer of apparatus at the

University of Glasgow, had taken the engine and made it economical and practical. Fitch thought that some such engine might be made to propel a boat. In 1786 he had produced a steamboat with paddles, a clumsy thing built in a blacksmith's shop of whatever materials he could collect. It was tried out on the Delaware and actually worked, though feebly. Five years later he had built a steamboat that ran from Philadelphia to Burlington, New Jersey, a distance of *twenty miles*. After that he constructed one that plied regularly as a freight and passenger vessel on the Delaware. Advertisements in a Philadelphia paper called this vessel simply 'The Steamboat,' for it was likely the only steamboat on earth.

Fitch had begged financial aid from Congress, from state legislatures, scientists, and capitalists, so that he might build a steamboat that was not patched together of odds and ends, but he could get no help. Finally he formed a small company that paid his way to France, where he hoped to arouse some interest in his experiments. He failed in this and had to work his passage home, leaving his designs and descriptions with the United States Consul-General in France, Mr. Vail. Vail had later handed the material to a young American artist, Robert Fulton, who visited him. Fulton kept the drawings several months.

John Fitch was penniless now, but persistent. He built another steamboat out of an old yawl. It was driven by a screw propeller and steered with an oar. The boiler was a ten-gallon iron pot covered with a thick plank which was fastened down by an iron bar; the cylinders were wooden and strongly hooped. When Fitch tried out this boat on the Collect Pond at New York City, he was elated to have as a passenger the wealthy Robert Livingston, Chancellor of New York, who was greatly interested in the possibility of driving boats by steam.

The vessel made several trips around the pond. Spectators ashore laughed uproariously. Mr. Livingston was polite, but he made no offer to help the inventor. Nothing came to John Fitch from this successful test except ridicule. He drifted to Kentucky, took new hope and built a three-foot steamboat model with paddle-wheels. He ran this on a stream at Bardstown. Onlookers were amazed — and amused. Fitch felt beaten and sick. He saved the opium pills given to him from time to time by his doctor to make him sleep, and when he had a dozen, swallowed them in a Bardstown tavern and washed them down with whiskey.[5]

That had been twelve years before, but people still talked of Fitch around their firesides, and of men before him who had tried to propel boats by steam. In the seventeenth century there had been an inmate of a Paris madhouse who called through the bars of his cell to passers-by in the streets, protesting that he was not insane, but had made a valuable discovery: ships could be driven by steam. He had come from Normandy to present his findings to his king, Louis XIII. Underlings had repeatedly ordered him away from the palace gates and at last had him confined. Lord Worcester, of England, happening to pass the madhouse, heard the man's pleas and determined to visit him. When he had worked through the red tape of petty officialdom and got a permit to visit the asylum, so much time had elapsed that the imprisoned man was indeed mad. Worcester declared hotly that short-sighted dolts had stricken the greatest genius of the age.

There had been others: Dennis Papin of France had invented a steamboat and run it on the Fulda in Germany in 1707. The vessel was so derided that he tried to flee the country in it, but boatmen had attacked and demolished it. Thirty years afterward, Jonathan Hulls, of Campden, England, designed a steamboat, then escaped the laughter of his townsmen and hid in London to starve. Urchins in Campden still sang a jeering doggerel about him. In 1802, William Symington, in Great Britain, built a steam vessel and used it as a tug. Two years later, Robert Fulton visited Symington and took a trip in his vessel on the Forth and the Clyde Canal.

In America, James Rumsey, a Maryland bath-tender, constructed a steamboat and plied it with some success on the Potomac; he went to England, built a steamboat there, but died before it won any substantial notice. One of his letters home mentioned frequent visits to him from a young American in England, Robert Fulton, who had quizzed him minutely about his designs. Elijah Ormsbee, a New England carpenter, borrowed a longboat and a copper still and fashioned a steamer that was paddled by mechanical goose-feet. He made several river trips in it, but attracted no capital and returned the still and the longboat to their owners. Nathan Read, of Massachusetts, built a boat model with paddle-wheels driven by a high-pressure engine. Samuel Morey, of Connecticut, constructed a steamboat with a stern wheel and sailed it from Hartford to New York City, with Chancellor Livingston aboard. Soon after that, Fulton visited Morey, studied his boat models, then began designing his own steamboat, the *Clermont*. Morey never recovered from Fulton's perfidy.

Colonel John Stevens, of New Jersey, was another

steamboat inventor. And there was Nicholas Roosevelt, who, in partnership with Chancellor Livingston, had built a steamboat in 1798 and run it successfully. Oliver Evans made an engine in Philadelphia and a boat in Kentucky and floated them to New Orleans to assemble for the Natchez trade; a hurricane destroyed the boat, and the engine was set to work in a sawmill. Fitch, Rumsey, Read, and Stevens were the first to take out American patents, but little came of their efforts.[6]

When Fulton began to build the *Clermont*, he procured a Watt-Boulton engine from England and adapted it to the propelling and steering devices that he had culled from various inventors. Robert Fulton was an attractive man, with dark curling hair and appealing eyes, an artist and sophisticate with a talent for making influential friends. Observant rather than inventive, he made the *Clermont* only of parts that others had originated, but he used these parts more impressively than the others had. He was accustomed to pleasing the eye, to playing up to a public. When his steamboat sailed on its trial trip from New York to Albany in August of 1807, it was no shabby, makeshift thing, but a handsome vessel, shaped like an ocean ship and decently painted. It had been financed generously by Chancellor Livingston. The *Clermont* was a hundred and thirty feet long, its uncovered paddle-wheels each had twelve huge blades, the smokestack rose majestically thirty feet above the deck. And, quite practically, the steamer had two masts and large sensible sails. It was convincing.

Without the help of its sails the *Clermont* had made only five miles an hour up the tranquil Hudson. The rumble of its engine was awful to hear. Its machinery had to be patched every mile. But it had such a proud look as it started off in a wide flourish that the laughter of the spectators turned to awe. Fulton had lent taste and dignity to the madness of propelling boats by fire. That was his great service to steam navigation.

The Livingston-Fulton Company secured from the New York legislature an exclusive right to run steamboats in the waters of the state, driving out the boats of other builders and discouraging invention. The Fulton boats became a common sight on the Hudson. But Robert Fulton still had only a faint vision of the possibilities of steam in navigation. In January of this very year, 1811, he had written to an inventor, Doctor Thornton, 'I do not see by what means a boat containing one hundred tons of merchandise can be driven *six* miles an hour in still water. . . .' He declared that he would give Thornton a hundred and fifty thousand dollars for the patent on a boat that could perform such a stupendous feat.

In spite of his pessimism, Fulton, in collaboration with Nicholas Roosevelt, was building a steamboat to run on the Mississippi. It would soon sail for New Orleans. If it could run back upstream to the Ohio, it would revolutionize inland navigation.

As Shreve walked the cabin top like a restless cat, he visioned a day when he would command a steamboat so powerful that it would stem the heaviest current. Just now he had to be satisfied with a strong barge and a sinewy crew. At Louisville he was greatly interested in the rumor that a Fulton steamer was coming to the West. When fast boats began to bring cargo up the Mississippi, Louisville would become a great port, its citizens boasted, a key port to the whole country, north, east, south, and west.

'JOLLY FLATBOATMEN'

From the painting by George Caleb Bingham
Reproduced with the permission of the St. Louis
Mercantile Library Association

Shreve's barge passed over the Falls amidst the usual shrieks and curses of the boat-hands and floated on between greening hills to the chalky Mississippi. A Fulton steamboat was coming to conquer this raging stream, Shreve exulted as he walked his strip of deck. Other steam vessels would follow, and this middle country would become the richest and best place on earth.

Summer glided out of the south and met the New Orleans-bound barge. Magnolia perfume filled the air, mockingbirds poured out their songs after dusk, and the great black bat was a fluttering blot in the night. A flock of the vanishing native swans that rode the river reminded the boat-hands of an eccentric fellow who had a small store at Henderson, Kentucky. Instead of minding his store, he was always wandering about the country painting pictures of birds. He was a French Creole, born in Santo Domingo, and looked sensible enough, but he could go on like a child over the swans as they floated on the river, dipping their black bills in the water. It was too bad! His name was Jean Jacques Audubon.[7] Had the *patron* heard of him?

The *patron* had, but he was thinking of a steamboat breasting the Mississippi. If one steamer could come up the river, others could — flotillas of them, graceful as swans. The day seemed very near.

The river at New Orleans was like molten glass. Heat quivered above the busy waterfront. Shreve sold his cargo, stowed a new one, and turned the heavily laden barge northward. The crew, disconsolate at leaving port, was soon diverted with breaking in the new men who had been taken on for the upstream pull. The evenings resounded with bragging and fights — the boat-hands were getting acquainted in the customary way.

Shreve and his crew sailed and rowed, poled and bush-whacked. Where the current was heaviest, the men had to walk the bank with the *cordelle* over their shoulders. If the bank was too rugged or swampy, they 'warped' the boat along. Two cables were used in warping, one end of each left aboard and the other ends carried ahead by two yawls. The rope in one yawl was tied to a tree or snag far ahead; then the men on the barge pulled on the rope, drawing the craft forward. By the time that cable length was exhausted, the second rope had been fastened about a tree still farther on. Even with a crew of forty, it was grueling work to make headway against the current.

The days were hot and glaring. At night a brilliant comet moved across the sky, giving an eerie light. The head of the comet was like an orange star with a halo of green; its long tail swept in an angle toward the horizon. The boat-hands had been awed by it on their downstream trip; now they were worried. Strange bodies in the sky were portents of disaster; the Indians were uneasy over this thing.[8] But weeks went by with no especial misfortune, and one autumn day the barge passed the Falls and reached Louisville.

Moored to the Louisville bank was a steamboat, the *New Orleans*, that Fulton had built for the Mississippi. The high-sided hull was painted sky-blue; the long bow-sprit was like that of a schooner. It had portholes and two cabins, one fore and one aft, in the seven-foot hold. The smokestack and two masts, rearing above it, gave the steamer an imposing look against the flat hand-boats around it. The *New Orleans* had left Pittsburgh on October 20, and reached here four days later. It would have to wait for a freshet to lift it over the Falls, for, in spite of

Nicholas Roosevelt's careful soundings of the shallow Mississippi, Fulton had designed this boat on the familiar lines of an ocean ship.[9] Shreve, knowing the Mississippi as he did, felt some qualms about the *New Orleans*. Anyway, steam had come to the Valley.

There was much excitement in the town over the steamboat's arrival. It had come after nightfall and awakened everyone with its terrific chugs. Half the populace had run into the streets. The sky was full of smoke and sparks. It was thought that the comet had fallen into the river.

Rash men who dared near the bank made out the boat's hull, its vitals still roaring. They had expected a steamboat, but who could have thought it would be like this? The town folk gave a complimentary dinner for Mr. Roosevelt and he gave a dinner aboard his boat. Louisville looked forward to a greater day when the steamer should arrive here from New Orleans.

Shreve hurried his trading and pushed on up the Ohio, in haste to get home. The weather was chill. Birds winged in long triangles southward. At this time there occurred a peculiar animal migration: a horde of squirrels, moved by some common impulse, pressed forward from Indiana over a wide front, poured into the river, swimming, clutching at driftwood. Some reached the other shore, but thousands of lifeless little bodies floated downstream. The boathands were grave over it, for they connected it with the comet. Something was wrong, they insisted; something tragic was going to happen.[10]

But Shreve's voyage finished safely. He sold most of his cargo at Pittsburgh and sailed on up the Monongahela. He had beaten a river freeze and would not be going out again for a while.

The home-coming of a bargeman was a town event. He had actually survived the river perils, and he brought news from every port. The country was so large and varied that its people could get a grasp of the whole only by piecing fragments of news together. To a tired and anxious bargeman home was an interlude of comfort and safety. To his family, his return was a reprieve from on high. Mary Shreve, only twenty years old, showed the somber fear that haunted the eyes of women whose men sailed the Valley streams.

On the twenty-eighth of November, at the time that custom had set aside for a general thanksgiving, Mary Shreve gave birth to a daughter. Half the terrace folk came in to see the baby, for the young father had come to be the town's most vivid figure. He owned one of the largest boats in the Valley; he was daring and original, and had a way of doing things *first*, for others to follow. His lean, sinewy body and abrupt motions gave a hint of his strength and driving energy. The little he said was so fundamental that older men pondered it, wondering what he might do next. Just now, however, he seemed to be concerned about nothing but his bright-haired wife and infant daughter, Mary.[11]

Midwinter set in. Ice stilled the little streams and crept down the rivers. Snow covered the hills. Through the day Shreve busied himself with his river findings — endless observations of currents, shores, and channels to be worked into new charts. In the evening he liked to sit before the fire and talk in blunt, disconnected sentences about his last voyage.

He described days of floating through a canyon of pale green forests, sweltering weeks with the heat beating back from the opaque water, the green-gray light in the swamps where the sun shone through vines and moss festooned from tree to tree. He told of the steamboat's waiting at Louisville, of the glow of the comet on the river, of the willows bending as if to study their reflections in the unusual light. He smiled over the superstitions of his men. They had believed that the comet and the squirrel migration were signs of coming disaster, and later they had decided to include the steamboat among the evil portents. They were so convinced that something terrible was going to happen that their fights and swearing almost ceased.

In January the news reached Brownsville that something terrible had happened. On December 16, a severe earthquake, centering at New Madrid in the Missouri country, had rocked the mid-Valley. Shock followed shock, the ground rose and sank in sickening waves, the earth opened fissures a half-mile long, sulphurous gases poured out, geysers of mud and water shot into the air. When the fissures closed, they had swallowed fields, houses, woods. The ground shuddered in billows, hills sank, the river rushed in and formed deep lakes. Islands dropped from sight, boats and crews were sucked up. Now treeless ridges stood where once there had been streams; fish and turtles swam in and out of submerged canebrakes and inland trees. The shocks still recurred at intervals, but were less violent.[12]

Shreve's mind leaped to the steamboat — what had become of it and of earnest, kindly Nicholas Roosevelt? He went to the wharves to question boatmen who had ventured home up the ice-crowded channels.

The steamboat? Nothing had happened to that cursed thing, boat-hands replied. Just before the earthquake a flood had lifted it over the Falls with only five inches to spare. It had turned down the Mississippi, slapping and snarling. Dozens of worthy flatboats, keels, and barges had gone down with their men, but that devil's-craft was not touched. The Indians said it was the beating of its paddle-wheels that had roused the earth to fury. Who knew? Nothing like this had ever racked the Valley before.

When later reports came in, the disaster loomed even greater. The tremors still went on. It was said that this was the most severe earthquake of non-volcanic origin of which any record existed.

Nicholas Roosevelt and the *New Orleans*, having escaped the havoc that lay all about them, went on their way,[13] reaching New Orleans on January 10, 1812.

Spring opened. Shreve manned his barge and headed it for the Mississippi. At each port he inquired whether the *New Orleans* had returned upriver to Louisville, for on such a voyage depended a new era for the Valley. There was no news of the steamboat. All that anyone talked about was the likelihood of war with England, into which the Government seemed to be drifting headlong. With England and France so far away, how had the United States become embroiled in their quarrel with each other? Americans had believed that they were well through with Europe.

Shreve, always thinking of river traffic, foresaw that if war came, a steamboat able to come up the Mississippi would be of great value in the country's transportation of supplies or troops. The *New Orleans* might yet make the test and succeed.

At Louisville there was news. The steamer would not come north of Natchez because its engine was too weak and its draft too deep.[14] Nicholas Roosevelt, who had recognized these faults, had studied the Mississippi, and was himself a steamboat inventor, freely lending his knowledge and experience, had been ignored. Now, tired of Fulton's obstinate clinging to an impractical design, Nicholas Roosevelt was going to abandon boat-building, and no one knew how long the Mississippi might have to wait for a steamboat that could ride against its heavy current.

When Shreve reached New Orleans, he found that port avid for a steamboat that would carry cargoes to Louisville for distribution in the East. With shipping demoralized on the seas by England's war with France, warehouses crammed, and business facing ruin, it was vital to get merchandise to domestic markets. Shreve's roomy barge found an especial welcome. There were too few upstream vessels of any kind, though what they needed was steamboats, the New Orleans merchants insisted. Shreve, proud as he was of his good barge, agreed.

Before he had labored the barge up to the Ohio, boats floating downstream hailed him with big news: War! War with England: since June nineteenth. Men were marching in the East . . . War — it would not last but a month or so. War. Shreve could not help but tingle at the word.

It was not Henry Shreve's Quaker upbringing that kept him from going off to war now, for he was to show no scruples about it later. It is more likely he believed that he was serving his country better by transporting goods than he could by fighting. He was convinced of the prime importance of keeping merchandise moving between the scattered ports of the Valley. Certainly fighting would be far easier and safer than plying a barge on the Mississippi.

Anyway, Shreve continued to run his barge to New Orleans and back to Brownsville, with only brief stays at home.[15] On one of his trips downstream in the summer of 1814, he sighted a steamboat well above Natchez, its deep hull listed against an island, no smoke coming from its funnel. When he got nearer, Shreve saw that the grounded vessel was headed upstream. It was the *Vesuvius*, the second steamboat that Fulton and Livingston had built for the Mississippi and recently sent down to New Orleans. Evidently it was on its way up to Louisville. Again Fulton had ignored the findings of Nicholas Roosevelt — this was a typical ocean ship. Only a flood could lift it afloat.[16]

When Shreve docked at New Orleans, he found that usually vivacious city depressed over the plight of the *Vesuvius*, and many other things. Indian uprisings had seethed through the Gulf country for a year. Andrew Jackson, sent down from Tennessee with a handful of troops to subdue these tribes and keep them from joining the British, had ragged, mutinous men that quit as soon as their short terms expired. Defiant Choctaws swaggered, drunken and insolent, through the New Orleans streets. The police dared not touch them for fear of setting off a massacre. There were rumors that Spain might invade Louisiana from Cuba and West Florida. A British fleet was said to be on its way from Bermuda to seize the mouth of the Mississippi. New Orleans had only a few troops and almost no arms. The English would surely take the city and from there conquer the whole Valley.

For the Valley itself, New Orleans people cared little or nothing whether the British or the British-Americans owned it. What mattered most was the stagnated com-

merce, the ocean trade routes cut off, the newest Fulton
boat lying helpless on its side halfway to Louisville. The
New Orleans had been impaled on a stump at Baton Rouge
in July while on a government errand and efforts to get it
off had sunk it.[17] The little steamboat *Comet*, built by
Daniel French in the East, had puffed in here not long ago,
its hind wheel kicking up such a wave that all the boats in
the harbor bumped together. The Livingston-Fulton
Company had chased it out with threats.[18] Anyway, the
Comet could not get above Natchez. Its engine was taken
out of it there and put to running a cotton gin. Here,
where steamboats were most needed, they were failures.

Shreve could have given the unhappy New Orleans shippers encouraging news, but it was a guarded secret. Daniel
French, of Brownsville, was about to complete the *Enterprise*, a far better vessel than the *Comet*, and Shreve had
arranged to run it down here — and back up the Mississippi if possible.[19] He would slip into New Orleans with
the steamboat, and get it out again the best way he could,
threatened, not by the British, but by the Livingston-
Fulton eighteen-year monopoly privilege in Louisiana
waters.[20]

This firm had applied to the legislatures of the inland
river states and territories for an exclusive right to navigate steam vessels on their streams, long since having such
a privilege in New York State. But the Ordinance of
1787, forming the Northwest Territory, had impressed
upon Valley Americans the idea that the rivers should be
'common highways, and forever free.' The settlers had
contended stubbornly with Spain for a free and open Mississippi, and would not hand over the cherished rights of
free passage to anyone. Only the Territory of Orleans,

later to be the State of Louisiana, had granted the monopoly.

That was enough to bottle up the Valley. Unless the Fulton Company could devise steamboats able to stem the Mississippi, the Valley's southern outlet to the sea would be barred to steam navigation. Robert Fulton, although he had been able to compile the steamboat inventions of others, had not originated anything, and likely would not. (Fulton's sympathetic biographer, Robert Thurston, admitted of him, 'He did not invent the steamboat, or, so far as is known, any part of it.') He had, indeed, applied for only one steamboat patent. This paper, drawn up in 1809, concerned the vertical paddle-wheels, which Nicholas Roosevelt claimed to have invented. Fulton knew he had no right to make the patent request, and 'neither subscribed nor swore thereto in the manner prescribed by law.' His name was placed on it by a Mr. Fletcher. Fulton had later withdrawn the application.[21] He and his partner, Robert Livingston, would continue, however, to sweep all steam craft but their own from the Mississippi's outlet port unless their unwarranted monopoly could be broken.

Henry Shreve had resolved to make the attempt. He believed that the *Enterprise*, with the new oscillating cylinder, recently invented by Daniel French, could breast the upstream current. Full of eager plans though he was, the only one to whom he would confide his intention to bring a steamboat into these forbidden waters was an attorney. He called on A. L. Duncan, a prominent lawyer of New Orleans.[22]

Shrewd, sophisticated Duncan listened in surprise to this soft-voiced young river man who planned so confidently to free Mississippi navigation from all restrictions.

Evidently Shreve did not know how much influence and money bolstered the monopoly, or how ruthless was its New Orleans legal representative, Edward Livingston, brother of Fulton's partner. Edward Livingston had come here from New York just ten years before and had forged his way by strong-arm devices to a commanding position. Men so feared and obeyed him that few would undertake to run counter to his will. Duncan told Shreve what he could expect: Livingston would try to frighten him out, and to prevent him from taking cargo when he went; if Shreve refused to run, the Fulton Company could have the boat seized. That power was written into their exclusive grant.

Shreve made it plain that he had no intention of running, and when he sailed north again in the steamboat he would take a cargo with him. If the Fulton people seized his boat, he would fight them in the courts. A stand would have to be made against the monopoly sometime, and he proposed to do it now. He argued that the grant had been made by the Territory of Orleans in 1811, but that when this territory was admitted into the Union the following year, it was on condition that its waters be free to all. This cancelled the privilege.

Duncan conceded that the state's authority should dominate, but in Louisiana it had not — at least, not when Edward Livingston saw fit to flout it. In a recent scrimmage with the New Orleans public over a section of waterfront called the Batture, Livingston had ridden over the state's courts, and then over federal decree.[23] Few men cared to come to grips with such a despot.

Shreve did. He paid Duncan five hundred dollars down and gave his personal note for fifteen hundred more.[24]

Lawing would not be cheap in New Orleans. The attorney pondered his client curiously. This young river man was strangely arresting, determined, abrupt, his motions unpredictable. His eyes were luminous — except that he was a mere Valley bargeman, they might have been the eyes of a crusader, or a genius. He was in deadly earnest about this matter.

When he had collected his new cargo, Shreve got away on the long, slow trip upstream. The crew set the sail and furled it, had the *cordelle* ready, sprang from oar to pole, staved and swore, fought and sang, and came with the sharp November winds to Pittsburgh. Here, rumors that had been shouted from passing boats were confirmed — Washington had been invaded and burned by the British. Shreve went into one of his rare furies about it.[25] He was bent now on giving his utmost aid to defend the country.

His stay in Brownsville was shorter than ever. New Orleans might be attacked at any time, and it was in need of many things.

CHAPTER

Four

O N DECEMBER 1, 1814, Henry Shreve sailed the *Enterprise* from Pittsburgh with a cargo of ordnance and ammunition for New Orleans.[1] He was buoyant with the feel of a steamboat under his feet. It was a vessel of only forty-five tons,[2] about half the size of his barge, but it would make up in speed what it lacked in size. Its parts chattered busily and it had a willful head at times; still it went right along, the stern paddle-wheel splashing the water impressively.

The Ohio had seen it before when Captain Gregg made two voyages with it to Louisville, while Shreve was in the South with his barge. No steamboat would arouse much excitement now unless it came *up* the Mississippi. The general feeling was that this boat would fail just as the *Vesuvius* and the *Comet* had. It was still a visionary fool's errand to try to run a mechanical boat against the Mississippi current.

The *Enterprise* sputtered and chugged, devouring an enormous amount of fuel. Twice a day it drew up while the crew went ashore, sawed wood, and carried it aboard to stoke the gluttonous engine. On dark nights, in the river stretches where snags reached from every bank and shoal, the boat was moored until daylight.

Meanwhile, the situation of New Orleans had grown more serious. Warning of the danger of attack had been sent in all directions. Andrew Jackson hurried from Pensacola with his sorry army to organize New Orleans for resistance. He found the prospect alarming. The French people were hazily divided in their allegiance. Many were Bourbon royalists, hating Napoleon — Britain was the enemy of Napoleon, and, therefore, their natural ally. Some were refugees from a recent negro uprising in Santo Domingo and had slight interest in the United States; they were loyal to New Orleans, but cared little what remote national government claimed it. The Spanish inhabitants were another doubtful element. The pirate horde of Jean and Pierre Lafitte at Barataria, well equipped with boats and arms, might prove menacing at a critical moment.[3] There was no financial credit in any quarter. Governor Claiborne, eager to do what was necessary for defense, feared his hands might be tied by the legislature, which was hostile to him.

If Jackson was dubious about the loyalties of the New Orleans people, they, in turn, were not confident of his ability to handle the crisis. This newly created major-general was experienced only in quelling Indian rebellions, a very different thing from standing off a highly trained foreign army. He was brusque and irascible, giving sharp commands to persons who had never been ordered about before and were offended.

Word came that the reinforced British fleet of fifty ships, bearing twenty thousand men, was sailing from Jamaica toward the mouth of the Mississippi. On December tenth, the fleet anchored off Lake Borgne, an arm of the Gulf east of New Orleans, and three days later cap- tured the American gunboats stationed there.

The following day, December 14, 1814, the *Enterprise* steamed up to the wharves of the frightened city.[4] The streets, cheerless in the mist-dimmed winter sunlight, were thronged. Men and women talked excitedly: How close was the British army now? When would it attack? These English, were they not for the new French king, Louis XVIII, and against the usurper, Napoleon, now exiled to Elba? Ah, if only by some blessed chance the city could be turned over to the French monarchy! Strains of the *Marseillaise* and *Ça Ira*, sung in bravado to the thud of feet on the board walks, disputed this point of view. A cry of discovery broke across the din. A steamboat, a new steamboat! It might have brought help.

Men swarmed to the river edge. The boat had brought much-needed cannon and ammunition. The British with endless ships, their masts like a forest, were at Lake Borgne — had the *Capitaine* heard? The city might be invaded tomorrow. Or tonight.

News of the steamboat sped back through the town, to Edward Livingston among the first. Another steamboat! And the luckless *Vesuvius* now grounded on the Batture north of town![5] After lying for six months against an island above Natchez, it had been freed by a flood only two weeks before and returned to New Orleans, where General Jackson had commandeered it. In a few days its deep hull had stranded it again. Livingston took imme- diate steps to have the *Enterprise* seized under the monop- oly's ban.[6]

But, when General Jackson heard of the steamboat's

arrival, he sent for its captain and ordered him to take it back upriver in search of three keelboats loaded with small arms. They had sailed from Pittsburgh two months ago for this port.[7]

Shreve was making necessary repairs on the boat the following day when several officers came aboard, read a court document to him in halting English, and ordered him to debark and leave the steamboat in custody, on a plea of the Livingston-Fulton Company. Shreve informed the officers briefly that the *Enterprise* had been commandeered for government service. Their seizure would have to wait.

A few hours later, he started on a hunt for the missing keelboats. He found them north of Natchez, dawdling along, doing a little trading by the way. Taking their cargoes and masters aboard the steamer, he tied the boats on behind and returned to New Orleans, the first instance of steam towage in the Valley. Shreve had been gone six and a half days and had run six hundred and fifty-four miles.[8]

Excitement had risen sharply in the town when British troops began to march on New Orleans over a ridge of ground between the river and a swamp. Jackson sent an advance guard against them, and there had been fighting. Now both sides had paused to put up barricades, the British building theirs of convenient sugar barrels, the Americans theirs of cotton bales. The odds against the city were appalling, though Jackson was doing his utmost to meet them. He had extended the bounds of the debtors' prison to the limit of the American lines so that the inmates could come out and swell the army of defense. He had even accepted an offer of aid from the Baratarian pirates, after shouting, with a torrent of oaths, that he would never deal with the filthy rabble. The street lights were put out at nine o'clock to discourage a British night attack. Ladies of the city provided themselves with daggers for a tragic escape in case the invaders reached them.[9]

Christmas Day there was no feasting from house to house, no cabriolets driven through the streets by dainty, sleek-haired women: the horses had been seized for military use. High-wheeled carts, drawn by oxen or mules, creaked out of town with loads for the battlefield near Chalmette Plantation. Ill-clad reinforcements had straggled in from Tennessee and Mississippi Territories. All day Shreve loaded arms, men, and supplies on the steamboat, ran it down to Chalmette, unloaded and returned. He came back from his last trip to a silent, lightless town. It seemed to him that the people, lately so divergent in their loyalties, were drawing together in the darkness.

Every hour of the next day was filled with commissions for the *Enterprise* and its captain. British shore batteries, which had been set up on each side of the river well below the city, had routed two American gunboats, peppering them hotly. And on Christmas Day, as a gift from Heaven to the enemy, Sir Edward Pakenham, brilliant strategist and brother-in-law of the Duke of Wellington, had suddenly appeared in the British camp to lead attackers to victory.[10]

Hardly had reports of this spread when the British were seen advancing. The Americans sallied to meet them and there was a skirmish. Meanwhile, fresh apprehension swept the city. Rumors got around that the legislature was about to meet and surrender Louisiana to the enemy rather than have New Orleans shelled. A. L. Duncan, Shreve's lawyer and one of General Jackson's aides, hunted the General out on the battlefield during a light engagement and gave him a message about these rumors. Jackson bellowed an order to have the meeting prevented. When members of the legislature arrived at the Government House, they found their entrance barred by a sentinel with fixed bayonet. Indignantly they met elsewhere, but if they had had any intention of surrendering the city, they abandoned it.[11]

Panic was growing in the city. As Shreve drew the *Enterprise* to port after one of his errands, he was met by a group of men who begged him to take their wives and children somewhere to safety. He agreed, provided they got permission from General Jackson to use the steamboat.

Envoys hurried to headquarters and appealed to the distracted general. He gave preoccupied consent. Presently mothers and children began to assemble near the steamboat. Shreve was taking them aboard, crowding them into every nook, when a courier came and ordered him to headquarters. Shreve, carrying out one command, had no time for another. He went on loading refugees.[12]

Shortly, a file of soldiers boarded the steamer and arrested its captain for disobedience. The passengers protested, but he was marched away. In Jackson's office the two men faced each other: the forty-three-year-old soldier, gaunt, choleric, his hair bristling above his thin face and piercing eyes; and the twenty-nine-year-old river man, tall, slim, bronzed, his mouth stubborn, eyes furious.

'By ——, Captain Shreve, do you dare disobey my orders?' Jackson demanded, as reported later in the Cleveland (Ohio) *Review*.

'Yes, by ——, I do dare!'

The General was outraged. He demanded an explanation. Shreve gave it. Jackson had forgotten giving the order to carry the women and children to safety. The prisoner was dismissed. A few hours later, Shreve pulled upstream with his crowded boat.[13]

Edward Livingston, who had married the beautiful Madame Louise Moreau de Lassy, a fugitive from the negro rebellion in Santo Domingo, did not send his wife and seven-year-old daughter on the disputed steamboat. Instead, he entrusted them to an unusual guard in their flight to safety: the pirate Jean Lafitte.[14]

Governor Claiborne had, some time before, offered a reward of five hundred dollars for the capture of Jean Lafitte, terror of the Gulf. Thereupon Lafitte, who called himself the Emperor of Barataria, had published a proclamation in New Orleans newspapers offering fifteen thousand dollars to anyone who would capture the Governor and deliver him to the pirate's base. Soon after this, Pierre Lafitte was caught, jailed, and denied bail. Jean, in quest of legal help to free his brother, approached Edward Livingston and his partner, John Grymes. Livingston knew more tricks than any other lawyer in the South; to him, any means likely to prove successful was righteous means. Jean Lafitte admired him greatly.[15]

Although not squeamish, Livingston balked at representing the Gulf outlaws and received the pirate coldly. Lafitte was not discouraged. He stood before the attorney in his habitual gray-green uniform, arms folded, head back, a black lock falling from his cockade over one eye. He was insolently imperious, but engaging. He had a way of making men forget how preposterous he was — and he had forty thousand dollars in cash to turn over to the two attorneys as a retainer. In short, he was irresistible.

Livingston pocketed his half of the fee and tried diligently to get Pierre released on the ground that confinement was bad for his health. The courts dallied, and the lordly pirate had to endure the boredom of a prison cell all the summer of 1814. When New Orleans was threatened by British invasion, the Lafittes, through Mr. Livingston, had offered the Governor and General Jackson their men, arms, and ammunition in exchange for complete amnesty. Now the pirates of Barataria strutted the streets of New Orleans as patriots. Their chief gallantly offered to conduct the exquisite Madame Livingston and her daughter to safety — he was always chivalrous if he could make it dramatic.

After Shreve had left his load of refugees fifty miles upstream at an appointed haven and returned, he was again ordered to headquarters. The General had a very different task for him:

'Captain Shreve, I understand you are a man who will always do what you undertake. Can you pass the British batteries on the river nine miles below, and with your steamer bear supplies to Fort St. Philip?'

It was important that this American fort, about sixty miles down the river, be relieved before the enemy advanced; but it was extremely hazardous to attempt passing between the British shore batteries that commanded the whole width of the stream. They could shell a vessel to fragments.

Shreve considered the question. 'Yes, if you will give me my own time.'

'What time do you require?'

'Twenty-four hours.' [16]

Jackson agreed. Back at the waterfront, Shreve began to cover the sides of the steamboat with cotton bales held on by large hooks. In the late afternoon, the supplies stowed, he dropped downstream a few miles and waited just above the British batteries for the mist that usually rises about midnight over the river. Then, with engine closed down and wheel muffled, he passed the shore sentinels unnoticed and reached the fort by morning. That night, on his return trip, the British sentinels heard the boat engine and gave an alarm. The batteries fired furiously, but only a few spent shells hit the protecting cotton bales.[17]

When Shreve started on his dangerous mission, he had left a desperate people behind him; now he found the whole city buoyed with hope. Both the British and Americans, after their battle from behind sugar barrels and cotton bales, had paused to set up better barricades, and in this breathing-spell a cheering thing had happened — the Kentuckians had come. Two thousand riflemen! To be sure, only a third of them possessed rifles; all of them were in tatters. But the town ladies had collected cloth of various kinds and were busy making pants for them. The men who actually had rifles would be dressed first and placed in the front lines. The others, armed with picks and spades, would bring up the rear.

Early and late the *Enterprise* transported war *matériel* to the battleground. By January seventh, the last cannon had been set up, the last ammunition stores delivered on the field. Shreve now went to headquarters with a request of his own. He wanted permission to leave the steamboat and take his place with the other men in the coming battle.

A steamboat navigator was too rare to risk lightly, but the General finally gave in and stationed Shreve in Colonel Humphrey's battery, near the river, in charge of gun number six, a long twenty-four-pounder.[18]

January eighth, which dawned in a heavy mist, was to witness the strangest battle ever fought on this continent. On one side were the splendid British troops, many of them seasoned in Wellington's army; on the other side were skilled veterans of Napoleon's campaigns, untrained city civilians and hardy but undisciplined American backwoodsmen. England, France, and America were at war along the waist-deep marshes of Louisiana.

At the first faint daylight, two British columns advanced. American artillerymen spied them and fired. A fog lowered over the field; the enemy came on under its cover. When it lifted, the British, crisply uniformed, moved in a rhythmic mass over the meadow of M'sieur Chalmette's plantation. They seemed to cover two thirds of it. Suddenly men in the British front lines began to drop. They had come in reach of the long-range rifles of the Kentucky and Tennessee men.

The invaders marched ahead into the slaughtering fire, their short-range muskets ineffective. Fog swept across the field again. Troops on both sides were confused and retreated. Officers rallied them. Pakenham, his right arm shattered, hat grasped in his left hand, waved his lines forward. Grimly they came on into the hell of rifle and artillery fire. A shot tore through Pakenham's thigh; he fell. His men gave way. Only the British artillery remained to be silenced. The sky blackened, a dismal rain fell. The murderous battle, only three hours long, was over.

Two weeks before this, statesmen of America and Eng-

land had officially ended the war with a peace treaty
signed at Ghent, but news of this had not reached Louisiana. The siege, the panic, the slaughter, had been un-
necessary.

With the mud of the marshes still clinging to him,
Shreve went aboard the *Enterprise*. He had hoped by now
to head it up the Mississippi, but a long series of government tasks lay ahead of him. Stores had to be transported
from the battlefield, and British prisoners taken down the
Balize to the Gulf and exchanged for American soldiers
held on British gunboats. There were five errands, in all,
down the Balize and nine to Natchez.[19] Shreve went about
them in a growing tension. Mary expected to give birth to
a third child in April, and April was passing. Still there
was another mission and another.

When the end seemed in sight, there were American
troops to be returned to their post at Red River Rapids.
Shreve got them aboard, steamed up the Mississippi, and
turned into the dull red stream. The transport caused a
flutter along the shores of Red River, for no steamboat had
penetrated this remote country before. Caddo Indians and
Acadian planters stared at the puffing little steamer in dis-
taste. It picked its way around shoals of rotting logs to
the Rapids, and chugged back to New Orleans.

The *Vesuvius* had been lifted off the Batture by a freshet
and now could take over the remaining government tasks.[20]
Shreve, working hard to put his boat in order for its long
run north, braced himself for a hostile move by the Fulton
Company. It came on May sixth, just as he was ready to
start upstream. Officers boarded the *Enterprise* and took
it over. The war for a free river was on.[21]

As news of the seizure traveled over town, men shook

their heads. The young boat captain could never cope
with the shrewd attorney. There was no chance for an
open river, or for anything against which Edward Livingston had set his will.

Brilliant, resourceful, Edward Livingston was an out-
standing, if unloved, figure in New Orleans. He had been
a member of Aaron Burr's remarkable counsel of defense.
Early in his career here, 'his talents and supposed rapacity
gave great uneasiness to the community.' [22] One *coup* of
Livingston's proved especially bitter to New Orleans
people, causing a succession of riots that echoed in Washington. It concerned the Batture. This strip of shore,
built by alluvial deposit along the Faubourg Ste. Marie, a
north suburb of town, had always been considered a public
common; earth was hauled from it to repair the Levee or
streets. The ground came to be mildly claimed by John
Gravier, and in 1807, Edward Livingston had bought it
from Gravier's son.

The townspeople, amazed and angry at the sale, insisted
that the land had belonged to New Orleans long before the
unhappy cession of Louisiana to the United States. They
threatened to appeal, 'not to American authorities, but to
France.' One newspaper declared: 'It is well known that
Napoleon will think himself bound in justice and honor to
see that the treaty be not violated. The Emperor of the
French did not cede his subjects to be devoured by the
harpies of chicane.'

Livingston, brazenly engaging, as one of his numerous
counsel, the Attorney for the United States at New Orleans, Mr. Brown, succeeded in getting a favorable decree
from the Superior Court of Louisiana Territory. This put
him in possession of the property. He set some negroes to

digging a canal across it. Citizens, alarmed lest the canal should change the waterline of the river and disturb navigation, drove the negroes off. The following day Livingston again put workmen on the Batture. A crowd gathered to protest.

Governor Claiborne returned from a trip at this time and found the people in a furor. Livingston appealed to the Governor to protect his rights; the city council begged the Governor to defend the claim of the United States to the Batture ground. Claiborne was distraught. He appealed to Secretary of State Madison, declaring that he feared blood would be shed in the dispute. He held that the Louisiana court had made an error in awarding the land to Livingston.

Two weeks later, while the question was hanging fire, Livingston set a dozen white laborers to work on the canal. At four o'clock that afternoon a drum was beaten in the streets, men gathered to its call, and several hundred marched on the Batture to challenge the work on it. A messenger was sent to the Governor, who hurried there to appease the outraged townsmen. He got their attention, and promised them he would take the matter up again with the federal authorities. Then he wrote to Secretary Madison, asking for advice and help.

Not waiting for Madison's reply to the Governor, Livingston set a hundred and fifty men to work on the Batture. On January 24, 1808, President Jefferson sent the United States Marshal to take possession of the property. Three regiments of militia paraded to lend force to the mission. The delighted populace saw Livingston's workmen driven off.

Thereupon, Livingston went to Washington to see the

President, and in March, Jefferson sent a message to Congress submitting to that body the settlement of title to the Batture. Congress failed to act on the question. Livingston then brought suit in the Louisiana District Court against the United States Marshal for seizing the land at the order of the President; and in 1813, in the midst of war alarms, New Orleans had been aghast to hear that this court had declared the interference of President Jefferson illegal and had restored the land to Livingston. Following his triumph in this decree, Livingston brought suit against Jefferson, now retired from office, and went out of his way to hold the ex-President up to public ridicule, saying, in one instance, ' . . . he pants for the wreaths of Hancock, Adams, and Otis.'

The people turned again to the Governor, pleading with him to appeal the dumfounding court verdict. Claiborne wrote to ex-President Jefferson: ' . . . Mr. Livingston has found means either to neutralize or to make partisans of most of the lawyers of the State. . . . I entertain strong hopes that we may yet be enabled to maintain the rights of the public.'

The litigation went on. Livingston, despite mandates and injunctions, had occasional work done on the disputed ground. In 1814, when Indian uprisings had drawn the eyes of New Orleans from all else, he took possession of the Batture.[23]

It was this practiced and ruthless opponent whom the twenty-nine-year-old river man was to face. While Shreve had been steaming the *Enterprise* here and there on government errands, Edward Livingston was busily putting his usual technique into play — going to every lawyer in New Orleans to engage him as an aide in the steamboat suit. He hoped to make it impossible for Shreve to get counsel.[24]

His plan had a slight setback when A. L. Duncan admitted that he had been retained by Shreve long ago. But Livingston had a way of handling such emergencies — he offered Duncan three thousand dollars to desert his client. Duncan need not line up in the counsel against Shreve, he was told; he was merely to drop the case. Duncan declined the offer.[25] Livingston was amazed and indignant. Duncan and his client would be taught a lesson.

Shreve had expected the seizure of his steamboat, but that probably did not keep him from going into one of his infrequent blazing tempers over it. It seemed to him outrageous that any private firm could shut off a public water-road to American commerce.

He made for Duncan's office with the news: the monopolists had had the boat taken into custody. Duncan was ready for the move, having arranged bond. The steamboat would be bailed out within a few hours. Shreve could go on his way with it, but that would not be the end of the affair. The Fulton lawyers were drawing up a suit against the *Enterprise*.[26]

The suit would have to wait, Shreve decided firmly. He was sailing as soon as he could get up steam.

At last Shreve started the *Enterprise* on the test voyage he had waited so long to make. No steamboat had run up the Mississippi to the Ohio. The *New Orleans* and the *Comet* had not attempted it; the *Vesuvius* had tried it and failed. This little boat might answer the question of fast Mississippi navigation.

The river was rising steadily. By the time Shreve reached Natchez, water was spilling over the lowlands.

This overflow eased the channel current, but the boat engine still labored and groaned. The flood gained until it lay over the prairie in a quiet, currentless sea. Shreve turned out of the river whenever he could and sailed over deeply submerged flatlands. He reached Louisville the last day of May, the limping vessel hardly able to make the last miles.[27]

In Louisville it was an historic hour. A steamboat actually had reached it from downriver. Shreve knew that without the helpful flood, the *Enterprise* could not have got here. The inadequate engine would have been helpless against the Mississippi's usual drive; the keel, which had managed to glide over the sandbars going downstream, would have scraped them coming up. It had taken unbelievable détours to make this port. The problem of upstream sailing was not yet solved.[28]

Shreve loaded cargo and pulled away with the hastily repaired craft. He could feel no great elation over having run a steamboat up the flooded lowlands, but he had learned much from the experience. Even the smallest vessel built on the model of an ocean ship would not be practical on the Mississippi; a weak, low-pressure engine could not stem a savage current. Slowly there shaped in his mind a boat different from any craft ever dreamed of before. It would be broad, tall, but of shallow draft, and powerfully driven — a Mississippi steamboat.

All along the way now the *Enterprise* was hailed with interest. It actually had come up from New Orleans! Up the Mississippi! Shreve did not explain that it had ridden a placid overflow; he let the little steamer have its hour of triumph, the Valley its new hope. Disillusion would come soon enough to these eager ports, unless Daniel French built a boat totally different from this.

At Pittsburgh Shreve left the last of his cargo and turned up the Monongahela. The Brownsville *Telegraph* commented: 'Arrived at this port on Monday last, the steamboat *Enterprise*, Shrieve, of Bridgeport, from New Orleans, in ballast, having discharged her cargo at Pittsburg. She is the first steamboat that ever made the trip to the mouth of the Mississippi and back. She made the trip from New Orleans to this port in 54 days, 20 days of which were employed in loading and unloading freight at the different towns on the Ohio and Mississippi. So she was only 34 days in actual service in making her voyage which ... must be made against powerful currents and upwards of 2200 miles in length.'

Niles' Weekly Register, published in Baltimore 'next door to the Merchants' Coffee House,' told the story thus: 'The Steamboat, *Enterprise*, worked up from New Orleans to Bardstown, nearly 1500 miles in 25 days. ... How do the rivers and canals of this old world dwindle into insignificance compared with this, and what a prospect of commerce is held out to the immense regions of the West by means of these boats! It is thought that the freight from New Orleans to Louisville ... will soon be reduced to $3.50 per c.'

The freight rate in hand-boats was $6.75 per hundredweight from New Orleans to Pittsburgh.[29] The passenger fare for the same trip was $160. Steam reduced this fare, finally, to about $30.

Shreve gave the *Enterprise* over to Daniel French with a full report of its performance, which in some respects had been remarkable. But the boat could not, Shreve admitted, come up the Mississippi when the water was at an ordinary stage. To produce a steamer that could run successfully on the Mississippi, certain drastic changes would have to be made in the design of both engine and hull.

Daniel French believed in his own theories and declined the suggestions, to Shreve's great disappointment and bewilderment. Fulton had clung obstinately to his errors; now French would hold to his. It dawned upon Shreve that if his dream boat for the Mississippi was to be built, he would have to do it.

For a little while rivers and boating took second place in his mind. He was back with his little family: Mary, frail and pretty; two bright-haired daughters, Mary and Rebecca, four and two years old; and an infant son born on April eighth,[30] while the *Enterprise* chugged up Red River. Mary showed traces of the anxiety she had suffered as months passed without bringing her husband home. Word had come by boatmen that New Orleans was besieged, that battles were fought, boats shelled, crews taken prisoner. And a voyage up the Mississippi in a steamboat would be as hazardous as war. It had been whispered at the Friends' meeting-houses that young Henry Shreve had at last taken one chance too many. He was not likely to return.

Now he was back, and the town made much ado over his latest exploit. Neighbors came in to greet him, placid women in gray dresses and bonnets, thoughtful men with longish hair and short breeches. Shreve recounted his trips in the *Enterprise*, but said little to these Quaker folk about the war, and nothing at all of the hours he had spent behind gun number six, plugging twenty-four-pound cannon balls at the enemy.

Before long, Shreve became absorbed in sketching and

figuring, day and night. The thing he pictured on paper was fantastic. His friends were dismayed over it, but Shreve was not disturbed. This was a logical Mississippi steamboat, he insisted, and he intended to build it.[31]

CHAPTER
Five

HENRY SHREVE laid the keel of his first steamboat on September 10, 1815, at Wheeling.[1] The hull, built partly of timbers from old Fort Henry, took shape rapidly. Loafers who watched the work carried sensational reports up into the town. The boat was outlandish. It was exceedingly shallow of draft, but reared aloft with *two decks, one above the other.* A layer of cabins would fill most of the space between the decks.[2]

Talk of this odd hull never died. Traders from the neighboring villages and gentlemen from Philadelphia took time from the cockfights or from political arguments at the pillory to have a look at it. Wits gibed at it and sober men deplored it.[3] The vessel defied every principle of shipbuilding; it would rock like an eggshell for a rod or so and turn over. Then, one day, as though the thing were not already absurd enough, its hold was boarded over, leaving no place for machinery.

Shreve was not often in Wheeling to hear the laughter. He spent most of his time at Brownsville, where the machinery was being constructed. This was a sight, too. It included twin engines totally unlike any other steam engine, not large and impressive like the single engine that Fulton had imported from England; this pair looked as though they could hardly propel a keelboat. And yet the vessel being built at Wheeling was said to be enormous — nearly a hundred and fifty feet long.

Shreve was not bedeviled by ridicule in Brownsville as he was at Wheeling; Quakers, in all moments of doubt, kept silent. The only ones whose criticisms disturbed Shreve were his partners, four daring gentlemen — Messrs. Neal Gillespie and Robert Clark, of Brownsville, and Noah Zane and George White, of Wheeling [4] — who had invested in the venture and worried about it ever since.

The gray skies of winter lifted. Flatboats and barges, keelboats and *pirogues*, stacked with tinware and dishes, flour or cotton prints, began to pull out from every haven to float downstream. Shreve watched them with interest and hope of relief. There was glamour in hand-boating, and misery. When these barges and keelboats came back upstream, men would drudge like beasts to bring them. Here and there a man would fall under the torture of the *cordelle* and not rise again; stoical companions would bury him where he crumpled and mark the grave with piled stones or a hasty cross. The riverbanks were strewn with these graves.[5]

One day Shreve took his incredible engines down to Wheeling to install them in the unbelievable hull. The curious gathered to see where, in such a boat, he could place the machinery. Shreve set them agog by putting the engines on the lower deck and the four boilers on the upper deck.

There was lampooning by the town wits, but it died out shortly. How such mistaken machinery was placed did not greatly matter. The cylinders in Fulton's boats were upright and stationary, and in French's boats were upright and vibratory; in Shreve's steamboat the cylinders, twenty-four inches in diameter, with six-foot stroke, were *horizontal* and stationary, the vibration being given to the pitman rod. The cranks were at right angles. The boilers, which had flues to them, were on their sides, too.[6]

However the Wheeling waterfront might feel about the strange vessel, Shreve was immensely pleased with it. All the machinery weighed only one twentieth as much as that in a Fulton steamboat, but the high-pressure twin engine — entirely different in design from the original high-pressure engine produced by Richard Trevithick, of Cornwall — furnished many times the power. David Prentice had previously employed a cam wheel for working the valves to the cylinder, 'and Shreve had added his great invention, the cam cut-off, by which three fifths of the fuel was saved.'[7] The fuel was wood, and cheap, but it cost time to stop and saw it and get it aboard.

Though the citizens of Wheeling had no great faith in this unusual boat, they were enthusiastic over the young inventor's determination to sail into New Orleans in spite of the Louisiana monopoly. The Livingston-Fulton Company had lost its suit against the *Enterprise* in the inferior court at New Orleans, in a decision stating that the legislature of the Orleans Territory had exceeded its rights in making the privilege grant. The company had then carried the case to the State Supreme Court, where it now awaited a hearing.[8] A few weeks before, the monopolists, although a verdict stood against them, seized a new Daniel French steamboat, the twenty-five-ton *Dispatch*, while it was loading at New Orleans. They forcibly removed the cargo of sugar and molasses, and ordered the boat out of Louisiana, never to return, on penalty of confiscation.[9] The Mississippi outlet, so obstinately defended from alien powers, had been closed by an American firm which had not been able to build steamboats that could master the Great River.

It was well known in Wheeling how seriously the Livingston-Fulton monopoly in New York State had hampered eastern shipping. All inventiveness was hounded out. Aaron Ogden, lately governor of New Jersey, had made a hard fight against the syndicate for the right to run his own steam ferry from Elizabethtown, New Jersey, across to New York City. He claimed that Fulton had not originated anything, and had, therefore, no occasion to set up restrictions.[10]

Fulton thereupon vigorously defended his use of other men's inventions. In a letter to Ogden, he accused that gentleman of having 'departed from that noble candor, that respect for truth, which marks the moral man.' He further declared: 'Every artist who invents a new and useful machine must compose it of known parts of other machines. So in patent medicines — Lee's bilious pills: he did not invent their elements, but combined certain ingredients in certain proportions to make a useful medicine.'[11]

Ogden contended that he had a right to employ, in his own original way, the same ingredients that Fulton had so freely used. But the monopoly beat him down and forced him to pay an exorbitant price for the ferry privilege.

Every man who had ever opposed Fulton was broken by him. There was Nicholas Roosevelt: after his invention, the vertical paddle-wheel, had carried the *Clermont* to victory (and Fulton, in 1809, had tried to get a patent on it for himself with an application signed by Mr. Fletcher), Roosevelt applied for and received a patent on it in December of 1814. In January, 1815, Roosevelt appealed to the legislature of New Jersey for protection of his patent. Fulton then appeared before that body and submitted a copy made of a letter he claimed to have written while in Europe in 1793. The letter, addressed to Lord Stanhope, mentioned vertical paddle-wheels. When examined, this copy was found to be newly made, and on American paper. After an embarrassed moment, Fulton hastened to explain that the original copy was worn and dim, and that he had made a fresh one.

Roosevelt then called attention to the fact that Fulton, long after 1793, had still been hunting a practical contrivance with which to propel vessels with steam, and had built several experimental boats which employed much cruder devices than the paddle-wheel. Fulton, however, was backed by so much influence and wealth that the New Jersey legislature coyly decided it was 'inexpedient to make any special provision in connection with the matter.' Roosevelt, betrayed and weary, retired from the fight.[12]

And there was Benjamin Latrobe, eminent engineer and architect, builder of the Capitol at Washington: he had undertaken to construct the Fulton steamboat, *Buffalo*, at Pittsburgh. Fulton sent to him, from New York, the most minute details of how the building was to be done and what each item should cost. He insisted that what he dictated should be rigidly carried out. Labor and materials were expensive at Pittsburgh, and Latrobe soon faced a mounting deficit. When he explained this,

Fulton grew tyrannical and abusive. Latrobe threw his own resources into the deficit, hoping that Fulton would finally appreciate this and reimburse him. It was a vain hope. In his *Journal*, Latrobe disclosed that 'the pressure of circumstances and constant mental suffering' had worn him out. He had a serious breakdown, and was never really well again.[13]

No one had ever run counter to the Livingston-Fulton Company without being crushed by it. Yet here was Henry Shreve making ready to fling himself against it. Neither Wheeling nor Brownsville believed that he had a chance to win, but the attempt was valiant. Brownsville ladies had woven a silk banner for Shreve's new boat, and embroidered it with the inscription: 'Our friends shall not take from us what we have wrested from our enemies.'

On June fourth, Shreve's steamboat, the *Washington*, turned out of Wheeling on its long journey, and for its inevitable legal battle. It sat the water like a great aquatic bird. The challenging silk banner curled from its jackstaff. *Niles' Weekly Register* (Baltimore) described it thus:

'She is 148 feet in length. Her main cabin is sixty feet; she has three handsome private rooms, besides a commodious bar room. She is furnished in very superior style. Gentlemen from New York who have been aboard of her, assert that her accomodations exceed anything they have seen on the North [Hudson] River.... Her steam power is applied upon an entirely new principle, exceedingly simple and light. She has no balance wheel, and her whole engine possessing the power of one hundred horses, weighs only nine thousand pounds. It is the invention of captain Shreve.'

Shreve steamed his boat down the familiar river

stretches, noting its smooth performance with satisfaction. Settlers along the shores were too amazed at the strange craft to halloo it. At Marietta, citizens came down to the river and looked over the vessel curiously. They had known its young captain since he had come as a lad in sober gray and broadbrim hat. Shy and reticent then, he was commanding and reticent now. He had filled out some, and grown more cosmopolitan. So he had contrived this bizarre vessel! It remained to be seen what it could do.

The *Washington* lay there two days taking cargo, then dropped below Marietta to Point Harmar. On the morning of July ninth, the fires were rekindled and the boat pulled out. Knots of men stared after it. In spite of its heavy load it handled easily. At last, perhaps, practical steamboating had come to the Valley.

Then suddenly the boat was struggling helplessly to head downstream, completely out of control. The current carried it toward the opposite shore, where the haze of distance closed it out. Men stared at where they had seen it last. Then the earth rocked under their feet, there was the heavy roar of an explosion — the steamboat had blown up.[14] They hurried aboard any craft at hand and paddled downstream.

They came upon a pitiable scene. To keep the *Washington* from running aground, it had been necessary to throw out a kedge anchor astern, and later when all hands were aft drawing in the kedge, a boiler had given way on that side, blasting a hell of steam at the crew. Tossed and huddled forms lay on the upper deck, eight of them dead. Of the others, six would soon be out of their agony. The disaster had been caused by the disarrangement of the safety valve, which had become immovable by the accidental slipping of the weight to the extreme lever. The captain had been thrown into the river and severely injured; he was dragging himself along the deck now, sobbing unashamedly over the dead and dying.

It was an ugly accident and the chorus of croakers were aroused again: it was sure to happen, they had known it would; the boat was too different. 'Different' was the key word in all the denunciations. Shreve was stricken by the tragedy to his men and passengers. His heart was sore at the apparent failure of the boat into which he had built so much faith. He had been confident that he could lift the pessimism that had settled over Valley shipping; instead, he had laid a heavier pall on it. Still he believed that the boat would make good. Its design was sound.

As soon as he was able, Shreve began repairing the boiler and damaged parts so that he could resume his trip to New Orleans, bent on two things: that the Mississippi should have boats that could run easily against its current and above its sand shoals; and that its outlet should be free from special privilege.

In the early fall the *Washington* was ready to sail again. Curious crowds boarded it at each port to look it over. The Cincinnati *Gazette*, commenting on the interest excited by the *Washington*, said: 'Notwithstanding the great inconvenience Captain Shreve must have experienced from the continual round of visitors, he was uniformly polite and obliging to all.' [15]

To Shreve, it was the Valley's boat that the people were inspecting and they had a right to be curious about it. Interest in its unusual design and handsome fittings was freely expressed along with skepticism of its practicability. It was generally believed to be just another downriver boat, if that. Even the brave little *Enterprise* had not been able to make a second trip to New Orleans; sent out under the command of Captain Worley, it had been wrecked on the rocks near the Ohio Falls.[16]

At Louisville, the *Washington* picked up a few more passengers and on September 24, 1816, glided easily over the Falls.[17] Now for eight hundred miles the shores were a hardly touched wilderness. To the eastern passengers, this trip was strange and exotic. Bronze forests along the Ohio gave way to a sunlit sea of prairie grass and tall bright flowers, to stone cliffs, and again to forested banks. Jays, blackbirds, and parroquets chattered in the trees. Pelicans swarmed the islands. Cranes rose from low banks with whooping calls. Occasional Indians darted their canoes along, intent on small flocks of the vanishing swan whose fine down, so fashionable in Europe, was in demand with the traders.

Fleets of flatboats dotted the river at times, laden at this season principally with cider, corn, hemp, cattle, hogs, and fowl. A tumult of lowing, trampling, cackling, squealing, and barking wafted from them. There were floating retail stores, too, with goods on shelves and a polite clerk to show them; there were floating smithies, dramshops, and dives — all on their way to tie up at any promising settlement and remain as long as business was good. Sometimes the steamer met a barge or keelboat laboring upstream with cargo, men doubling to the poles or oars.

The *Washington* offered a striking contrast to these hand-run craft. Until now boats, even the western steamboats, had been designed to run as best they could and carry all they could, with no extra frills of comfort or taste. It was universally accepted that when one set out on the rivers, he left comfort behind. Shreve had made the *Washington* a luxury boat, finished with the finest of woodwork and mirrors, and provided with handsome carpets and furniture. The meals equaled those in the best hotels and were served with much formality. To Shreve, nothing was too good for the rivers.

The few women passengers sat on the forward deck against the blue sky and tawny water, gossiping in groups as the panorama of shore glided past. Their cashmere shawls or long Carrick capes fell back from light-colored dresses made full of skirt, with short waists and half-sleeves. Large bonnet-shaped hats lined with ruching and trimmed in ostrich tips framed the face.

Their talk was mostly about the national capital. Washington was so gay that one would hardly believe there had been a recent war. There were many enticing items about what Mrs. Madison had done and worn ... she used rouge and pearl powder ... she even snuffed. Things never got dull around her. The government circle was quite gay, and the embassies were small, brilliant foreign courts.

The gentlemen passengers who were not in the barroom stood in knots on the deck. The skirts of their long walking-coats were cut back, leaving tails to be whipped by the breeze; tight pantaloons were strapped under the instep — men never stood so much and with such self-conscious grace as in these early years of pantaloons. The high beaver hats were so narrow of brim that they barely shaded the eyes. The gentlemen tried to remember that this was a pleasure trip, or adventure, and to keep away from the bitter subject of politics. Still, with James Monroe, the Republican-Democrat, running for President against the Federalist Rufus King, and election hardly more than a month away, talk got around to dangerous ground. Tempers flared and voices rose to shouts. Generally, though, conversation turned on what the Fulton Company would do to this boat of Shreve's; and whether the *Washington* would be able to get back upstream against the Mississippi current.

Shreve, watching his engines and the violent stream, knew how much depended on his winning a free Mississippi and conquering it with steam. He was thirty years old now, and seasoned with experience; he believed that he could solve the problem, though it would take all his wits and courage to do it.

The *Washington* sailed southward, devouring the wood that was hastily chopped and brought aboard. The current slowed, canebrakes twinkled by, cypresses waved their mantles of long moss drowsily. There were fewer songbirds. Alligators, resting against islands like stranded logs, slid into the water. The sky was a deeper blue. At night the starlight was so tangible that it seemed like a bright mesh hanging on the tree-tops. A whitened channel wound between the dark shore forests. Music drifted from the cabin — music and the rivers belonged together.

On October seventh, the *Washington*, with sunlight gleaming on its many windows and new paint, floated into the bay at New Orleans.[18] Men on the bank and Levee stared in astonishment at the strange craft sitting so lightly in the water and bearing up such a superstructure of cabins and decks. Where had it come from, how had it kept afloat? Was it a Fulton boat? Would it be allowed to take cargo?

Traders, merchants, boatmen, sailors, negro roustabouts, and carters crowded toward it. Some of the townsmen went aboard and looked about them wonderingly. Almost no hold, machinery and cargo on the lower deck, engines and boilers lying on their sides! Then there were the handsome cabins, and an unbelievable upper deck. New Orleans had seen craft from everywhere, but nothing like this. It had come all the way from Wheeling without turning over. Shreve had built it — young Shreve, who had sailed the *Enterprise* all about here during the war and had got himself into trouble with the steamboat monopoly. He would be in trouble again. The monopoly would go on forever; if it finally made successful boats, rates for steam transportation might be whatever it decided.

The news was hastened to Edward Livingston, who now represented the Livingston and Fulton heirs. Chancellor Livingston had been dead for two years and Robert Fulton for a year and a half, but the monopoly lived on. Edward Livingston made for the waterfront.

He took in the boat hull, dumfounded. There was nothing about it to suggest the traditional ocean-ship type of the Fulton boats. He went aboard, studying the craft shrewdly, missing no item of its radical but practical design. It was an odd vessel, he realized, only because no one had ever before built a steamboat for the Mississippi. He could foresee that it would be the Valley steamboat of the future. In some respects it would be the ocean ship of the future. There was honest admiration in his grim remark to Shreve, who stood by, watching him coolly:

'You deserve well of your country, young man, but we shall be compelled to beat you if we can.' [19]

Livingston went ashore and put the law in motion. He had the boat seized and turned over to the marshal, to be held in ten thousand dollars bail. Shreve had expected to have to raise this amount, but Duncan decided not to bail the boat out, but to come back at his opponents with an unexpected move: he secured a court order demanding a ten-thousand-dollar bond from the Livingston-Fulton Company to cover any damage or loss caused Shreve and his partners by the detention of the *Washington*. The monopolists would be exempt from damages, however, if they won a suit they were launching against the boat.[20]

This was a jolt to Edward Livingston and his associate, John Grymes. They were most uneasy at having their weapon of heavy bail turned against them. This court suit they were instituting was all right as a device to frighten or heckle Shreve, but it was a poor gamble for a ten-thousand-dollar stake. They released the *Washington*. The suit appears to have been dropped.

Shreve loaded his boat with cargo and passengers, and eight days after his arrival in New Orleans he started back to Louisville. It was not a propitious season for the first Mississippi steamboat's trial upstream trip. An early and very severe winter had set in; the Ohio was freezing; [21] Louisville was shut off. Shreve edged through the ice to a berth at Shippingport, below the Falls. Here the *Washington* lay for three months, waiting for spring. Louisville had taken the steamboat's victory over the Mississippi casually. With the rivers ice-locked, other ports heard little of it.

This was a bleak, sad winter of family tragedy for Henry Shreve. Soon after he had had Mary and the children come to Louisville, where he would make his home, his infant son, Zane Hampden, died.[22]

It was a tense winter for Shreve. Public irritation was growing over the Fulton monopoly. In January a resolution had been introduced in the Louisiana legislature by one of its members to repeal the monopoly grant. The committee appointed to investigate the matter condemned the resolution with much vigor and eloquence.[23] In the same month, the Kentucky legislature adopted a resolution against the seizure of non-Fulton boats in Louisiana waters.[24] Shreve knew it would devolve upon him to make effective this paper protest. The Fulton Company and its army of lawyers would be waiting for him to dare to go back to New Orleans; they would have ready some new move against him. Week after week ice crunched against the side of the boat with which he hoped to free the Valley outlet to the sea.

At last spring opened, the ice above, hurled downstream, belaboring the craft along the banks. Shreve began to put the *Washington* into condition and to gather cargo. On March 3, 1817, he started his steamboat,[25] with a full load of goods and adventurous passengers, for a round trip to New Orleans, 'the voyage from which all western historians date the commencement of steam navigation in the Mississippi Valley.' [26]

The passengers found it a pleasant excursion down the two rivers. The comfortable cabins, broad decks, excellent meals and formal service provided the most luxurious holiday they had ever known. The willows were in pale leaf; white dogwood and crimson redbud bloom showed against dark tree-trunks. Migrating birds swarmed the islands; a clamorous twitter mingled with the cries of pelican and brant. From the shore came the call of farmers to their oxen. Music played on deck or in the salon.

The captain had foreseen the worth of giving western river travel a social value; he kept a casual eye on the service. Above all, he studied the engines and the channel. He was intent on having this round trip prove that steamboating on the Mississippi was practical.

Near midnight, on March twelfth, the *Washington* came in sight of a long grove of masts — the first glimpse of flat New Orleans. The boat docked among the inland craft. The town was still awake. Candlelight twinkled from tavern and poolroom.

The arrival of a steamboat aroused slight interest — steamers often returned from Natchez. The new Fulton steamer, *Aetna*, had even come back from two trips to Louisville. Its first voyage up to Louisville had taken sixty days; the second one, with the use of sails, was made in thirty-one days. It arrived each time at its upstream destination on one wheel, and was long laid up for repairs.[27] A barge could do as well.

The boat that had just come into New Orleans was the fast *Washington*, bulletins persisted. It had made the trip down from Louisville in nine days.

Then excitement spread through the streets. The *Washington* had dared to come back to New Orleans! No other non-Fulton boat had come here a second time. What would Mr. Livingston and his friends do to it? There was a growing clack of feet on walks leading to the wharves. The *Washington* was back, and if it could get free of custody as it had before, it would take another New Orleans cargo north.

The Louisiana *Gazette* of the following day carried this item in its ship news: 'Last night the Steam-boat Washington, Shreve, Falls of the Ohio in *nine days*. Left Shipping port Monday, March 3, at one o'clock P.M. and arrived at N. O. Wednesday at 12:00.... The Washington will sail again for Shipping port on Sunday 23 inst.'

Edward Livingston had the boat seized. Again Shreve's attorney demanded bond for any resulting damage. The monopoly's lawyers appealed to the court to have this order for bond set aside, but their plea was denied. Livingston and his colleagues released the *Washington*, then held a conference. New measures for dealing with Shreve would have to be adopted.[28]

Henry Shreve was a strong-willed young man and had no thought of backing down, Livingston pointed out. He had built a remarkable vessel, powerful and light, so radical that only genius could have devised it. Compared to the fast, trim *Washington*, the *Aetna* was a clumsy thing. The Fulton Company had no one who could match Shreve's inventiveness. He was a dangerous man against them, but would be a highly valuable one with them. He had solved the problem of a steamboat for the Mississippi — the only sensible thing to do was to buy him over.

It was decided to go ahead with a suit against Shreve, but to offer him a half-interest in the monopoly if he would instruct his lawyer to conduct his case in a way that would cost him the verdict. Livingston argued that the monopolists had nothing to lose in taking Shreve in with them; their boats could do little for them. Rather, they had much to gain by the gesture. They would enjoy the fruits of Shreve's originality. He would doubtless take up a golden offer of partnership, for he was said to be much in debt. Envoys went to the waterfront with a proposition that they believed no sane man would decline.

They found Shreve and confided to him that they had concluded it would be profitable to both sides of the controversy to cease hostilities and co-operate. In fact, the Livingston-Fulton Company was offering him a half-interest in the monopoly. The privilege grant, given for eighteen years, had twelve years more to run. There would be an extension of its term, up to a final accumulation of thirty years, for each steamboat produced that met certain requirements. During this time the Valley trade, which would multiply immeasurably, would be virtually in their hands. Besides this partnership in the company, Shreve was to be accorded equal credit with Robert Fulton for the invention of the steamboat. All Shreve needed to do, the persuasive argument went on, was to lose this suit.[29] It could be arranged without his appearing to have changed front — such things were done all the time.

Shreve listened in amazement to the offer. Under the artful reasoning a vista of wealth and honor opened before him. He was an obscure inventor, in financial straits. He had his family to consider. He had toiled on the rivers for nine years, slept wet and cold, sweated in the burning sun, fought off fevers; he had spent months of intense labor designing an engine and hull. All he had for this was debt and a long, precarious legal fight ahead.

Debt ... riches! With his good steamboat, and the privilege grant behind it, who knew how powerful he might grow in the Valley? He would be the inventor that the monopoly would henceforth coddle, his name would ring with fame. All he needed to do, the insistent voice repeated now, was to direct his lawyer to ease him out of his fight.

Shreve roused. His fight — the Valley's fight! It would go on. He made the point clear. The conference was over.

'The temptation was powerful,' wrote Judge Samuel Treat, of St. Louis, 'but he [Shreve] had commenced the controversy for other objects than private gain. He felt the force of his position — that on him hung the right of free navigation — that his companions on the waters of the West looked to him as their leader and representative in the struggle; — and he was equal to the occasion. He had dared risk his fortune in a contest, single-handed, against the most powerful monopoly of the times, and the same spirit which prompted him to resist at first, impelled him to spurn the base bribe, although it promised boundless wealth.' [30]

On Saturday, the day before Shreve was going to sail, all was in readiness for the passengers to come aboard the following morning when, down the waterfront, officers marched crisply toward the *Washington*. A queue of traders, idlers, and boatmen fell in behind them. They came aboard and made for the captain. One of them unfolded a paper and read this order of arrest:

'District Court of U. S. For the Louisiana District.
'The President of U. S. To the Marshal of the Louisiana District or to his lawful Deputy, Greeting:
  'You are hereby commanded to take Henry M. Shreves and him hold to bail in the sum of Ten Thousand Dollars, that he be and appear at a District Court of the United States, for the Louisiana District, to be holden at the

City of New Orleans on the third Monday of April next, to answer to the complaint of Edw. R. Livingston [31] and Elizabeth his wife ... and that he do file his defence or answer with the Clerk of said court, on or before the meeting of the same, or judgement will be given against him by default; and have you then and there this writ.

'Witness the Honable Dom. A. Hall, Judge of said court etc. 22 March 1817, and 41st year of the Independence of the U. S. (Signed) R. CLAIBORNE, Clk.' [32]

Edward Livingston and his partners had for some time been drawing up a petition of the heirs of Chancellor Livingston and Robert Fulton; and now, their bribe having failed, they were bent on bringing Shreve to trial. The petition showed that the Territory of Orleans had, on April 19, 1811, granted to the deceased partners the sole privilege of impelling vessels 'by fire or steam within the jurisdiction of the said Territory for and during the term of 18 yrs. from and after the first day of January ensuing.' The petitioners further showed 'that one, Henry M. Shreve, a citizen and inhabitant of the State of Ohio, did on the 7th of Oct, One Thousand Eight Hundred and Sixteen use, employ or navigate a boat or vessel called the "Washington" urged, impelled or driven through the water by the force of steam and fire, within the jurisdiction of the said Territory'; and also 'that the said Henry Shreive, on the twelfth day of March, One Thousand Eight Hundred and Seventeen, did again use, employ and navigate the said steamboat Washington within the jurisdiction afore-alleged.'

The officers came ashore with Shreve, towering and indignant, between them. The waiting crowd closed in after them. Men left their boats or carts to join it. What was going on? newcomers demanded. There was a babble of answers: they had taken the young captain off his boat; they were marching him to jail. *La prison — non, non!* Let him go! It was Shreve! In the war he had taken the children to safety. He had run the British blockade to Fort St. Philip, he had fought at Chalmette. *C'est le monopole — toujours le monopole!*

The crowd milled and clamored. The officers ordered it away. The roar only grew louder. For some reason, Shreve was led to Edward Livingston's office,[33] and when the mob saw where he was bound, it blazed to fury. Livingston, *Duc de la Batture!* By what right did he order a free citizen brought before him?

'At the request of Captain Shreve no outbreak occurred.' He was used to being obeyed. The crowd halted in its angry surge about the officers.[34]

If Edward Livingston had meant to furnish Shreve a chance to reconsider the monopoly's fat offer, after having been treated to a sound scare, he had miscalculated. Shreve's stand was taken. 'He could not be intimidated into a compromise.' It has been often written that the officers, alarmed at the temper of the mob, prudently released Shreve, but recently unearthed court records do not bear this out. Under the order for Shreve's arrest, on the court books, appears this item:

'Served and held to bail in the sum of 2000 Lb.
   '(Signed) M. REYNOT, Marshal.'

Then, in A. L. Duncan's handwriting, with his client's name at last correctly spelled, stands the following:

'R. R. Livingston et al vs. H. M. Shreve.

'Sir: Please take notice that I will apply for defendant's discharge on common bail tomorrow morning at 11 o'clock, the Judge having ordered the hearing in open court.

'A. L. DUNCAN, for Deft.' [35]

After all, the hearing probably did not take place at eleven o'clock. A further record shows that one of the attorneys for the plaintiffs could not be reached for a personal service of the summons until four o'clock Sunday afternoon, March twenty-third. It would seem, in the face of these court entries, that Shreve was held in custody for more than twenty-four hours.[36]

It was not until Tuesday [37] that Shreve sailed, two days behind his schedule. With a case coming up against him in less than a month, he had had to make arrangements to appear by attorney, as the Fulton and Livingston heirs must do.

The delay was not likely a hardship to the passengers. The arrest of their captain had furnished drama to fill the wait. His decks were lively with chatter about it and about New Orleans sight-seeing. There had been visits to the foreign-looking churches and to the negro pagan rites in Congo Square; glimpses of the chastely supervised Creole doorstep courtships; peeps into walled gardens; dancing and gaming; and shopping for baubles from Europe and the Orient. Now there was the long, luxurious trip ahead.

Besides a full list of passengers, the *Washington* was laden with a hundred and fifty-five tons of freight.[38] And there was no freshet to lift it along. A few months ago, Shreve had made this upstream voyage and the country had not roused from its apathy to note it. This trip, he hoped, would give the Valley new heart. Through the bright, warm days he listened to the pulse of his high-powered engines, and searched the river for swirls made by hidden snags. God had given the Valley this great roadway, but he had not made it safe to travel.

Even above Natchez, where the river flung its current headlong, the *Washington* skimmed easily. There were moonlight dancing and sunlit games. The cypress and cane gave way to oak and walnut. The prairie chicken, or pinnated grouse, strutted the prairie in great flocks, moaning its hoarse call. On the twenty-fourth day, the *Washington* pulled up to its home berth at Shippingport.[39]

Twenty-four days from New Orleans, heavily loaded, and with no aid of flood! Louisville had not believed that a large boat could make such time up the Mississippi. Then, too, the *Washington* had finished the trip without being shaken nearly to pieces, as the *Enterprise* and the *Aetna* had been. Its passengers made much of its smooth sailing and unusual comforts. They told of Shreve's arrest and the suit pending against him, and tales that had leaked out about the bribe offered him by the Fulton Company. In the East, Aaron Ogden had given up his battle against the Livingston-Fulton monopoly and was now hand in glove with it. Shreve was fighting on.

Louisville was more enthusiastic than ever about this fight, now that there was a large, fast upstream boat on the rivers. A new order was at hand. The Mississippi steamboat had come at last. Henry Shreve had created it. This tall young river man, retiring but forceful, with his swift, penetrating glance and reticent smile, was keenly original. He was honest and stubborn. There was a chance he might free the Mississippi outlet from the monopoly.

Louisville citizens decided to give Henry Shreve a public dinner and hail him as the ranking benefactor of the Mississippi Valley. When a delegation called on him and broached the plan, he was astonished. A banquet for him? Shreve was appreciative of the honor his townsmen wanted to show him, but he was far more concerned with getting away again to New Orleans. He would sail, he told his callers, the first day he could get his old cargo unloaded and a new one stowed. That would be about the twenty-seventh of April.

While banquet committees worked and the town buzzed, the suit against Shreve was heard in the District Court at New Orleans on April 21, 1817. Judge Dominick A. Hall presided. The heirs of Fulton and Livingston, citizens of New York, and Henry Shreve, of Kentucky — not Ohio — were represented by their attorneys. According to a court entry: 'It appearing, after arguments of counsel and the examination of the record in the case, that the court has no jurisdiction of the same, it is therefore ordered, adjudged and decreed that the petition of Pltffs be dismissed with costs.' [40]

The news of this favorable decision had not, of course, reached Louisville when the testimonial dinner to Henry Shreve, the most elaborate demonstration Louisville had ever witnessed, was held six days later in Union Hall. The ladies of the town had provided their finest napery and silver, china and crystal. Mulatto cooks turned out their magic dishes. Gentlemen had donated prize old wine and whiskey from their stores. Negroes bore heaping platters and kept the plates and glasses filled. Speeches were made with true Kentucky eloquence. Toasts were drunk to several Presidents of the United States; to the nineteen states of the Union; to the Mississippi and Ohio Rivers; to the states of Louisiana and New York; to Robert Fulton and Henry Shreve; and to Captain De Hart of the *Aetna*, who was greatly respected, even though he did run one of the monopoly's boats.[41]

When the guest of honor was asked for a speech, he stood up, tall and grave. Everyone had been very kind to him, and it had touched him, he said. But his achievement was small. The time was not far distant, he stated, when steamboats would make the trip from New Orleans to Louisville in ten days.

Ten days! After a gasp of incredulity, smiles were exchanged over the young captain's optimism. Shreve remained serious. He had been too conservative. He would himself build far better boats than the *Washington*. He had several improvements in mind now.

The celebration over, Shreve hurried to his boat. It was loaded with cargo; passengers were streaming aboard. A steamboat was a good investment, Shreve had assured business men. The *Washington* had paid for itself on its first two round trips, and left seventeen hundred dollars to divide among the owners.[42] Other builders should come forward.

The first real Mississippi steamboat pulled out, a crowd cheering it from shore. Keelboatmen and 'broadhorn' pushers eyed it with suspicion. On board, men lounged at the bar, drinking toddies and mint juleps. Ladies, gowned in French silks cut in the French mode that prevailed in Louisville, promenaded the upper deck. The captain had taken up his vigil. He scanned the channel for shoals or snags, and wondered whether, at the end of the trip, he would find a favorable or adverse court verdict.

When New Orleans sighted the *Washington*, alarm spread through the town. Merchants who had sent their goods north by it were dismayed and hurried to the wharves, crowding about the boat as it moored. What had happened? some demanded of those aboard. What ailed the boat? Why had it turned back? How far had it got upriver? [43]

How far? Louisville. In less than twenty-five days. It lay there ten days.

That heavily loaded vessel had made the upstream trip in little more than three weeks, and it was back for another cargo! Shippers went wild. A tremendous possibility of commerce and trade opened before them. Goods from the oceans of the world would pour through New Orleans and sail up the fifteen thousand miles of navigable Valley streams; produce from Canada, from the East, from the Rockies, would pour down through New Orleans to the Gulf. New Orleans would rule an inland empire of trade. Its port would outstrip New York, Philadelphia, Boston. It would grow into a great city. For, besides the achievements of this grotesque vessel, the Fulton monopoly had lost its suit against Shreve. Talk of all this rippled along the waterfront and Levee; it was enlarged on in the Market and on the verandas. There had not been so much excitement since the battle of New Orleans.

Meanwhile, word had been carried to Shreve by many eager messengers that the Livingston-Fulton case against him in the District Court had been dismissed. Shreve was well pleased, but he knew the struggle would go on. The monopoly would still claim its special privilege; boats might be seized or driven off without cargo. Edward Livingston did not let loose easily. Neither did Shreve. He would come here with steamboats again and again, in placid Quaker persistence, until the Mississippi was free.

When the *Washington* left Shippingport on its next trip down to New Orleans, on June twenty-fourth, it received a courtesy gun from the *Vesuvius*. This Fulton boat, after having burned to the water's edge at New Orleans, had been so reconstructed that it was able to run up the Mississippi [44] — given time enough.

The log of the *Washington* on this trip down showed the following entries: 'June 28. Met the s.b. *Aetna* at the foot of Buck Island under full sail. Met *Harriet* at No 54 lying among the willows. Met s. b. *Buffaloe* at the head of No. 57 aground. . . .' [45]

The Fulton steamboats still relied upon sails. Fulton himself had never believed that steam alone was adequate. He even boasted of the sails, claiming as his invention and exclusive right: 'the combination of sails with a steam-engine to drive a boat.' Chancellor Livingston, too, apparently considered steam as a partner of sails.

The *Washington* traveled upriver and down, and found freight and passengers waiting for it at every port. At the news of Shreve's court victory over the monopoly, optimism spread through the country. Other men began building steamboats, using the type of engines and hull that Shreve had originated. He had not patented any of his devices; they were free for anyone to use in furthering the development of the Mississippi trade.

In the East, all this while, the famous Ogden-Gibbons

suit over steam navigation simmered in the courts. Thomas Gibbons, a wealthy Georgian, had bought a summer home at Elizabethtown, New Jersey, and there had become interested in steamboating. He acquired a small steam ferry to run on the Raritan. It connected with Aaron Ogden's ferry which crossed the Hudson to New York. Ogden had paid a round price to the Livingston-Fulton Company for his permit; Gibbons had paid nothing, as he kept out of New York's forbidden waters. Gibbons's ferry fed trade to Ogden's line, so for a while all went well. Later — some time after Shreve's *Washington* suit at New Orleans — Gibbons decided to run his ferry to New York, in defiance of the Fulton special privilege. Expecting trouble, he persuaded Cornelius Vanderbilt, who owned a fleet of sailing vessels plying Long Island Sound, the east coast, and Hudson River, to take command of the ferry.

Vanderbilt, a big blond Dutchman, blustering, profane and hearty, was a man of vision. He saw far ahead into an empire of steam navigation, and knew that a battle must one day be fought with the Fulton monopoly. He liked a fight. He startled his friends by selling all his sailing ships to take the insignificant post of master of a steam ferry. Under his command, the ferry paid Gibbons handsomely. In another year, a second boat was put on the run.[46]

Aaron Ogden, who had dearly bought the right to cross the Hudson, was indignant over Gibbons's unpaid-for invasion. He secured an injunction against the rival line. Gibbons appealed, but the injunction was upheld. Nevertheless, Vanderbilt's lusty spirit, impressive size, the reputation of his ready fists, and his cleverness kept the Gibbons boats running. Deputy sheriffs were often waiting on the New York side to arrest Vanderbilt, but he eluded them by, it was said, hiding in a secret compartment of the boat. Gibbons and Vanderbilt in the East, and Shreve in the West, were fighting for the freedom of the country's waters. The rest of the nation watched its favorite arena, and hoped.

As Henry Shreve captained the *Washington* up and down, he studied its every whim to find how better steamboats might be designed. A year after his record trip to Louisville with the *Washington*, Shreve finished a new boat, the *Ohio*, of 443 tons. In this one, he provided double flues; and the boilers were supplied through the 'aftstands,' thereby further reducing fuel consumption, and also preventing those stands from being burned out every few months. In the same year (1818), Shreve, in partnership with Messrs. Miller and Breckenridge, of Louisville, built the *Napoleon*, of 332 tons. In 1819, Shreve built the *Post Boy*, of 200 tons, to carry mail between New Orleans and Louisville; this was the first mail steamer on western waters.[47]

Although the Livingston-Fulton Company still claimed the sole right of steam navigation in Louisiana, Shreve ran his steamboats into New Orleans. Edward Livingston and his splendid legal support could do little but threaten. Their appeal from the *Enterprise* verdict in the inferior court appears to have been still drowsing in the Louisiana Supreme Court.[48] Shreve held over the monopoly his bludgeon of heavy bond for damages if they seized his boats. Edward Livingston at last had encountered a will that matched his own. Shreve was as relentless as himself, and more dynamic. His energy was terrifying. He brought

down another boat and another. The monopoly's contention and helplessness grew farcical. Nothing could stop
Shreve. In 1819, the Livingston-Fulton Company withdrew all claim to an exclusive right of steam navigation in
Louisiana.[49]

News of this surged up every stream. The Mississippi
was free! Henry Shreve had battered the barrier down.
'At this day,' reported Judge Samuel Treat in 1848, 'the
enthusiasm with which the news was received cannot be
duly appreciated ... the western country owes a vast
debt to Captain H. M. Shreve.'

The Valley sprang into new life. Men who had lacked
courage to sail in the teeth of the monopoly began to
build steamboats. In the following two years, sixty were
built for the Valley rivers. All were patterned on Shreve's
models. Remote St. Louis, once so inaccessible, was now
a convenient port; it was growing rich and substantial.
New Orleans was one of the most important cities in the
nation. The wilderness was settling rapidly, comfort and
ease replacing pioneer privation and toil.

Five years after the Mississippi outlet was freed, the
Hudson threw off its shackles. The fight of Gibbons, with
Daniel Webster among his counsel, against Aaron Ogden,
had a hearing in the Supreme Court of the United States
in 1824. Chief Justice Marshall gave the court's decision
that under the Constitution all waterways of the country
were free to all men.

Meanwhile, owing to Henry Shreve's determined rout-
ing of the monopoly in Louisiana, the West and South
had gained a distinct advantage over the East in the development of river navigation and trade.

Shreve improved his designs with each boat he built. He provided more private cabins and began to name these compartments for the states of the Union. Concerning this, Winston Churchill, in his novel, *The Crisis*, put these words into the mouth of one of his characters: 'There was an old fellow named Shreve who ran steamers before Jackson fought the redcoats at New Orleans. In Shreve's time cabins were curtained off.... The old man built wooden rooms and named them after the different States ... and from this river the name spread over the world — stateroom.' Shreve was, at the time indicated, about thirty-four years old.

Others too have claimed that Henry Shreve originated the term 'stateroom,' but sailing ships had long designated the cabins provided for passengers of rank as 'State' rooms. Shreve in calling his cabins for Kentucky, Delaware, and so on, may have been making a play on this expression. From the Mississippi steamboats 'stateroom' came into general American use. Later it passed to sleeping compartments of steam trains.

The life of a steamboat was short, often no more than four or five years, even if it met with no accident. John James Audubon wrote, in November, 1820, from near Chain of Rocks, on the Ohio just above its mouth: 'The old *Washington* Steam Boat came along side of us Took 70 barrels of salt rais*d* steam and made herself fast about 2 miles below.' [50] The *Washington* was then four years old. It was discarded in 1822, as worn out. Although its model had come to be accepted by the Valley as the inevitable type of Mississippi steamboat, Shreve had found it inadequate. In 1824, when he began to build the *George Washington*, he made radical departures from his earlier designs.

The side-wheel boats, preferable to the stern-wheelers in most respects, were less flexible to steer; in order to turn, they had to describe a large circle. Shreve now proposed to connect each side wheel to one engine only — thus, one wheel would be able to go forward while the other went backward, and the boat could be turned in its own length. The boat would be almost flat of bottom, and have *two more stories of cabins and decks* than his other steamboats had.[51] His boats needed to be roomier. He was going to provide a setback story of cabins, and the pilothouse would sit atop that.

Shreve's associates argued that such a vessel would be so topheavy that it would sway from side to side, then turn over; and with each wheel connected to a different engine, the steering could not be controlled. Shreve showed mathematically that none of these misfortunes need be feared. The boat would float easily on the water, it would steer as if by magic. He wore down all opposition.[52] The construction of the *George Washington*, at Cincinnati, proceeded.

As had happened when the *Washington* was building, river men and landlubbers came and saw and croaked a pessimistc chorus: the thing was preposterous; a Tower of Babel, cabin upon cabin. It was dubbed 'Shreve's Folly.' To Shreve, his new boat was beautiful. It would sit the water like a swan with arched wings. It would be safe and fast; it could turn out alertly for driftwood or shoals. Its fittings would reach a new high mark of taste and comfort.

On the day set for it to sail a curious crowd gathered from near and far. A spectacular disaster had been prophesied. The sensation-hungry waited breathlessly for it

They were cheated; nothing untoward happened. The towering steamboat moved easily away and glided down the river. The spectators stared after its lofty structure as upon a miracle.

A description of the *George Washington* was written by W. Bullock, an Englishman, who traveled on it two years later while on his way home from Mexico by way of New Orleans: [53]

'On the third of April we left New Orleans in the beautiful steam-boat George Washington of 375 tons, built in Cincinnati, and certainly the finest fresh-water vessel I have ever seen. River boats, like these, possess the advantage of not having to contend with the ocean storms, as ours have, and are therefore built in a different manner, having three decks or stories above the water. The accomodations are much larger, and farther removed from the noise, heat and motion of the machinery; wood being the only fuel made use of, they are consequently not incommoded by the effects of dense smoke, so annoying in some of our steam vessels. The accomodations are excellent, and the cabins furnished in the most superb manner. None of the sleeping rooms have more than two beds. The principal are on the upper story, and a gallery and verandah extends entirely round the vessel, affording ample space for exercise, sheltered from the sun and rain, and commanding from its height, a fine view of the surrounding scenery, without being incommoded by the noise of the crew passing overhead. The meals served in these vessels are excellent, and served in superior style. The ladies have a separate cabin, with female attendants, and laundresses; there are, also, a circulating library, a smoking and drinking room for the gentlemen, with numerous offices for the servants &c. &c. They generally stop twice a day to take in wood for the engine, when fresh milk and other necessaries are procured and the passengers land for a short time. The voyage before the introduction of steam, was attended with much risk and labour, and occupied ninety days from New Orleans to Cincinnati, for small vessels, the same voyage (1600 miles) is now performed with the greatest ease and safety, in eleven or twelve days, against the stream, and the descent . . . is done in seven days; each vessel taking several hundred passengers besides her cargo of merchandise. . . . We paid 8 l. each from New Orleans to Louisville, (1500 miles) which includes every expense of living, servants &c. . . . The traveler is now enabled, without the least danger of fatigue, to traverse the otherwise almost impassable wilderness and wilds, that bound the western States of America, and this, without leaving his comfortable apartment, from the windows of which he can enjoy the constantly varying scenery, so new to European travelers.'

When Bullock made this voyage, the Valley steamboats were being modeled generally after the *George Washington* instead of the earlier *Washington*. All side paddle-wheels worked independently; all western boats sat nearly on top of the water. Shreve was quite undisturbed by imitation. He expected steamboat-builders to use the most practical design they could find. The Valley needed fast, capacious boats — its needs were his consuming interest.

Soon Henry Shreve was to give his whole attention to a problem that had bedeviled him since he brought his keelboat down the Ohio and up the Mississippi on its first voyage: the accumulated driftwood that choked the waterways. Turning from his packet boats, he spent fifteen years in a struggle to clear the Valley streams of stacked and planted timbers. It was a gigantic task. Shreve's performance of it stands as one of the myriad forgotten sacrifices of great and simple men.

CHAPTER

Six

THE inland rivers teemed with luxurious steamboats;
freight rates were reasonable and trade had quickened. Men from the eastern seaboard poured westward.
Slowly the eyes of the Government turned to the middle
country. The Valley could no longer be treated as a
remote hinterland — it was the full lap of the nation.

Great areas of the Valley's million and a quarter square
miles held the richest soil in the world. No other great
river valley was so habitable. It touched frozen winters
and endless summers, yet all of it lay within a temperate
average of climate. Its stream-edge forests furnished
timber for building; its limestone was inexhaustible. The
supply of iron included two mountains of it in the Missouri country. Lead ore was abundant. Coal cropped out
of its slopes. Hemp, wool, cotton, leather, and fur were
at hand for clothing. Every cereal of a temperate zone
could be raised. The apple, pear, peach, and plum of the
North were supplemented by the orange, banana, and fig
of the South. Berries grew wild in thickets as far as eye
could see; the grapevine twined wherever it could find a
hold. Sugar-cane and tobacco flourished. A variety of

nuts fattened myriads of small animals; deer and game fowl abounded. The native grass would furnish sustenance for any number of cattle, horses, and sheep. Medicinal herbs could be found for every Valley ill. There were the natural roads, the rivers, on which men could transport their produce. And there were the broad, light steamboats, so suited to these rivers that they might have sprung by magic from the waters.

The fact was well known at Washington that travel on these river roads was made extremely dangerous by the uprooted trees that were embedded in the channels or stacked at islands and bars. For years, boat-owners and settlers who had lost their craft or goods had pleaded with Congress to do something about the driftwood menace. The bewildered statesmen could offer no help. It was considered impossible to dislodge the enormous timbers: trees, whose roots had dug deep into the stream bottom and become planted, were packed down by tons of silt that had caught against them; those piled against bars were snarled together in great masses. Only a race of giants could cope with them.

These timbers were not only a bane to commerce, but had hampered troop movements in time of war. Both General Jackson and General William Henry Harrison had complained that the driftwood, especially in the Mississippi, had hindered them in their military campaigns.[1] It was essential, army heads insisted, that the inland rivers be cleared of obstructions, so that troops and supplies could be carried swiftly and without suffering more loss by river accidents than by enemy fire. In 1824, about the time that Shreve launched the *George Washington*, the United States Government took a hesitant step toward improving these rivers. John C. Calhoun, Secretary of War, sent a circular letter to all western steamboat captains, putting the question:

How could the Valley streams be cleared of their transplanted forests of dead trees and age-old accumulation of logs?

A mad and futile question to be posed by any government, most of the river captains believed. They did not reply to the query. Others who responded were pessimistic: men could never tear out the huge forest trees that had thrust their roots deep into the stream beds; no human strength could untangle the ancient log piles. A few thought that something possibly might be done to clean the rivers, but they could suggest no method. Fewer still made suggestions without much conviction that they would work. One captain offered a definite solution. This was Henry Shreve.

Shreve stated without reservation that the Mississippi could be entirely freed of obstructions. He outlined a method for doing it. The means would be a steam vessel which he had invented for that purpose three years ago. He offered to submit a model of it to the War Department.[2]

To this enthusiastic letter of Shreve's, answering the question in an explicit way and offering a definite solution, the War Department did not trouble to reply. Months went by. Then another circular letter was sent out to steamboat captains. This one offered an award of one thousand dollars for the best plan of removing timbers from the Valley rivers. Shreve, having waited eagerly for any interest shown in his reply to the first circular, ignored this one. The award went to Mr. Bruce, of Kentucky.

Bruce entered into a contract with the Government to remove, at the cost of sixty-five thousand dollars, all obstructions from the Ohio River, and from the Mississippi between the mouth of the Missouri and New Orleans.

Bruce had designed a machine with which he proposed to do this work, and now went to Pittsburgh to build it. Before he had gone very far with the construction, he realized that it was not practical. He abandoned it and began his campaign in the Ohio with manual labor, saws, levers, and chains, working from pole-driven flatboats. His attempt was brave, but inadequate. At the end of two years of hand-to-hand struggle with huge logs and spreading branches, his appropriation was exhausted; and there was little to show for the effort and money spent. Bruce had taken only a small portion of the driftwood from the Ohio. He had failed to remove a single timber from the Mississippi.[3]

Meanwhile, Henry Shreve went his way, running the sensational *George Washington* and his newer boat, the *President*. He spent much thought on further improvements for steamboats. In each of his successive models the engines had proved more capable, the draft shallower, the cabins more commodious; and each design had been readily adopted by other boat-builders. The Mississippi steamboat now surpassed any other craft on earth in efficiency, comfort, and service. Men of means had formerly avoided river trips — now they haunted the steamboats. (The French, however, were still inclined to send their goods and remain ashore.) The Valley had forgotten that it had ever considered Shreve's boats, with cabin on cabin and deck above deck, grotesque. These now familiar vessels floated on the water, broad and secure, towering and light. The sun gleamed on their white woodwork and many windows. At night they twinkled with lights like hospitable palaces set adrift.

As Shreve carried his passengers, mail, and freight up and down the Mississippi, he was increasingly rebellious about the driftwood that slowed his runs and constantly imperiled his boats. He was positive that this menace could be removed by means of the powerful steam device that he had invented, which would tear out these planted dead trees and jammed logs, but he was also convinced that it was hopeless to offer his invention to the War Department, now under the Whig administration of John Quincy Adams. Shreve was particularly unpopular with the present government. John Quincy Adams's ticket had defeated that of Andrew Jackson, and Shreve had been one of seven men in Louisville who had raised the first demonstration to have Jackson nominated for President.

The water forests would wave unmolested and logs would thrust from packed masses of timber. Boats, moving ever so warily, would be ripped — a sudden wrench, the rush of sucking water, a clanging of bells, terrified screams, and the current would sweep over another tragedy. The large quantity of sand borne along in the Mississippi made any accident on that river disastrous. Men who went down in its torrent were seldom seen again; sunken boats were soon embedded. But an inventor's politics was wrong — the rivers would have to wait.

The demands of farmers, merchants, and boat-owners continued to bombard Washington. Mr. Bruce's efforts to clear the streams with human labor had failed. A lately appointed successor to Bruce, Judge Samuel McKee, died within a few months after undertaking the work. The office of Superintendent of Western River Improvement was an exhausting and thankless post. Secretary of War James Barbour knew of no one who could or would fill it. When the Valley complaints grew more vehement, Barbour appealed to his predecessor, John C. Calhoun, who was now Vice-President: Did Mr. Calhoun know of anyone in the whole country who might be able to grapple with the problem of river clearance?

Mr. Calhoun did know of someone. He had been well aware for nearly two years that Henry Shreve, a friend of Andrew Jackson's, had designed a steam timber-removing boat with which he had proposed to clear the rivers. Calhoun had been content, however, to see everyone and everything else tried instead. He told Secretary Barbour now of Shreve.

And so, as an unexpected Christmas present, Shreve received an appointment, dated December 10, 1826, to the vacant post.[4] It was not a gift calculated to bring cheer to the season, an office demanding the most intensive work, bearing with it a traditional bombardment of public criticism, and paying only five thousand dollars a year, less than could be made on a single trip of a good steamboat to New Orleans. The job already carried a bleak record of futility and despair; it had broken the men who undertook it. Shreve would have to leave the luxurious background of his steamboats and the comforts of his Louisville home to go into the water wilderness for weeks or months at a stretch. Still, he was elated over getting the appointment, seeing his odd timber-clearing boat pulling the giant trees from the Mississippi and untangling log piles.

He had accepted eagerly the task of cleaning out the rivers and waited impatiently for instructions, but when his orders came, he was justly indignant over them. In his written acceptance of the office, he had made it plain that he would undertake this tremendous work only with the aid of the steam timber-removing vessel, or snag-boat, which he had invented. He had never thought for a moment that the massive forest trees deeply planted in the Mississippi bed, or the great shoals of wedged logs, could be dislodged by human muscle.

Shreve wrote an emphatic protest to the Engineers' Office of the War Department. He begged to have the snag-boat built. His superiors held flatly to their original order.[5] Shreve was tempted to throw over the whole project and go on with his steamboating, but the waving dead forests and endless graveyards of prostrate trees marshaled before him in a gloomy panorama — river navigation could never come into its own while the streams were half-choked. He decided to do the best he could with the task. Hastily he improved the hand-machine makeshifts of flatboat, windlass, chain, and lever, and went to work on the Ohio.

These poor devices got along in a laborious way here, but they would be worthless on the Mississippi. Again Shreve wrote to the Engineers' Office at Washington, urging that a steam snag-boat be built. Its cost of twelve thousand dollars would soon be saved by the speed and economy of its operation, he argued. The Valley's losses from snags had amounted to a million and a half dollars in the last five years. The annual commerce of fifty million dollars on the inland rivers needed protection; it needed speed. The snag-boat that he proposed building would be able to remove the most massive trees from the Mississippi, no matter how deeply they were embedded.[6]

His claims of what his snag-boat could achieve were looked upon in Washington as the boasts of a crank. The War Department firmly decided that no government money would be squandered upon such a theoretical contraption as had been described. The Engineers' Office sent Shreve an impatient command to proceed in his work without further protest, and by proved means.

The means had been proved, indeed, Shreve admitted sourly — proved hopeless. He returned to the futile flat-boat and hand-windlass method.

As the slow, ineffective effort went on, Shreve's impatience with it grew. There were twelve hundred miles of half-submerged forests in the Mississippi, the nation's greatest roadway. This vital trade route could never be cleared without the aid of steam.

Again Shreve wrote to his superiors, asking that they authorize him to have the snag-boat constructed — it was the only device with which he could hope to take the immense timber deposits out of the Mississippi. This plea again brought no result. Then Shreve made such a boat on a small scale, at his own expense, and tested it.[7] It performed exactly as he expected. He sent an enthusiastic account of this test to Washington, insisting that the full-sized vessel be built at once. With this boat, Shreve repeated, he could break off embedded trees, of any diameter, well below the river bed; or he could uproot loosely planted trees. All timbers would be cut up and floated off, or disposed of in some other manner. He would be able to clean the entire length of the Mississippi, from the Missouri mouth to the Gulf. He had seen his snag-boat work, and he knew.

Shreve did not expect to profit by his invention beyond using it to earn his modest salary as superintendent, yet his offer of it to the Government was met with the utmost suspicion. He had not patented any of his inventions,[8] he had merely set them to work. All he asked now was to set this one to work.

The coldness of the War Department did not discourage him. Just as the New England Quakers had returned with serene persistence to forbidden meeting-places, assembled outside their barred doors or among the ashes of their ruins, Henry Shreve came calmly back, again and again, with his insistent demand. His superiors were annoyed, disgruntled, bored or threatening. In time they were worn down. Wearily they agreed to have the snag-boat built.

Their agreement, however, bristled with such defensive caution on the part of the Government that any failure of the device would throw the entire expense of its construction upon the inventor, a cramped and sorry acceptance of a generous offer. But Shreve was satisfied. He willingly shouldered the risk that the Government would not bear, and placed his own moderate means and credit behind his resolution to clear the Valley rivers.[9]

After he began the construction of the snag-boat at New Albany, Indiana, a few miles below Louisville, opposition to it sprang up from some of the Valley folk themselves. As soon as rumors of the new device drifted about, indignant protests began to assail the already dubious Washington officials. One letter insultingly declared:

'It is said the present Superintendent [Captain Shreve] has in contemplation to construct a large and powerful steamboat for the purpose of cutting out the snags and pulling them down by force of steam. Now, those projects are only calculated to get through the appropriation, without anything like the object contemplated. *All machinery, whatsoever, whether used by lever or steam power,* is considered by persons who are well acquainted with the Mississippi River navigation, as a *useless expenditure of time and money.'* [10]

So gusty were these critics that it looked for a while as though Shreve might be retired and the cause of the rivers lost. But there were a few steamboat men anxious to have any means tried to make the rivers safer, and these petitioned the Government to let Shreve go on with his project.

It had taken him a year and a half to gain the War Department's consent to have the snag-boat built — permission had been sent him June 27, 1828 [11] — and it would take almost another year to complete the vessel. Meanwhile, Shreve further improved the hand-run boats and worked them in the Ohio and in cleaning off some of the island and sandbar edges in the Mississippi. Even with the stoutest efforts the hand-boats could not be made to lift any of the large trees planted in the Mississippi's bed.

While he waited for the snag-boat to be finished, Shreve eased his impatience by inventing a marine battering-ram for harbor defense. He submitted this design to the War Department. Officials there brought it to the attention of Andrew Jackson, the lately inaugurated President. Jackson requested Shreve to file accurate descriptions drawings, and complete details of this proposed military machine with the Navy Department, and to construct a model of it. Shreve filed the drawings and descriptions, but, with the demands of the rivers pressing him, he could not find time to make a model.[12]

This battering-ram, Shreve believed, would be able to sink an enemy vessel in twenty minutes, and be ready for another. Its machinery and propelling power would not be exposed to enemy fire, nor could a point-blank shot strike it. Later, a patent on such a machine was taken out by a distinguished naval officer who, it would seem, had given Shreve's material careful study.

The snag-boat, which Shreve had named the *Heliopolis*, was finished in April of 1829. Although it had a draft of only five feet and one inch, the boat could not then come down the Ohio.[13] That river was at its lowest stage for many years; the sandbars stretched high above it and glistened in the spring sun.

Throughout the summer the sandbars baked. Shreve, busy with hand-machine boats on the Ohio, waited impatiently for a freshet. It looked as if it would never rain again. Then August brought a deluge. The Ohio surged about the parched islands and over the sun-cracked bars. Shreve hastened to get the snag-boat, which now seemed almost mythical to the Washington office, across the river to Louisville.[14]

A crowd gathered on the New Albany shore to watch the peculiar craft pull out. Some men were indignant about the absurd thing, others shook their heads. At Louisville, townsmen, and traders who had ridden the freshet down from the east, gaped at the snag-boat as it drew into port. It was more startling than Shreve's radical river boats.

The snag-boat had twin hulls placed side by side about eleven feet apart, and connected abaft midships. The bows were connected at the waterline by a heavy wedge-shaped beam. This stout protruding beam was to be the main weapon against the giant trees embedded in the Mississippi. Besides the warlike beam, there were ingenious windlass, lever, and roller devices.[15]

On the whole, though, the boat was trim and innocent-looking. It could never, the spectators agreed, dislodge the massive drift-timbers in the Mississippi. Its first blow against one of them would jar its machinery to pieces. As the rumors from New Albany had insisted, this craft was a waste of government money. Louisville people regretted it. They liked Henry Shreve. He was a strange, deep man, with long silences and sudden enthusiasms. He was enthusiastic about this twin-hulled boat, but he would soon be disillusioned. The trees would still stand half-buried in the Mississippi. Boats would still crash against them and sink.

Perhaps Shreve took in the grave faces of these men and heard their prophecies and warnings, but he was too anxious about hiring a good crew for the *Heliopolis* to be concerned over anything else. It was getting harder all the time to persuade men to work at river clearance. There was no adventure in it; the government pay was small; and lately malignant fevers had followed the streams. When he finally had the boat manned, he sent it to Trinity, Illinois, at the Grand Chain of Rocks, where the hand-machine boats were working. He followed a few days later, bringing for the *Heliopolis* a missing iron shaft of 7354 pounds' weight, which belonged 'to the machine for raising snags.' The shaft, difficult to cast and turn on account of its weight, had not yet arrived from Cincinnati.[16]

On an August day Shreve sailed the snag-boat out of Trinity and down the hot, glassy Mississippi. He was buoyant over the coming test, although no one but himself believed in the *Heliopolis*. He had chosen Plum Point, halfway down the Tennessee State shore, for this trial. Here was the worst timber-clogged passage on the whole river, the terror of boatmen. As the unusual double boat made its way downstream, men on steamboats, keels, broadhorns, and barges shouted questions at it. The answers that were shouted back were taken as a joke. A steam snag-boat to pull the deep-planted trees out of the Plum Point channel! Ha ha, that was a good one!

Some of the boats fell in behind. When Shreve stopped at Plum Point, he had for an audience the crews of a short line of craft. Jeering quips were bandied from boat to boat. Raucous laughter came in gusts on the breeze.

Shreve knew that if his test failed, a cheer of cynical elation would ring from these very men who would benefit by its success. Not only this small group, but his countrymen all up and down the Valley, would feel a bitter exultation. Even the officials at Washington would find a certain satisfaction in a failure that they had persistently foretold; the cause of a cleared Mississippi might suffer a severe setback. He poised the *Heliopolis* for its first onslaught.

The twin boat drove head-on at a massive 'planter.' There was a booming impact, and crash. It seemed to the onlookers that the boat must shatter to pieces. But there it was, still intact, and the huge tree toppling into the water. A spontaneous cheer went up from the audience. The boat chains caught the tree, the windlass pulled it up until it lay on a series of fore and aft rollers. It was dismembered, cut into lengths, and pushed into the channel to float off.

In this headlong encounter there had not been a quiver in the boat's machinery, so perfectly was the shock distributed over the whole vessel. Repeatedly the boat attacked the thicket of large trees, vanquishing it. Of those who witnessed this battle, only Shreve was not astounded. He wrote simply to Brigadier-General Charles Gratiot, Chief of Engineers, of the War Department:

> Mouth White River, Arkansaw Tery,
> 23 August 1829
>
> Sir
>
> I have the honour to inform you that I have made some successful experiments with the U States Steam Boat Heliopolis. I got underway from Trinity, Ill, on the 19th instant at 9 A.M. and proceeded down to Plum Point (the Most dangerous place on the Mississippi River) where I arrived at 12 M. There I made the first attempt to remove snags with the boat & am prout to say that the performance far exceeded my most sanguine expectations. In eleven hours that whole forrest of formidable snags, so long the terror of the Boatman (many of which were six feet in diameter) were effectually removed. All of them were broken off several feet below the surface of the sand at the bottom of the river. . . .

From Plum Point Shreve had sailed to another danger spot, Islands Number 62 and 63, below Helena, Arkansas.

Here many of the planted trees were completely under water and could not be struck by the bow beam. For such as these Shreve had provided a method which he described in a report:

'When snags are invisible except by the breakers made by them, they are removed by a large chain, the two ends of which are made fast to the two bows of the boats, the middle bite of it is taken thirty feet abaft the main beam, where it is fastened by a line to the gunwale of each boat. In this manner the boat passes over the breaker in such a position as to bring the breaker between the two boats, when the snag or breaker is a few feet abaft the bows of the boats, the lines are let go, the bite of the chain falls below the surface of the water and either breaks the snag off in the mud or sand, or throws the end of it above the water where it is held by the headway of the boat, being kept between the wheels, until the chain from the main windlass is fastened to it, it is then thrown on deck and disposed of as before described.... I have no longer a doubt of being able to take every snag out of the river — should the Government continue the work.'

Shreve did have a doubt, though, that the War Department would believe his claims, and got his crew to back his statement. The following certificate, not in Shreve's handwriting, but its wording typical of him, was signed by his boat officers:

Mississippi River 10th Septr 1829
We the Undersigned, officers of the U. S. Steam Boat Heliopolis, do hereby Certify that we have succeeded, Under the direction of H. M. Shreve Sup...

&C in improving the Channel of the Mississippi Riv at two points that have for many years been Considered the Most dangerous, Namely at Plumb Point, and at Islands Nos 62 & 63 So as to be as Safe to navigate with any discription of Boat, as any other part of Sd River — And it is our belief, that Sd Boat is Capable of removing Any discription of Snag in the channel of the Mississippi; And upon trial we have found that She has more than answered our Most sanguine expectations.

On his way back up the Mississippi, Shreve removed all the timbers from the most dangerous passages. He trained his men to meet various emergencies, and, at the Ohio, turned the *Heliopolis* over to them, instructing them to go back down the Mississippi and take out every snag they could find. He himself had to be at Grand Chain of Rocks to superintend an important piece of work he had begun there.[17]

Grand Chain was a broken reef that reached nearly across the Ohio, about twenty miles above the river's mouth. Many boats came to grief here. Shreve had undertaken to remove enough of the ledge fragments to leave a safe channel. It was not a light task. The rocks were immense — one was forty feet long and twenty wide. Some of the stones rose high above the water, others hid just beneath it. Here Shreve had gathered flatboats that had been fitted up as living-quarters for the laborers; canoes from which the drilling in the rocks could be done; mess boats and blacksmith boats. The stores of black powder were kept ashore — dynamite had not yet come into use. A large crew of men was needed for this work. One of Shreve's voucher lists of supplies showed, among other items, ten dozen knives, forks, and spoons; six hogsheads of bacon; two barrels of mackerel; fourteen barrels of pork; one hogshead of molasses; and seventeen barrels of whiskey! [18]

Work at Grand Chain could be done only at a low-water stage, and was, therefore, much interrupted. Eventually, Shreve made a channel twelve hundred feet wide. He had removed 3375 tons of rock. With this rock he then constructed a dam which ran out from the Illinois shore, deepening the channel. [19]

All the winter of 1829–30, and the following summer, the *Heliopolis* worked up and down the Mississippi, from the Missouri mouth to Bayou Sara, just north of Baton Rouge. Monster sycamores, oaks, and cottonwoods were broken off at their points of leverage beneath the river bottom. Loosely planted trees were drawn up. Log masses were pulled from banks and sandbars. On Sundays, the snag-boat would put in at one or another of the many wood-yards that had been established by settlers to supply steamboats. Here repairs were made and boilers cleaned. By the end of 1830, the age-old drowned forests had vanished from the Mississippi. Shreve reported to General Gratiot that, during the past year, there had not been a single loss, through driftwood, of any kind of boat. [20]

Much work remained to be done. Trees, growing on bend banks that were undermined by the current, had to be felled to prevent their crashing into the stream at the next flood. Bars and islands were not entirely clean of timbers. There were other dams to be built in the Ohio. Wrecked boats must be lifted from channels — twelve boats had been drawn out of the Ohio below Louisville in a single month.[21]

Shreve had seven crews of men working now, each with a fleet of keelboats, scows, small steamers, skiffs, and flatboats. He traveled almost constantly from base to base, up and down a thousand miles of the Mississippi and nearly another thousand of the Ohio.[22]

Every time he stopped at Louisville, the weary superintendent found letters from his chief, General Gratiot, demanding more minute monthly reports. Each report was to list all work done in the past month, money spent, men employed, and supplies purchased. A description was demanded of the condition of boats and all other government property in the superintendent's charge. Accompanying the report was to be a detailed estimate of the cost of the next month's work. Shreve wrote repeatedly to Gratiot, explaining the great distances between points of operation, the slowness of communication, the tardiness of bills coming from distant supply ports, the carelessness of merchants in providing vouchers. He emphasized the impossibility of forecasting the extent or cost of work a month ahead — an estimate made for one water stage would be too great or small for another stage; often projected work had to be abandoned for months on account of floods or drought.[23]

On August 10, 1829, Shreve had written Gratiot that he could not devise any plan for making correct monthly reports. 'However,' he went on, 'I hope you will make great allowance, when you compare the operations under my charge with that of any other public work that is now in progress in the U. S., which on comparing will be found to be more complicated and attended with more difficulty than any other.'

Later, Shreve wrote to Gratiot, 'I find the responsibility of my station very great and the labour severe, therefore I hope some allowance will be made.' He promised to conform to the rigid rules as nearly as the nature of his tasks permitted. Still the demands for minutely detailed reports heckled him.

In October, Shreve sent a somewhat irritable reply to a request that he fill out form sheets in his monthly reports. The forms, designed for other types of public work, evidently did not perfectly fit his case. He wrote: 'If I was so situated as to be at one point with all my work under my eye & all my laborers within the compass of a Fort & all my papers in an office, I could then comply with all the rules and regulations of the Engineer Department as laid down . . . but the work under my charge, is of an entirely different character, attended with more casualties and more complicated in its operations than perhaps any other work under the direction of the Department. Each individual who has preceded me in the Superintendency of this work has been disgraced. For myself I undertook it with some confidence of success, but with little prospect of credit to myself. My whole time has been devoted to the service, my Machines for doing the work (which on examination will be found to be entirely new inventions well calculated for the execution of that work) have all been furnished from the exertions of my own mind. I have always hoped that I should be able to satisfy my Government and go through with that improvement without fault; how that may terminate time has to test.'

Shreve was conscientious and sensitive. He had an optimistic pride in his work. He was devoting himself, at a financial sacrifice, to river improvement because his heart was in it. He could not open a letter without a wistfulness for a word of approbation, or of confidence in him. This word never seemed to come.

Although the Engineers' Office approved each proposed operation before it was begun, the funds for it were sent with apparent reluctance. In the resulting waits, the boats, manned and provisioned to start on the new assignment, had to be held ready. Often, before the funds came, a flood would surge down the rivers or the water would fall too low. The projected work had to be abandoned, for the time. The crew was paid and released. A season's opportunity had been lost. Shreve, chafing and restless over one of these costly delays, protested to General Gratiot:

'I am led to believe that the Department suspects that all things relating to my business are not correct; if this has been the cause of the delay I am wronged by that suspicion, my labour has been faithfully bestowed and all the economy has been strictly used for the benefit of the work under my superintendence. What I have done for the improvement of the navigation is to be seen and speaks for itself. I hope you will be so good as to explain to me what you deem is incorrect in my proceedings.'

A lesser annoyance to Shreve arose from his traveling expenses. He found it nearly impossible to get these allowed, and was, himself, frequently out of pocket on their account. For every ferry trip over to New Albany, when the *Heliopolis* was being built, he had to produce a voucher. Vouchers had to be the first and last things in his mind, no matter how rushing the emergency.[24]

As time went on and the frequent losses of boats, cargoes, and crews had all but ceased, the heckling from Washington lessened. Funds were rarely delayed. Another snag-boat, the *Archimedes*, of shallower draft, was built for use in low water.[25]

Shreve had gained the grudging confidence of the War Office, but not of the public. Some settlers still sent up a protesting cry over each new phase of river improvement. They complained to Congress about everything that the superintendent and his crews did or failed to do. When the snag-boats were busy, thrifty citizens deplored the expense of their operation; if a flood or drought stopped the work, there was a volley of accusations that the snag-boats were lying idle on government time. Each tree that was not felled, but toppled from a caving bank, proved the futility of Shreve's efforts; each tree that was felled seemed to have its champion. Captain Lewis Bissell, of Missouri, complained to the Engineers' Department that trees on his waterfront had been cut down by one of Shreve's crews. General Ashley, Representative from Missouri, brought the grievance to the floor of Congress, charging that Bissell had been damaged to the amount of six or seven hundred dollars. After a lengthy correspondence between Shreve, Bissell, and General Gratiot, the matter was dropped. The most lasting furor was caused by a cut-off Shreve had made in 1830–31 where Red River flowed into a great circle of the Mississippi. Every water rise south of there was blamed on the absence of the circle. Emerson Gould, a veteran river man, later labeled the popular belief in the ill effects of this cut-off as a probable fancy.

Through the persistent, nettling criticism, Shreve went his determined way. He feared only one possible misfortune: that the Government, for some reason, might check his efforts to make the rivers safe and easy to navigate. No labor was too severe for him to spend on the rivers. He was jealous of every interference with his work on them. When one of the snag-boats was ordered by the War Department to tow a disabled government steamer, and when it was detailed to remove the Choctaw Indians, assembled at Memphis and Vicksburg, to the mouth of the Arkansas in an enforced migration, Shreve sent the Department a bill, in favor of river clearance.[26]

Henry Shreve is described as being, at this period, 'a man of fine appearance, with a face marked by indomitable energy and resolution; reserved and rather strange in manner; temperate in habits; brooking no disobeyance of orders or interference with his duty.'[27] He had one driving intention: to establish safe, fast river travel and transportation. It dominated him, it made him dominant. He swung out at a lax government, and at careless boat-owners and captains. He demanded that strict rules be put in force to prevent boat collisions at night, then drew up the rules himself and belabored government officials with them.[28]

In November of 1832, Shreve wrote to the Honorable C. A. Wickliffe, Chairman of the Committee on Public Lands, House of Representatives: 'I have witnessed four fatal accidents of this description [collision] — consequently I have thought much on the remedy to be applied. The one on which I have determined as most simple and effectual is to compel the boat bound down stream to stop her engine and drift in the stream when she has approached within a half mile of a boat bound up stream. . . . The penalty might be to make the descending boat liable for all damages if she did not stop her engine in time. . . . All boats descending should be prohibited from passing down the narrow and short channels of the Mississippi river, which is attended with great danger in case of boats meeting. Another subject of importance ... steamboat owners are in the habit of running boats that are worn out and rotten. If Congress will make provisions to inspect them, it will be a beneficial arrangement.'

Shreve urged the testing of steam boilers to prevent explosions. And since there was no adequate means of making such a test, he invented a hydraulic pump for the purpose. He wrote Mr. Wickliffe of this:

> Sir:
>
> A hydraulic pump, of sufficient capacity for proving the strength of a steam boiler, so constructed as to be portable and at the same time, applicable to every description of a boiler, can be manufactured at Cincinnati, O., for about $300, the entire operation can be moved from place to place on a common wheelbarrow....
>
> Your obedient Servant,
> H. M. SHREVE

In February of 1833, Shreve returned to Louisville from one of his river inspections and found an unusual letter from General Gratiot. It did not concern reports or form sheets, estimates or vouchers. It was an order to undertake a new and heavy assignment. Shreve read it excitedly, paced the cheerful living-room, and paused to look out at the bleak Ohio that flowed dully between ice strips. An occasional loose ice cake bore down against a passing boat. Ice was the only thing that might obstruct the Ohio now; the stacked driftwood and the channel rocks had been cleared away. The Cumberland River, too, had been improved. The Arkansas was opened nearly to Indian Territory. The Missouri was so well renovated that boats were, according to Shreve's reports, 'enabled to run ... in the night which was not attempted by any of them previous to the commencement of the work.' Above all, the Mississippi no longer pushed in and out of trees transplanted in its bed; it plunged along, open and broad, and could be kept that way merely by removing trees tossed into it by recurring floods.

Now ahead of Shreve rose his most gigantic task: a battle with the Great Raft of Red River, that jumble of piled timbers extending intermittently for, it was thought, a hundred and sixty miles, many stretches of it forming solid bridges from bank to bank.

CHAPTER

Seven

THAT singular stream, Red River of the South, rose in the western part of the Mexican province of Texas. A clear rill, beginning in a cavern, grew and rushed through a tortuous stone gorge. The cliffs that towered above the stream were carved by erosion into fantastic forms, like a double line of castles and battlemented walls against an intensely blue sky.[1]

Spreading away from the cliff summits in every direction lay the Staked Plain. This was a barren platform of rock, about two hundred miles wide, whose sides, often sheer bluffs, reared eight hundred feet above the rest of the country. The high tableland was a nearly uninterrupted desert. Animals shunned most of it because it lacked water. Indians ventured across it only at a few short angles between basins that filled with water in rainy seasons. Mexicans had marked a trail that touched at these scant pools. The stakes they used for this gave the desert its name Llano Estacado.

The rivulet had cut its gorge down through this tableland to the level of the rest of the surrounding country, which was itself sixteen hundred feet above the sea. For a brief time each day, the sun reached into the dusk of the narrow canyon, showing the layers of red and gray sandstone and white limestone of the walls.[2] The stream wound for a hundred miles in this cut, then tumbled down a rapid drop for seven hundred miles more. After this, it meandered beside the north border of Texas, entered a lower corner of Arkansas Territory, and turned sharply southward.

The river, dull red now with marl washed from its banks, flowed lazily into Louisiana and came to the head of the Great Raft. A little water seeped through the barrier, or a flood sheet might pass above it. The rest of the stream's volume spilled over the banks, submerging hundreds of thousands of acres.

The Great Raft grew slowly upstream, by driftwood lodged against its head. As it grew, the adjoining country was overflowed. Where substantial Indian villages had once clustered, the morass now stretched. Lofty dead oaks stood rotting in it. Swamps deepened to lakes, bayous linked lakes to marsh. After much wandering, some of the overflow found its way back to Red River before that stream came leisurely to the Mississippi, halfway down the eastern side of Louisiana.

For many years, much of the lower Red River country had been disputed ground between French Louisiana and Spanish Florida. Settlers in that region called it No Man's Land. When the United States bought Louisiana, it acquired this chronic wrangle. To get information about the newly purchased ground and the dispute over it, President Jefferson sent down an exploring party, headed by Thomas Freeman, a government surveyor, and Doctor Peter Custis, a naturalist.

In April of 1806, the party descended the Mississippi in two shallow barges, entered Red River and pulled upstream to the French village of Natchitoches. Above there the trip became difficult. The boats worked past one pile of driftwood only to encounter another. Presently the way was completely blocked by the lower end of the Great Raft. The explorers hired a Caddo Indian guide to take them on a détour through bayous, lakes, and swamps that were half-choked with timbers and willows. The guide lost his way in this maze of waters. Another Indian was engaged to lead the party to the open river above the head of the Raft.[3]

When the explorers set down their findings about the disputed region, the Great Raft, with willows, cottonwoods, broomstraw, and vines growing on top of it, was the most remarkable feature they had to report. They recommended feelingly that the Red River route be improved, and the Administration agreed that this water-road should be bettered. Later administrations echoed this. Now and then, schemes were proposed for doing it; attempts to carry the plans through were made and abandoned.

Eighteen years after the Freeman-Custis exploration, it became urgent for the United States to place a garrison on the upper Red River, against the border of Texas. Fort Towson was built on a high, healthy site at the mouth of Kiamichi River, more than five hundred miles above the head of the Raft. Stores for this outpost had to be sent down the Mississippi, up Red River, around the Raft through swamps and bayous, and then on. At a low-water stage, this détour could not be made. For one whole season the garrison at Fort Towson received no supplies.[4] The

War Department insisted that the Red River route be improved.

In 1828, Congress appropriated twenty-five thousand dollars for this purpose. Engineers and surveyors were sent south to look over the Raft region, in order to make recommendations and estimates. The investigators paddled into the swampy wilderness, in and out the littered bayous and brush-infested lakes. Now and then they turned back to the river, but met either a barrier of driftwood or a dammed and brimming pool.

The Indian guides said that the Raft had always been there. Their oldest tribal stories mentioned it. Each year it grew upstream, the swamp creeping beside it. Where their ancestors had once had their largest village, Caddo Lake now rippled. This cursed barrier would always crawl on and on, devouring the river, ruining the country, and driving out the game. The gods themselves could not stop it.

The tired and fever-ridden party echoed the hopelessness of the Indians. The engineers reported that it was impracticable to attack such a tremendous obstruction as the Raft. Any earnest attempt to remove it would cost from two to three million dollars, and have little chance of success. They advised that that idea be abandoned.[5] Perhaps the détour could be improved.

It had cost the Government a good share of the appropriated twenty-five thousand dollars to get this discouraging report. The War Department relayed the findings to Congress: *The clearing of Red River was all but impossible. Any attempt at it would cost millions and likely end in failure.*

The Great Raft would never be removed, the people of the Southwest heard. Gloom settled over Louisiana and

Arkansas Territory. Another canal or so might be cut to improve the détour around the Raft, but the planters and traders refused to be appeased with makeshifts. They had begun to hear how the driftwood was being miraculously swept out of the Mississippi by Shreve's snag-boat, and allowed themselves to envision an open Red River and a drained swampland. The richest soil in America lay under that stagnant overflow. Its fate would grow more hopeless as the river's silt, settling where the current was sluggish, built up the river bed until the stream would refuse what little drainage it now accepted from the countryside. Malaria would remain rampant, trade would be stifled.

The Southerners pelted Congress with demands that Red River be opened. Military experts added their insistence that the road to Fort Towson and the Indian posts be cleared. These pleas worried their way to the Secretary of War, General Lewis Cass. He studied them dubiously. The impossible was being asked of him. He put the question to his engineers: How could the Great Raft be taken out of Red River? The engineers had no solution. Henry Shreve had entirely cleared the dead forests out of the Mississippi, but the Red River obstruction was a much graver problem.

General Cass decided to throw the decision of this troublesome matter on Shreve and sent a letter to him, asking him what chance there was of opening Red River. The reply would be disheartening, no doubt, but every possibility would have been examined.

Shreve read the General's query without surprise. He saw nothing unusual in a project to wrench the Great Raft from its ancient bed. His reply was so confident that the War Department, after lengthy, puttering discussion, ordered him to proceed to Red River and undertake the colossal task.[6]

Now, on February 24, 1833, Shreve, with the coveted order in hand, stood looking out the window of his cheerful living-room at the wintry Ohio. He was planning intently. The light-draft *Archimedes* was to be in St. Louis on March sixth. He would meet it there and bring it back to Louisville. Here, meantime, would have been gathered three small government steamers, the *Java*, *Souvenir*, and *Pearl*, with their complements of keels and flatboats.

Shreve wrote at once to his chief, General Gratiot: 'I will leave here for the raft about the 15th of March. You will therefore please forward the whole amount of the Estimate as soon as possible. The great raft is in so remote a part of the Country that I cannot receive monthly remittances. It is therefore necessary that I should take with me the necessary funds.'

The entire appropriation for such a stupendous piece of work might seem to be a very large sum for a man to carry about with him. It was not, however, a great amount. Gratiot had already informed Shreve that the full allowance on hand was $21,663, or what remained from the $25,000 appropriation after the engineers' survey had been financed from it.

In another day, Shreve was on his way down the ice-edged Ohio to the Mississippi. He got the *Archimedes* at St. Louis and hurried it to Louisville. Here he manned and stocked the boats he had collected, and was ready to go on March fifteenth, the day he had set. But no money had come from Washington. Impatiently Shreve sent half of his men on ahead, and waited.

On March twenty-fifth, he wrote to General Gratiot: 'My preparations are all made for Red River. I started two Boats for the Raft with 80 men and only wait the arrival of the funds ... which should have been here 10 days ago — to follow in person.'

On March thirtieth, the money came. Out of the $21,663, Shreve paid for food, clothing, and medicine necessary for a hundred and sixty men during a long stay in the wilds, took what was left, and set out with the other boats and men down the Mississippi. He overtook the advance boats and reached Natchez on April third.[7] From here he wrote Gratiot that he expected to arrive at the Raft by the ninth.[8] The mouth of Red River was only about forty miles below Natchez as the crow flies, but not as the Mississippi twists. Still the channel was free of timbers, and Shreve was wasting no time.

He turned out of the lunging Mississippi into turbid Red River, whose drowsy current barely crept around the occasional heaps of driftwood. Cypress and cottonwoods of great size threw their reflections on the water. Where a vista opened between the shore trees, acres of palmettos could be seen. Swamp oak and hackberry trees grew sparsely. Grapevines had caught hold of sapling limbs and grown up with them, the twisted, thick bodies of the vines appearing to have reared unsupported a hundred feet in the air to grasp a lofty branch. An occasional clearing showed a log house, set high on stumps, looking secretive and blank without any window openings. Hollow cypress 'knees,' placed in a row against a shed, served for beehives. The inevitable hand-mill, in which corn was ground for each day's bread or mush, was nailed to a tree near the house. Farther upstream, the wilderness magically van-

'SNAGS
IN THE MISSOURI RIVER'

Reproduced from Charles Bodmer's hand-colored
drawings for Prince Maximilian von Wied Neuwied's
TRAVELS IN NORTH AMERICA, 1843

ished at intervals, and luxuriant plantations and spacious houses appeared.[9]

About a hundred miles up Red River, Shreve and his fleet came to Alexandria, an old and sophisticated town. It had a courthouse, three hotels, and a dozen good stores. Many of its houses were large and costly; their gardens had an Old-World conventional beauty. Planters on horseback from the countryside and ladies in small carriages kept the streets lively. The busiest places were the billiard rooms, and the racecourse at the upper end of the town.[10]

When Shreve's long line of boats came in sight, men left their games, women their shopping, and slaves their tasks, to gather at the riverbank and stare. Alexandria was accustomed to periodical swarms of boats, principally after the cotton harvest, but had never seen anything like this odd array. When the twin-hulled *Archimedes* was singled out, a cheer went up. Shreve had come! The Raft would be cleared out, Red River opened to the Spanish trade from the west! A navigable upper river, and land no longer swamped at flood seasons!

Soberer men among the onlookers doubted that the stream would be opened. They knew the Raft — trees were piled twenty-five feet deep and cemented together with centuries of packed silt and vegetation roots. There was nothing in this fleet of boats that looked as if it could break up that solid mass of timbers.

Shreve hurried his boats along. He was keen to get at his difficult undertaking. For seventy-five miles more, there were plantations, tiny settlements, and long stretches of lowland forest. Then the fleet neared the ancient town of Natchitoches, the last outpost of civilization, and called by the people south of it 'the jumping-off place.'

Natchitoches, a larger town than Alexandria, had once been the main village of the Natchitoche Indians, a tribe of the Caddo nation. The Spanish had made a settlement there before Philadelphia was founded. Its people were French, Spanish, and American, with a strong showing of Indian blood. It was the extreme end of steamboat navigation, and the last town toward the Spanish frontier. The Spanish came here from long distances to trade, paying for goods with silver bars and little mules. The Natchitoches people were easygoing, luxury-loving, and gay. There was always time to loll on the galleries of their houses, gossip, or play games. At candlelight, the tinkle of guitars and singing began in the taverns and spread through the town, keeping up well into the night.[11]

A few miles above here began the unbroken wilderness. Shreve noted that the shores were increasingly littered with fallen trees; the bars were piled with logs. Willows, leaning from rotten driftwood, scraped the boat sides. Beyond the banks, a shallow sea stretched among dead oak and ash trees. The scene had a vivid beauty. The sky was deep, bright blue; sunlight glinted on the marsh water, long black shadows of tree-trunks striped the shimmer. Vines and water-lilies, torn from their footing, floated about or caught at trees. Hanging moss waved idly. As the advance boat chugged forward, the gray logs in the snag piles appeared to lose long strips of bark — alligators slipping from their basking-places to sink in the opaque, silt-stirred stream.

The sun dropped early behind the trees, leaving a gloom over the marsh and river. The boats slowed, groping in a sudden dusk. Much later, a waning moon [12] slanted an orange light over the swamp and turned the black shadows of the trees like hands on a clock. In a while, the fleet was making good time on a whitened line of river between dark shores. Before long, the light would slip up the cypress trunks, shine a moment on the gray moss, and vanish. At daybreak, Shreve saw the solid mass of the Raft ahead.[13]

In places it reared jaggedly above the river; in others, it dropped below the surface. The water, now at very high stage, sucked against willows and cottonwoods that grew out of the Raft. Vine-draped logs thrust from the tightly packed timbers. This was the obstruction that closed off a thousand miles of Red River. Engineers believed that an attempt to remove this barrier would cost a titanic, but futile, effort. To Shreve, it was a challenging task that had fallen to his hand. He was impatient to start it. The laborers, on the bunk flatboats, were aroused. Breakfast was quickly served on the mess boat.

By good daylight, the *Archimedes* was steaming head-on into the Raft. There was a thud, a crackle as of artillery fire, and the groan of pulled timbers. Against the stillness of the swamp rang out another blow of the wedge-shaped beam; and another. There was the splash of wheels, clank of chains, grate of rollers, and rasp of saws. Men, naked to the waist, loosened a tangled chain, wielded axes, or handled the saw. Men in skiffs shoved the sawed timbers into the current, freeing a space behind the snag-boat for the next massive billets. A little steamer poked and drove the cut logs downstream in the sluggish current and herded them into the mouth of a bayou to close it. That would leave one less outlet to drain water from the river out over the land.[14]

The thud and crash, creak of hoisting-cables, and drone

of saws fell into a pattern. Calls, orders, curses, and warnings sounded through it. The white wood smoke from the
engine flues waved back and forth with the sudden movements of the snag-boat. Swarms of bees poured from
hollows in the disturbed timbers; men ducked under water
to escape them. Indians crept through the swamp to peer
from the shadows — the white men were crumbling the
mighty work of the Evil One. They were freeing the river.
The sensational news was hurried to the first Caddo village
back on high ground.

The sun set early behind the trees. Mosquitoes rose in
gray clouds. The battle of the Raft went on in the sub-
dued light. Later, the low sun sent copper streaks across
the marsh and drew them back; a chill ran over the earth.
Darkness fell quickly. Stars showed suddenly in the strip
of sky that wound above the river.

Lanterns twinkled on the mess boat. The forge fire on
the blacksmith boat glowed on the willows; the clang of an
anvil rang above the clatter of pots and heavy dishes as
broken chains and bars were mended for the next day's
work. The odor of strong coffee and roasted fat pork shut
out the dank smell of rotting logs. Men, still wet, but with
their shirts and jackets pulled on, shuffled to the benches
beside the long board tables. They ate voraciously and
with no talk, smoked their pipes, and turned in early,
drawing mosquito nettings about their bunks. The river
rocked the boats gently, an occasional loosened log drove
against them. While the tired men slept as though they
were dead, Shreve bent over his desk, making notes of the
day's work.

At dawn the whole colony was astir. Presently the bombardment of the Raft echoed through the marshes. On the

second night, after his men were abed, Shreve wrote to
General Gratiot:

> 12th April, 1833
> Grate Raft Red River

> I arrived at the foot of the raft yesterday at morn-
> ing. I am now about five miles through it. . . . The
> water is within two feet of the highest stage, therefore
> it is impracticable to clear the banks of the timber and
> willows that grow to low water mark. . . . I hope to
> effect more than was believed . . . possible, even under
> the disadvantages of commencing the work at a very
> unfavorable season.

The work on the Raft proved unusually hard and afflict-
ing. The steam of the swamp rose about the toilers. Vegetation, rotting where higher water had subsided, filled the
air with its stench. The midday sun beat down. Nights
were sultry, or chill with the slightest wind. Violent
storms swept the river. Sudden rains drenched the men
and boats; wet clothing would not dry. Still the *Archimedes* beat its way through the jammed mass of logs and
branches, chains and levers clanking and shrieking.

'In many places,' Shreve wrote in a report, 'the timber
was quite solid to the bottom of the river, which I found to
be on an average of twenty-five feet deep.'

At times, the boats came through the obstruction into a
dammed pool. In the shallower pools, wherever the willows left off, the water-lilies spread their flat leaves and
large white flowers so thickly on the surface that a bird
might walk on them from bank to bank. The boats plowed
through the lilies, stirring the red marl silt among them.

Then the onslaught of the snag-boat again silenced the twitter of insects and bellow of alligators.

A month after the first thunderous blows of the *Archimedes* shocked the wilderness, Shreve wrote to General Gratiot: 'I have the honour to inform the department that I have progressed through the raft fourty miles. . . . In that distance, thirty-one sections has been removed by drawing them out log by log.' Some of the willows and other trees that leaned over the water had been cut away. Islands had been cleaned of timbers by 'hauling the trees out by the roots.'

A week later Shreve reported to Gratiot: 'I have to inform you that my progress is yet continued in the same rate through the raft. I am now about fifty-five miles up from its foot.'

On June fifth, less than two months after he first attacked the Raft, Shreve reported: 'I am now within three miles of a point opposit Cado Agency. The distance from this place to the foot of the raft where I commenced operations is estimated by the settlers here at seventy miles. . . . I contemplate proceeding upwards fifteen days longer. I shall then retrace my steps and finish the work that may have been left incompleat from the hight of the water, which is now falling.'

The third week in June, Shreve ceased work on the Raft. His money was exhausted, and his men were falling prey to swamp fevers. Shreve wrote: 'The labour is severe, and exposes near the whole force to the heat of the sun, and constantly in the water.' He was disappointed that he had cleared away only seventy-odd miles of the huge obstruction in his two and a third months of effort. He had wanted to pierce twenty miles farther on his meager appropriation. When he wrote headquarters, he expressed the hope that he had at least been able to show that the Raft could be entirely torn out.[15]

The Red River was now open nearly to the Caddo Indian Agency, a matter of great satisfaction to both the Indians and the American traders. The route to Fort Towson had been greatly shortened — this alone was to save the Government eighty-five thousand dollars in the transportation of supplies in a single season. In that one item, the removal of timbers had paid for itself more than four times. Shreve had taken out this stretch of the barrier at the cost of about three hundred dollars a mile.

Where the Raft had been pulled away, the current multiplied in velocity twelve times — from a quarter of a mile an hour to three miles an hour. This vigorous current was digging the river bed ten feet deeper, not only to the former foot of the Raft, but for forty miles below it. The outlets, which had been draining the river, were stopped by filling the mouths with logs, packed in tightly by 'running a steamboat frequently against them.' Many of the sand islands were swept away by the current after the timbers on them had been drawn out.[16]

Shreve deplored that he had made poor progress in the unfavorable season. He insisted that the War Department allow him six months' more battle against the Raft, beginning at the low water in the autumn.[17]

Even another half-year's time was not to be enough for the task. The timbers were greener and stronger as the mass reached upstream, and the Raft was far longer than had been estimated. Shreve was to return to his fight again and again.

He started his fleet down through the cleaned stretch of

Red River late in June, and turned north in the Mississippi for his annual clean-up of new driftwood in that river. Before he got to Natchez, cholera, which was rife in the Valley, attacked his crew. The agonized victims had to be attended day and night. After the boats reached the Ohio, four of the men died. It had been an anxious trip. Shreve reached home exhausted and ill. He wrote casually in his report that it was fortunate that, in such a sickly season, he had lost only four of his hundred and sixty men. Of himself, he admitted: 'I am slightly indisposed, resulting from want of rest during the latter part of my passage up the river.'

Shreve settled back for one of his short stays at home. With the help of his brother-in-law, James Blair, who acted as his clerk, Shreve went over the reports from the captains of his various crews working up and down the rivers. These reports enumerated every snag drawn out, each tree felled, man hired, or lot of supplies bought. Following is an extract from the log of William Cooper, captain of a crew sent on the little steamer, *Java*, and two hand-machine boats to fell trees on the caving bend banks of the Arkansas River:

Sept. 12th, Fell on the Bank 250 trees Cut under the Bank 60 logs & removd 18 Snags.

" 13th, Fell on the Bank 174 trees Cut under the Bank 82 Logs & removd 13 Snags.

" 14th Fell on the Bank 28 trees Cut under the Bank 190 Logs removd 14 Snags & buryed William Allen who died at 6 o'Clock A.M.

Shreve, in turn, had to send on to Washington a report

of the total number of trees or timbers handled by each of his crews in the past month; of rocks blasted from the rivers, or yards of dike built. He listed the numbers of men employed, hours of work lost by them, damages to boats or equipment, repairs made, wages paid, provisions on hand, commodities purchased, bills settled and accounts disputed. Besides, he had to state his future intentions, chances of success, and estimated expense.

Then there were criticisms and accusations to answer. The people at Smithland, Kentucky, at the mouth of the Cumberland River, had objected to the building of a dam at near-by Cumberland Island for the improvement of the Ohio channel. Shreve wrote to his Department: 'During the progress of the work there [Smithland] there has been much clamour against it. . . . However, the clamour is now at an end.' The Smithland citizens, who had made it so hot for Shreve while the operations were going on, now sent a letter to Washington, dwelling on the great interest with which they had witnessed the work on the dam, and expressing much satisfaction with the improvement in navigation which it furnished.

Another complaint to be settled was from a Mr. Ewing, who demanded remuneration from the Government for damages caused to his land by the building of a dam at Cypress Creek on the Ohio. Shreve sent a map to General Gratiot, proving that Ewing's land was nowhere near the dam in question, and had not been injured by anything.

The Engineers' Department had sent Shreve a sharp reprimand for having had the crew of the *Archimedes* clean an accumulation of small timbers from an island chute at Horse Shoe Bend, on the Mississippi, without orders to do this. Shreve explained that the *Archimedes* had a broken shaft at that time and was being repaired. It seemed better to have the men busy than idle. The cleaning of this chute, with hand-boats, shortened the navigation route by fifteen miles. 'I did not consider at the time I had the work done,' Shreve wrote, 'that it was in the slightest degree a departure from the very letter of the law, much less from the intent and design of it.'

Gratiot had also sent Shreve a strict order to keep his funds in certain designated banks. Unfortunately, not one of these banks was within the range of his operations. The money might as well be reposing in Washington.

Most annoying to Shreve at this time was the storm of public disapproval, all up and down the Valley, of his attempt to remove the Raft from Red River. Men who had never heard of the Great Raft until a few months ago felt and wrote bitterly about the work being done on it. Letters on the subject had piled up at Louisville. The superintendent did not find much relaxation in his visits home.

On Sundays, Shreve went to the little Episcopal church of which Mary had become a member.[18] He appears to have remained a Quaker, although outwardly he wore no sign of it. His sister Rebecca, who had married James Blair, still conformed to the Friends' ways. Her letters were sprinkled with 'thees' and 'thous.'

Shreve, working on his reports or letters, found himself pausing, at times, to listen for the prattle of his little daughters. Their childhood had flown by in his long absences. All at once, it seemed, on one of his home-comings, he had found the small, curly-haired girls transformed into spirited young ladies, flitting about in a gay, youthful set. There were moments when he wondered if he had not sacrificed too much for the rivers. As in a dream he had witnessed the marriage of his elder daughter, Mary, to John Reel; and of Rebecca to Walker Randolph Carter, from Virginia. Both young men were steamboat officials.[19]

Louisville had grown into a handsome city. A lively succession of steamboats moved through the Portland Canal, that had just been cut around the Falls. It was a sophisticated city. Its intellectual life centered at the home of George Keats, brother of John Keats, the English poet. George Keats, 'a gentleman of fine address and literary tastes, respected and loved by all,' had come here twelve years before and opened a lumber business. There was fashionable society, too, a circle often graced by Henry Clay, of Lexington, Kentucky. An aura hung about Clay; he was acquainted with the great and near-great of two continents; he had basked in the very light of royalty while on foreign missions; above all, he had moved in the Paris realm of which Madame de Staël was queen. Louisville was fastidious, a little pretentious, but fundamentally democratic and independent.[20]

Shreve, forty-eight years old, had grown heavy, leonine, and more silent than ever. He is described in *Memorial History of Louisville*, by J. Stoddard Johnston, as 'a man of education and great force of character.' It is not known how much or little education he had, but it is evident that he had a peculiarly arresting personality. The elaborate attire of Louisville gentlemen of that time lost its importance on Shreve's big body. He forgot his clothes as soon as he put them on. His mind was usually intent on Valley navigation and its many problems. At moments he would rouse from his preoccupation to wonder at the respect in which his townsmen held him — he did not know that, with the might and sweep of the water wilderness clinging about him, he walked like a giant among them. He had fought for the rivers against foreign invasion, against cramping special privilege, and the forces of Nature. He was still fighting. The power he had hungered for was in his tense quiet and in his abrupt enthusiasms. It was for use, not display.

All summer of 1833, cholera had raged in the middle country. The dams Shreve was building at several points on the Ohio were delayed by lack of hands. He had great difficulty, in the autumn, manning his boats for work on the Arkansas River. After these boats finally were sent out, sickness invaded their crews. Men began to desert. Shreve combed the South for recruits, but there were almost no white workmen to be found. On December nineteenth, he wrote to General Gratiot describing the suffering of northern white men on the southern projects and asked permission to contract slave labor from plantation owners. It might make a political furor, but the river work must go on. He said:

'I would by no means recommend this as a general plan; because one of the great advantages of the expenditure of public funds for internal improvements is the distribution of the money among the free laboring men of the country. But in the execution of the work above alluded to, the case is different from most others. In that part of the country where the work is to be executed, there is no labour to be obtained, and makes it indispensable to transport laborers from a distance of twelve to fifteen hundred miles.'

The War Department promptly rejected the proposal to use slave labor on a government project. It would be like setting a match to tow. Moodily, Shreve made out with the handful of white workers he had.[21]

When he returned to Louisville for Christmas of that year, he found another accusation waiting for him. Apparently, a few stale facts had been embroidered with much suspicion and vilification and tossed into the War Department as a first-rate scandal: Shreve had hired incompetent men; he had let boats lie idle at government expense; he was guilty of buying provisions in St. Louis at a high price.[22]

In a letter to General Gratiot, dated December 21, 1833, Shreve made his reply:

'I have to acknowledge the receipt of your letter dated the 11th inst, accompanied by a copy of charges preferred against me by a Mr. John Simonds, Jr. of St. Louis Mo; also a copy of a letter addressed to Thomas B. Monroe Esqr, District Attorney of the United States, at Frankfort, Ky, requiring him to investigate that part of the subject relating to my integrity of character. I have this day addressed Mr. Monroe on the subject and only regret that it will interfere in some measure with my immediate departure to the Arkansas river. I have however requested Mr. Monroe to make as early a communication to me as possible in relation to the affair and will lose as little time as possible on acct of it. . . . I wish to have a full and satisfactory investigation of the whole affair.'

When the matter was hunted down, it was found that the incompetent men were sick with cholera, or dying; the idle boats were laid up for repairs; and when river clearance was being done near St. Louis, provisions were purchased in that city of somewhat high prices instead of at distant New Orleans, Louisville, or Wheeling.[23]

Shreve, upon his return to Red River, armed with another small appropriation, used the Caddo Agency house as his headquarters and a near-by bayou as his base. Here he grew close to that unusual people, the Caddo Indians, and watched their gathering tragedy with regret.[24]

The Caddo, or Caddoquious, Indians were not related to the tribes around them, but belonged to a larger tribal group on the western plains. They dwelt in the hill or bluff forests, in villages of tall, bullet-shaped houses which were constructed of woven mats, straw, and mud. All about these villages were fields of corn, potatoes, yams, and pumpkins. The Caddoes were diligent and thrifty. If the weather was too bad for them to work in the fields, they toiled in their huts. The men fashioned tools, weapons, and clothing; the women wove mats and molded pottery. The clothing was made of skins, to be worn in cold weather. In summer, except upon formal occasions, the Caddoes went nearly naked. They were skillful metal-smiths, and produced necklaces, ear-pendants, amulets, bracelets, and collars strikingly like those worn by the Aztecs. Their religion was similar to that of the Aztecs — the worship of a Great Spirit of which the sun was the symbol. In their devotional ceremonies of song and dance, offerings of bows and arrows, tobacco, corn, and buffalo fat were made to the sun god. Generally, these Indians were peaceable and mild; but they were harshly intolerant of laziness, and punished it severely.

The Caddoes had formerly lived about the great bend of Red River, where the stream turned south in Arkansas. Driven from this region by the Osage Indians, the Caddoes had moved down the river and settled on two ridges of land that ended at the water edge in steep cliffs. It was on one of these cliffs that Shreve had established his headquarters for work on the Raft. He found the Caddoes brave, diplomatic, and friendly. They boasted that they had never willingly shed a white man's blood.[25]

Ten years before Shreve first came to the Raft, these Indians had begun to grow discontented. The Choctaws and other tribes, whom the Caddoes considered thievish and indolent, when driven out of the neighboring country by the advance of white men, had encroached on Caddo territory. The Caddoes decided to sell their land to the United States, and accept an old, insistent invitation from the Mexican Government to move to Texas. The Mexicans thought that this industrious people would be worth luring into their country. The United States, reluctant to lose the intelligent tribe, refused to buy its land. Still the surge of white settlers drove alien Indians into this region; the whites themselves took bits of the Caddo ground without compunction. Fear and friction were increasing. The authorities finally decided to buy the Caddo territory and let these peaceable Indians go their way into Mexico.

Colonel Jehiel Brooks was sent as a government agent to treat with the Caddoes. He arrived at their agency on Red River early in June, 1835. Here he engaged elderly, weathered Larkin Edwards, long a friend of these Indians, to notify the chiefs and head men that he had come to buy their million acres.[26]

Larkin Edwards boated and plodded up and down the wilderness, carrying the message in the Caddo language. The Indians were relieved, yet dismayed. They had known for years that they were being crowded out of their land, but now that the time was at hand for them to part with their beloved country, the weight of tragedy settled on them.

Late in June, on an appointed day, the head chief, Tarshar, and the under-chief, Tsauninot, with twenty-three chosen councilors, made their way to the agency. They reached it at the hour when their god, the sun, blazed at zenith. It was a solemn procession. The Caddoes wore their most formal regalia. Each ceremonial cloak had a painted sun of many pointed rays on front and back; necklaces, bracelets, and earrings of cut stone caught the noon light. The Indians followed each other quietly into the large bare room of the agency house and took their places around the walls.

Colonel Brooks, seated at a table, looked them over with a shrewd eye. These were simple, trusting primitives, for all their careful dignity. Tersely, he stated the Government's willingness to buy the Caddo land. In the unwonted absence of old Larkin Edwards from a parley of these Indians with white men, his son, John Edwards, interpreted the statement.

Chief Tarshar stepped forward to address the room. With reserved eloquence, he told of the heartbreak of his people at having to part with their homeland. There was no alternative open to them, he admitted — the game had fled before the white men, and squatters were taking unlawful possession of the edges of their territory. It was better to sell what would eventually slip from them. He and his head men from the different districts had only just met here and had not had time to consult together; they would retire now, and come again tomorrow.

At ten o'clock the following morning, the Indians filed

back to the agency house. They had agreed among themselves to sell, on condition that they could reserve a square
mile of ground for their friend, Larkin Edwards. For
years he had been their champion and faithful interpreter.
He had never turned a red man hungry from his door.
Now that he was old and poor, unable to support himself
by the work of his hands, he must not be left destitute.
The Indians would not be here to care for him. When he
had been told that the tribe meant to repay him through
this sale, he had refused to be on hand. That was why his
son had to serve in his stead.

Colonel Brooks was well pleased that honest, stubborn
Larkin Edwards was not interpreting this deal. After the
first conference, Brooks had lost no time in having a
confidential talk with John Edwards. An understanding
glance between the agent and the young interpreter at this
meeting went unnoticed.

After a wearing silence, Brooks stated the Government's
price for the land. His voice was hard, his words blunt.
The Indians froze in their places. It was not in their code
to appeal or protest. They would have to discuss the offer,
their spokesman said. Stiffly, silently, they withdrew.

It was two days later when they appeared again at the
agency. They were stoical and resigned; they accepted the
Government's offer dully. The agreement was put in
English writing. Now John Edwards read the document
to the Indians in their own tongue: the United States con-
tracted to pay them eighty thousand dollars for the million
acres, or eight cents an acre for the richest soil in America.
Thirty thousand dollars would be paid at once in cash,
goods, and horses; the remainder was to be paid in five
annual installments of ten thousand dollars. The Caddoes,

for their part, were to move off the land at their own expense within a year.[27]

After the reading, the Indians were asked if they understood the document. They replied that they did. The ceremonial pipe was passed around and politenesses were exchanged. The Caddoes departed gravely. Colonel Brooks re-read the agreement with satisfaction. There was one clause in it that had been obediently skipped by the interpreter when he read it in Caddoan.

In the spring of the following year (1836), rumors came to Henry Shreve, at his camp on the bluff beside the agency house, that a trick had been played upon the Government by Colonel Brooks. Shreve traced the affair down. John Edwards, although he had been sworn to secrecy by Brooks, admitted to Shreve that the government agent had reserved a certain large area, a tract which had a river frontage of thirty-six miles, and contained 34,500 acres of rich land.[28] Shreve wrote a heated letter to President Jackson about it:

'The reserve was made to a half-breed Caddo, or his heirs,' Shreve revealed, 'without any knowledge on their part of the transaction until after the ratification of the treaty, when the agent came direct from Washington to Cample, the residence of the half-breed's heirs, and bought the whole of the reserve at $6000. It would have been sold by the Government for upwards of $150,000, if not double that amount. I am also informed that the principal Chiefs of the Caddos did not understand that such a reserve had been made. The witnesses to the treaty were also ignorant of such a clause having been made. The opinion that prevails here is, that it was a premeditated plan to defraud the Government, as the half-breed alluded to has no claim on the Caddo tribe. Not one individual of the heirs, twelve in number, lived within sixty miles of the Caddo boundary. They are the children of a negro woman. Under all circumstances, I am clearly of the opinion that an extensive fraud had been practiced on the Government by the Agent. . . .'

While the matter still rested there, Shreve was ordered north to the Upper Mississippi, to explore the Des Moines Rapids and Rock River Rapids, and to plan the cutting of canals through them. Steamboats persisted in going everywhere they could find a sheet of water a few feet deep, and were forever in trouble on these northern reefs.[29]

Shreve, in a small government steamer, sailed north of St. Louis, past the rearing white cliffs and misty hills, past the Des Moines Rapids, through which he had tugged his keelboat twenty-five years before and went on directly to Rock River Rapids. Here, the reefs, lapping past each other in midstream, made a steamboat hazard for eighteen miles. Shreve threaded these mazes until he knew every rod of them. He then planned a channel down the middle of the stream, by cutting off the lapping ends of the ledges.

The conditions at Des Moines Rapids were worse. The flow of water over the eleven-mile-long series of reefs was so shallow that freight often had to be taken off of steamboats and carried past the obstructions on lighters. Shreve charted a ninety-foot channel to be cut through the reefs near the west shore. 'The Des Moines Rapids can be so improved as not to require Buoys or Licensed Pilots,' Shreve reported.

Cutting these two channels would be a heavy but not

terrifying task, Shreve believed.[30] 'I have no hesitation in stating that it can be effected so as to remove all the difficulties that now exist, making the navigation as safe and easy over the Rapids as it is now above and below them,' he wrote to General Gratiot. 'The rapid sale of public lands in that section is a sufficient testimony of the importance of the navigation of that noble river.'

Shreve turned back to St. Louis, where another commission awaited him. For years the Mississippi had been cutting into the Illinois shore opposite St. Louis, and, correspondingly, receding from the Missouri side. Bloody Island had broadened, and another island was forming — a river that annually carried more than four hundred million tons of mud to the Gulf [31] dropped some of its burden on the way. The harbor of St. Louis was being destroyed; the port would soon be left inland. The citizens had appealed to Congress, and at last had obtained an appropriation of fifteen thousand dollars with which to save the harbor.

When Shreve arrived, the St. Louis people took heart. He had come to be looked upon as the miracle man of the rivers. Men watched him hopefully as he sailed back and forth, sounding, studying the current, planning. They were dismayed at his conclusions: fifteen thousand dollars would not restore the harbor; it would take four times this hard-won allowance. Dikes would have to be built at the Illinois side and at Bloody Island to throw the stream westward. Underwater construction was expensive. Shreve promised, though, that he would make a plea to his Department for fifty thousand dollars more for the project. It was too late in the season then to begin the work. By spring the necessary boats and equipment for this undertaking, as well as those for the channel-cutting in the Upper River, could be made ready.[32]

St. Louis set up a cry at this. How could they wait, with their port in danger? St. Louis always had to wait! Presently Shreve was under fire in Washington. The War Department debated his estimate of fifty thousand dollars additional cost. They noted, too, that he was again making an excuse of high water or low water, a late season or an early season, to postpone work. Perhaps a more alert and economical man was needed on the St. Louis project. In any case, Shreve was covering several thousand miles of river, and his hands were overfull.

A young West Point graduate, Lieutenant Robert E. Lee, on the staff of the Engineers' Office, overheard these discussions. He begged to be detailed to the St. Louis and Upper Mississippi work. General Gratiot agreed to it.[33]

Lieutenant Lee reached Louisville in July of 1837, where Shreve received him, and turned over to him all the equipment that he had ready for the St. Louis and Upper River improvements. He gave him, also, his charts and plans for both enterprises. Shreve was convinced that the rivers needed more men with engineering ability to work for them, and thought that this somewhat imperious, strong-willed young Virginian would do well by them.

Lee went on to St. Louis, arriving there August fifth. He was immediately discontented with the town and wrote in a letter: 'It is the dearest and dirtiest place I was ever in. Our daily expenses about equal our daily pay.' Nor was he overjoyed with his river work, writing to a friend later: 'I volunteered my services ... to get rid of the office in W[ashington].' He rented offices in a levee warehouse, had the riverbanks surveyed, and maps drawn. In general, he used Shreve's plan.

Lee reported to the War Department, in December, that the construction of the dikes at St. Louis would be 'attended with the greatest difficulty,' and their cost would be $158,554. He had added nearly a hundred thousand dollars to the estimate with which Shreve had dismayed his superiors.

So far, no work had been done on the harbor. Lee found that it was too late in the season to begin. He disbanded his force and went back East for the winter. When he returned in the spring, he sent a party to start operations at the Des Moines Rapids. The channels which Shreve had so optimistically planned to cut through the rock reefs seemed to Lee an appalling enterprise. He wrote to General Gratiot that this work, too, could be performed only with great difficulty. Shreve's casual tackling of these staggering tasks grew more amazing to Lee all the time.

The water at the rapids was rarely at a stage that permitted stone removal; there were months of waiting for a few weeks of actual work. The rapids channels developed slowly. The St. Louis project, too, dragged from season to season. The St. Louis public bickered over the delays; newspapers crabbed and insinuated; gossip darted about like wasps. Lee quivered before the stinging criticism that had always assailed river improvement, and wished heartily that the projects were finished so he could get back to Virginia. He suffered constantly under a sense of frustration; he was haunted by the dread that he might be sent to Red River, where Shreve battled with giant driftwood. In July of 1840, Congress adjourned without making any appropriations for the rivers, and in October, Lee abandoned his work in the West. The St. Louis harbor was in fair temporary shape; the work at Des Moines was well under way. Lee never returned.

During all this time, Shreve, busy on the Ohio, Arkansas, Red River, Mississippi, and Missouri, found his work often beside Lee's, or overlapping it.[34] There were occasional clashes of two steel-strong wills, but the determined, enthusiastic older man whose heart was in the rivers, and the temperamental young army engineer, enduring an uncongenial task, had grown together in mutual respect. To Henry Shreve, Robert E. Lee would always be, first of all, a man who had done his courageous part by the Valley streams.

CHAPTER

Eight

WHILE Henry Shreve was exploring the reefs in the Upper Mississippi and studying the St. Louis harbor, he did not forget the expensive fraud that he believed had been perpetrated against the Government when the Louisiana Caddo lands were purchased. His indignant letter to President Jackson apparently brought no result. It was incredible to Shreve that a federal agent should be allowed to prey so flagrantly upon the country he was appointed to serve.

When he returned to his work on the Red River Raft, early in 1837, Shreve found a deep resentment at the fraud among both whites and Indians. Presently, the Caddo chiefs and head men addressed a memorial to their white fathers in Washington, declaring that the treaty made with Colonel Brooks had lately been interpreted to them, and that they had discovered that the boundaries laid down in the document were not those understood by them when they signed their cross-marks in solemn ceremony. They had never owned the land reserved to the heirs of the half-breed, Grappe, and did not realize that a provision was being made for such persons.

The Government, apparently undisturbed by the costly

loss, flicked this evidence aside. Three years later, a Mr. Samuel Norris was to bring charges that the Grappe reservation had been fraudulently introduced into the Caddo treaty. The Committee on Indian Affairs tardily investigated the charges and recommended that they be referred to the courts. All interest in the matter seems to have dwindled after this.

Tragically, the treaty promise of the Caddoes to vacate the land they had sold could not be carried out within the year. Although Mexico had invited the tribe into Texas, the British-Americans of that province, who were now in revolt, very positively did not want among them a large body of Indians friendly to the Mexican Government. They threatened the Caddoes with extermination if they crossed the Texas border. A dearth of game in Louisiana finally drove the desperate Indians over the forbidden line. The Texans hunted them back. Hungry, forlorn, and shabby, the once thrifty, honest Caddoes learned to idle, steal, and to shed white men's blood.[1]

Meanwhile, Destiny shone on the legitimate but unlocated square mile of land reserved by the Indians for their faithful friend, Larkin Edwards. Traders had long fancied the cliff on which Shreve made his headquarters for the Red River work. It was the only lofty bank, except for one other, in a hundred miles. At this elevated point, the Texas trail reached the river. Along this high trail, from east and north, Americans were steadily drifting into Texas. Two Easterners, James Cane and William Bennett, recognized the importance of this cliff-top, squatted on it, and opened a store in a large log house. Business was excellent on 'Cane's and Bennett's Bluff.' The two traders wanted to secure a legal title to the ground.[2]

And so did one Angus McNeill. McNeill went to Larkin Edwards, and bought his unlocated square-mile reservation for the fair price of five thousand dollars. Then he persuaded Edwards to 'locate' this section of land on the coveted bluff-top. This was exceedingly hard on Messrs. Cane and Bennett; they might be evicted. McNeill let them worry a bit. He deliberated impressively, and sold them interests in the land.

His share lists were not closed yet; he was casting shrewdly about him. There was Bushrod Jenkins, who had gone about setting up a cotton gin, agreeing to furnish all the 'nessery timbers, sawn or hewn planks, shingles, nails, and mettle castings for the running geare'; there were James Pickett, from South Carolina, Sturgis Sprague, of Mississippi, and Thomas T. Williamson, of Arkansas, all substantial and farseeing — these gentlemen were taken into partnership. At last, Henry Shreve was invited to join them. Shreve felt that he had been a squatter on the ground for some time; he liked the commanding site, with the rich country spread about it and Red River winding past it. He accepted the invitation.

The Shreve Town Company was formed. A village, eight streets wide and eight long, was laid out. Each of the partners agreed to buy a lot and to use 'all proper means to encourage the settlement of said town.'

Not far above this town-site bluff was the other high bank on this stretch of river: Lower Coates's Bluff. On this second cliff, two men, Messrs. McLeod and Carr, although holding no title to the ground, had established a trading-post. The river made a great turn around the high point, circling nearly back upon itself. Where the current struck the cliff and veered, centuries of floods had carved

Bayou Pierre. This outlet carried half the water out of the river, not returning it to the main stream until a hundred miles below. Boats passing up and down Red River found the channel too shallow here. There had been trouble in getting dislodged driftwood carried away by the sleepy water in the circle, and Shreve had thought of cutting a canal across the narrow neck of land, disposing of the circle altogether. But he had discarded the idea. A. J. Bowman, a government engineer, sent to inspect Shreve's progress, strongly recommended that the canal be made. It would shorten the boat route, and would do away with the re-bound of flood waters from the bluff into Bayou Pierre.[3]

Shreve still hesitated to cut the canal. The citizens of the little town, which had come to be called Shreveport, were bent on having it done. They bombarded Shreve with pleas, arguing that boats could not run past here in the low-water seasons, and that, with the slow current not carrying the débris away, a new blockage would form.

The pleas rose to a hardy chorus. Shreve was thoughtful, and amused. At last, on a Sunday in May (1837) he took his newest snag-boat, the *Eradicator*, and dug a ditch across the forty-two-yard neck of the river circle. The water surged through the cut, digging it deeper and wider. Shreve, watching the ditch become part of the river, knew that it would accomplish all the beneficial things that his Shreveport friends had listed — and one thing more, which they had neglected to mention: it would leave the rival trading-post on Lower Coates's Bluff far inland, high and dry!

In his report to the Engineers' Department, he told of his Sunday foray briefly: 'A canal was also excavated across a narrow point of land through which the whole channel of the river now flows, and shortens the distance three miles.' [4]

Shreve closed the work for the season on May twenty-fifth. He wrote that he was within four hundred and forty yards of the head end of the Raft, but that the remainder was of newer timbers and would be hard to remove. He was again out of funds, and asked that another appropriation be made, and that it be not delayed until more timber had accumulated at the Raft's head. 'The Red River... will open a safe and easy steamboat navigation to the heart of the Indian settlements on the west side of the Mississippi river, as well as to an extensive line of the Texas frontier,' he argued. 'The country above the raft is also populating with great rapidity. Its settlers are now shut in from the market, which will be of easy access if the remainder of the raft is removed, which requires nothing but the means to carry on the work.'

Even with all but a fraction of the barrier cleared out, boats bound up and down Red River had to make a détour through almost impassable lakes and bayous. A journal kept by Robert Peebles a year before this (in 1836) describes the toil it cost to go around the then remaining twenty-three miles of the Raft. Peebles was aboard the small steamboat *Rover*, which had been engaged to carry stores from Pittsburgh to Fort Towson. Captain Benjamin Crooks was in command of the vessel.

The *Rover*, having reached Natchez, left that port for Fort Towson on December 21, 1835, with two keelboats in tow. It had no difficulty in the cleared part of Red River, and reached Soda, where Shreve's boats were operating, on December thirty-first. Shreve procured a pilot to guide the boats on their roundabout way. Hardly had the little steamer moved out of the cleared stream into Black Bayou when its troubles began. Trees, fallen across the bayou, must be cut away; brush and limbs hung over the narrow channel so that steam dared not be applied. The *Rover* had to be 'warped' along by cables and human muscle.

'No steamboat has ever passed through such navigation as the Steam Boat Rover has done this day,' Peebles wrote in his journal on January 2, 1836, 'as it took the greatest care and labor to keep the chimneys and upper works of the Steam Boat from being torn away.'

The keelboats, left behind while all hands warped the steamer up a piece, were brought along one at a time later. The stores were then removed from the *Rover* and placed on the keels, so the men could pull the steamer another few miles. Half the stores were put out of the keels on the bank, the keels drawn up to the steamer, unloaded, and taken back to bring the rest of the cargo. A little farther on, the bayou proved too shallow for the *Rover*. The crew built a dam of cross-timbers, pickets, clay, and prairie grass. This raised the water two feet, and the men 'hauled the boats up about 30 rods.'

After hanging trees were cut down and banks at the short turns had been dug away, the boats again moved 'a few rods upstream.' At the Falls, another dam was built. It failed to raise the water enough, and was rebuilt, taking three days' labor. The stores were set on land again, and the steamboat pulled by hand over the Falls. In several trips apiece, the keelboats brought the freight up. Going was better now. On January twentieth, the fleet 'got on two and a half miles.' The following day it made four miles more, and on the twenty-second, another two miles. The men warped the boats one at a time. On January twenty-third, the *Rover* moved only its own length. It waited while trees, standing in the channel, were cut down well below the water. Chisels were used for the felling, because the current was too strong for handling the saws — 'the day was freezing cold.'

There had followed other days of unloading, moving the boats a few rods, and reloading; and of digging down banks of 'the toughest kind of clay,' the men standing in the water. At last, Red River above the Raft was only a mile and a half away. It took eleven days to get all three boats and their freight through this distance. The trip around the Raft head, begun on December thirty-first, ended on February tenth, after forty days of exhausting toil. The voyage upriver was resumed.

The détour on the journey back from Fort Towson was nearly as difficult. The water had fallen. The boats were stranded in Red Bayou. A canal a hundred feet long had to be cut, 'labored hard at for a number of days.' The boats were tugged through it. The round trip from Natchez to Fort Towson had taken four months.

Peebles's diary came into the hands of Shreve, who later sent it to Washington. At the end of the journal is written: 'This Memorandum or Journal is left by Robert Peebles at the suggestion of a friend to enterprise and perseverance to comply with contracts and engagements.' It is catalogued in the National Archives as 'forwarded to the Chief of Engineers by Captain Henry M. Shreve in February, 1837.'

Part of Shreve's motive in putting this diary on file in the War Department doubtless was to pay a tribute to enterprise and perseverance, and to show what toil and expense it had cost Captain Crooks, of the *Rover*, to fulfill his contract. For the rest, he used it to emphasize the urgency of taking out the remaining Raft. He had had to beg for each successive appropriation. It was hard to impress his superiors with the importance of removing the last of the Raft at the earliest possible time. It had been harder still to explain to them the unexpected difficulty in the work on the upper end of the obstruction. The Red River undertaking had proved much larger than Shreve had at first thought. Government Engineer A. J. Bowman estimated the length of the Raft as having been, not one hundred and sixty miles, as earlier represented, but about two hundred and fourteen miles, and the upper stretches four times as troublesome to remove as the lower.

Bowman had written the Engineers' Office from Memphis, on April 16, 1837, that he was astounded by the herculean labor that had been performed. He reported:

' It is difficult to form a just conception of the magnitude of this work, or fully to appreciate the important results that are to flow from it.

'The river is navigable more than a thousand miles above the raft, and through a region not surpassed in fertility by any on the continent. . . . The indefatigable industry, zeal and perseverance of the superintendent have triumphed over difficulties well calculated to intimidate him; bayous have been closed by masses of timber, islands made of huge logs, for centuries embedded together, and covered with silt and living trees, have been removed. . . . Indeed, every mile in ascending bears evidence of immense labor bestowed upon its improvement.' [5]

It was in March of the next year, 1838, late spring in Louisiana, when one of the powerful snag-boats pierced through the head of the Raft, cleared the last of it away, and let the full current sweep down the stream! The first steamboat now passed up the river.[6]

The settlers were jubilant. They were, at last, in touch with the world, could travel with ease, take their products to new markets, and bring back comforts and luxuries such as they had never known before.

Shreve was satisfied to have conquered the stubborn barrier, but he was not elated. It was disappointing that the project had cost three hundred thousand dollars (a full tenth of what the Government engineers had estimated).[7] Moreover, the money and labor expended might all be forfeited by a piece of mistaken economy. Shreve had persistently begged the War Department to finance the felling of all trees on caving Red River banks, as far up as Fort Towson. Otherwise, each freshet would toss hundreds of large timbers into the stream. After the hard task of opening the river had been performed, the slight one of keeping it open should not be neglected.[8]

The tree-felling had not been ordered because the War Department could spend money only on extremely urgent ventures. The whole country was passing through a severe financial crisis and every government appropriation brought upon Van Buren's administration wails from a frightened public. No appropriation was made for keeping the channel of the Red River clear.

In July, about four months after the last of the huge obstruction had been torn out, a heavy flood threw trees from crumbling bend banks into the stream. They whirled down the river, tumbling against each other, and heaped in a mass three miles below where the Raft head had been. The current beat them together, working the roots down into the muddy bed, forming a blockage twenty-three hundred yards long.[9]

Shreve immediately asked his Department for orders to clear this mass away. By the time that the slow processes of Government had got the order to him, nearly four more months had gone by. Shreve sent the snag-boat *Eradicator*, with its auxiliary craft, south with Captain Tyson. The Red River flood had long since subsided. When Tyson got above Shreveport, on December sixteenth, he found only a thin copper rill in the channel. The bulk of the water was spilling over the lowlands above the lodged driftwood. The snag-boat could go no farther.[10]

Two more months elapsed. The water rose, and on February 15, 1839, Tyson pushed up to the now compact new raft. The great trees were lying at every angle, enmeshed together. The *Eradicator* picked them out, one by one. When it was nearing the last of them, violent rains set in. Streams raged into Red River, banks were torn out. The crashing down of trees filled the storm with terror. The whole river seemed to groan and shriek as oak and cottonwood hurled and beat together. After the flood had passed, another barrier, twenty-one hundred and fifty yards long, lay stacked where the recent one had been.[11]

Arriving at the Red River base at this time, Shreve found Captain Tyson in despair over the new driftwood. Two steamboats with cargoes of cotton waited above the barrier; five boats of various kinds, some with government stores for Fort Towson, had been stopped below the raft; three boats had left their cargoes in Shreveport warehouses and returned to New Orleans. Shreve wondered, for the moment, if human effort was, indeed, futile against the

terrible rages of Nature. All this misfortune could, however, have been spared by a campaign against trees on
undermined banks.

News flew back through the country that Henry Shreve
was here. Settlers paddled over their inundated fields or
down the flooded bayous to make their appeals to the superintendent: the river was their only road — these matted
timbers would isolate them again. It had swamped their
land. How soon could it be cleared away?

Shreve had to face these anxious men with depressing
facts. He showed them a letter he had received, some time
before, from Chief Engineer Joseph G. Totten, who had
replaced General Gratiot: 'Capt. H. M. Shreve — Supt.
Sir: No appropriations were made by Congress at the last
session for any works under your charge. . . . In Treasury
nothing, in agent's hands $7875.88. You will of course be
sure not to transcend amounts available in any of your
operations.' The seven-thousand-dollar remnant of the
Red River fund had been exhausted on the driftwood that
Captain Tyson had just removed.

The planters were stricken. Everything they had was
threatened by that mass of driftwood. Their very land
would be devoured again by the creeping marsh. Shreve
made up his mind — it might cost him his post as superintendent, but the river would be opened. He proposed to
the desperate settlers that they make a loan to finance the
clearing out of this new obstruction, and he would do all in
his power to get Congress to reimburse them.[12]

They agreed eagerly to this. In a short time, seventy-
one hundred and fifty dollars had been borrowed from the
Branch Real Estate Bank, at Washington, Arkansas. The
river work began at once. On May fourth, the last mam-

moth timber was drawn up. The *Eradicator* and its train of smaller boats sailed down the open stream on its way to St. Louis.[13]

Shreve again begged the War Department for funds to fell the endangered trees along Red River — not only for the sake of navigation, but to protect the land from over-flow. It was a country of great natural wealth, worth far more than the insignificant sum its protection would cost. The removal of the Great Raft had transformed the swamp into a succession of flourishing plantations, and had set up a substantial commerce. Before the Raft had been at-tacked by Shreve's powerful snag-boats, there had not been a single settlement, except the Caddo Indian Agency, from forty miles below the foot of the barrier up the whole seven-hundred-and-twenty-mile stretch to Fort Towson. Now, Shreve wrote with pride, this area was settled with 'a dense and respectable population. . . . There has also a town sprung up equal in population and surpassing any on Red River in amount of business transactions.' This was the town on Cane's and Bennett's Bluff — Shreveport. The rich Red River country, with its thousand-mile water-road kept open, would become one of the most valuable regions in the Union.[14]

The financial depression continued to weigh upon the nation. Shreve, with whatever was left of the appropri-ation for each river, continued his work. He especially de-plored the lack of funds for the Missouri. On an inspection trip up that river nearly to Westport Landing (later to be part of Kansas City), he had found the stream greatly bet-tered, but in need of much further improvement. He recommended to the War Department that an exceedingly light-draft iron-hulled snag-boat be built for the Missouri;

it must be of lighter draft even than the snag-boat *Henry M. Shreve*, recently placed in the Arkansas. A safely navigable Missouri River was of growing importance to the West, Shreve contended. He could not know then how important it was to be.[15]

For some time, the turbulent Mississippi below St. Louis had been neglected. New timbers had accumulated after storms and floods. Shreve besieged the War Office to have some work done on this stretch, but without success. St. Louisians felt personally ignored. They upbraided and criticized Shreve until he wrote Chief Engineer Totten: '... censure has been cast at me by the public on account of the situation.' This was a mild statement of the harsh and peppering comment.[16]

At last, with hard times squeezing the country dry, the river work all but ceased. The outcry of the ports was lost in the general murmur of discontent. In 1840, Van Buren paid the penalty of being in office when a long-gathering depression had settled over the country — he was not re-elected. William Henry Harrison rode into the Presidency on public reaction and a Whig ticket, died just a month after his inauguration, and was succeeded by Vice-President Tyler. In the general upheaval of Tyler's uneasy administration, there were many political victims. Henry Shreve was one of the earliest of these. To the consternation of the Valley, on September 11, 1841, Shreve was summarily dismissed from his post.[17] He was ordered to transfer the public property in his charge (which included the devices he had invented) to his successors, Captain John Russell, and Colonel Thomas T. Williamson, one of the founders of Shreveport.[18]

No work appears to have been done on the rivers for

more than a year after this. Colonel Williamson removed some later accumulations of timber from Red River, using, besides the snag-boats, the newly discovered explosive, nitroglycerine. President Tyler had little interest in the western rivers, and vetoed nearly every appropriation made for them by Congress. A bitter complaint of this was voiced by St. Louis delegates to a convention of shippers held at Chicago in July of 1847, more than two years after Tyler was out of office.

In the notice of dismissal sent to Henry Shreve, there were a few lines of regret:

'In concluding this communication, which finally dissolves your connexion with the Government as an Agent of this Department, I take occasion to say that the zeal you have manifested for the public interests, the ability you have displayed in conducting your operations, and the faithful manner in which for a series of years you have executed the various important trusts committed to your charge, entitle your conduct (so far as is known to this Department) not only to an avowal of satisfaction, but also to an expression of high approbation.'

The encouraging word, which Shreve had lacked all these years, had come at last.

His sudden discharge must, nevertheless, have been a severe jolt to him. It was not easy for a man of his dynamic energy to stop short. He had served the Valley rivers under three Presidents. He had given his inventiveness and fifteen years of his prime to the enormous task of tearing the timber deposits of centuries from the river beds. His efforts had made thousands of miles of once dangerous streams comparatively safe to navigate, and had reclaimed great areas of submerged rich land. Shreve had spent eleven earlier years devising steamboats that could sail those shallow, riotous streams.

Because of his labor and ingenuity, villages had sprung into cities. New Orleans, with its faster upriver transportation and multiplied trade, was the fourth city of the country in population; [19] its steam tonnage was more than twice that of New York. Jefferson had predicted, when he bought Louisiana, that New Orleans was destined to lead the world in commerce, [20] and many now believed it would. Louisville had prospered. St. Louis, once all but cut off from the world by the savage Mississippi current, was becoming important. Its population had tripled in the last ten years, and its steamboat arrivals, which had numbered eight in 1830, in the past year totaled more than two thousand. [21] 'The steamboat tonnage of the Mississippi Valley exceeded . . . the entire tonnage of the British Empire.' [22] The thriving, picturesque steamboat era was well on its way.

CHAPTER
Nine

WHEN Henry Shreve found himself abruptly set aside from the work that had been his first thought for fifteen years, he felt lost and frustrated. He had earnestly wanted to please his Government and the public. Now he could have leaned back and contemplated the middle country in pride and self-gratulation, for its clean, open streams and the vessels that floated on them, its growing ports and reclaimed land, owed an immense debt to him. Almost every mile of the principal trade routes showed the labor of his hand and brain. But he saw only that his task was unfinished. Others must take it up where he laid it down.

As for himself, he could go back to steamboating. Although he was fifty-six years old and showed the strain of the past fifteen driving years, he had not lost his zest for boating. Still, there was Mary — he had sacrificed her, as well as himself, to the rivers. It would be better, he thought, to find work that did not take him away from home. Idleness never occurred to him.

From his window he could see the Ohio slip by, dash over the stone ledges, and wind on between its brown banks. The rivers would glide their way through the Valley after this and leave him ashore. But the earth was good, too — across the Ohio, the hills were browning; beyond them would stretch the endless prairie. Shreve was a water man, but he was making a decision to go back to farming. He had happened into St. Louis five years before when parcels of the old Common Field were put up for sale, and he had gone, with curious others, to look over this relic of French days. The beauty of the Grand Prairie, which was the more distant part of the Common Field, with its woods and creeks and meadows, had tempted Shreve. He had bought three hundred acres of it then, and had added three more parcels to his tract within the next two years.[1] This land, four miles outside of the city limits, was wild and undisturbed; cattle wandered in it; outlaws took shelter in its gorges and stream thickets. Shreve had often thought of it as a retreat when he should finally be through his work on the rivers — a hazily remote time. Now, all at once, this time was upon him.

In a while, Henry Shreve, with his wife and little granddaughter, Harriet Reel, whose young mother had died when she was born, boarded a steamboat as a passenger, not master, on one of his last long river journeys.

Many on the boat knew him. 'That's Shreve,' they pointed him out. Already he was a legendary figure along the rivers. He was graying, dignified, erect. A long cutback walking-coat and tall gray hat of the period added to his height; the points of his collar stood out at angles from his chin. His brows had a way of pulling down over his keen eyes; his mouth closed in a determined line. Mary Shreve, like the other Louisville ladies of that day, wore a full-skirted dress with a tight, pointed bodice, a long narrow bonnet, and handsome three-cornered cashmere shawl.

Shreve invariably drew a crowd around him. He talked with great intensity and drive, or kept tight-lipped and silent. He had little to say on this trip. He was trying to realize that he was leaving the rivers — actually leaving them!

The boat stopped at many landings along the way. Bales and barrels were trundled ashore, crates and boxes were carried aboard. Carters and roustabouts sent up their needlessly far-flung cries. When St. Louis showed through the autumn river haze, passengers gathered their luggage and waited forward. The whistle — steam whistles had recently begun to replace the gun signals — shrieked its port call.[2]

St. Louis had grown phenomenally from the whitewashed village that Shreve had visited on his first trading trip, thirty-four years before. Now it stretched more than a mile along the river, and several blocks inland — a city of sixteen thousand people. An impressive line of steamboats reared their blunt, unenclosed bows above the levee. There were nearly three hundred steamboats on the Mississippi now, the largest and finest of them in the St. Louis trade. St. Louis might not become, as Pierre Laclede had fondly planned, the most beautiful city in America, but it was the principal port of the middle country. With boats the prime means of transportation throughout the world, only a port could hope to become a metropolis. A few visionaries dreamed that this place might some day rival New Orleans.

On his land in the rolling, virgin Grand Prairie, Shreve

began to build a substantial house. (This farm lay in what is now the north side of St. Louis, between Euclid and Taylor Avenues.) [3] He laid out gardens and fields, and called his home Gallatin Place,[4] probably in honor of that veteran Republican-Democrat, Alphonse Albert Gallatin, whose estate had adjoined Israel Shreve's farm in Pennsylvania. Gallatin had served in the Pennsylvania legislature, in Congress, as head of the Treasury Department, as Minister to France, and as Minister to England. Later he had become president of John Jacob Astor's National Bank in New York, where he found time to outline reforms of the penal code, to become an authority on Indian ethnology, and, at all moments, heartily to condemn a high protective tariff. For years he had been the ringing voice of his party.[5] It was growing common to name things for him.

Shreve farmed as he had boated — vigorously. Farming in the Missouri country had never been an art. The French had gone at it buoyantly in the spring, plowed — and nearly anything answered for a plow — sowed their seeds and trusted to the bounty of the *Bon Dieu*. The British-Americans had given earnest attention to hunting and grudging time to their fields. No one had bothered to develop better ways of farming. The crops grew well enough; the fertility of the soil seemed inexhaustible. Shreve, 'devoting his attention to improvements in agriculture,' [6] experimented in methods of planting and of soil conservation. His farm prospered.

For all that, his heart was out on the Valley streams. Whistled boat signals, riding the east wind, searched out Gallatin Place. Shreve's daughter, Rebecca, and her husband, Walker R. Carter, now lived in St. Louis, and

Shreve was soon deep in his son-in-law's steamboat enterprises. Gallatin Place became a favorite gathering-point for steamboat owners and officials. They liked to sit on the comfortable veranda or about the wood fire and talk of the greatness of river travel, and of its splendid future. The mid-Valley was a storehouse of natural riches. As these were developed, steamboating would grow.

Nothing, it was believed, could ever lessen the river steamboat traffic. The Erie Canal, opened seventeen years ago, and the later Welland Canal, had hardly dented Valley boating. St. Louis could still deliver grain and metal to Europe, by way of the Mississippi and New Orleans, more cheaply than they could be carried over any other route. As for the railroads, the few and insignificant lines in existence fed steamboat traffic; most of them had been constructed to carry ore, coal, or stone to the nearest navigable stream.

Railroads! The topic was always good for a round of humorous stories and indulgent chuckles. There was nothing more amusing than the efforts of railroads to establish themselves importantly. Shreve was not inclined to join in this mirth. He could see the railroad locomotives growing on the dim horizon where once the first crude steamboats had loomed. The railroads would yet be important, he thought — but only as servitors of steamboats.

Railroads were far from new. The first of them had appeared in England, near Newcastle-upon-Tyne,[7] nearly two hundred years before. In all this time they had gained little foothold in the transportation world. The Newcastle road had had parallel rails of wood, over which a horse could draw an unusual load of coal to the river barges.

Such roads were built by a few other collieries. But England had for some time been more intent upon canals, digging them wherever possible. The canal boats were generally pulled along by horses on a towpath. Railroads developed slowly. It was not until 1738 that cast-iron rails were used. These broke under the heavily laden wagons. It took thirty years more to discover the weight-distributing device of linking several small wagons, one behind the other.[8]

In the same year that Shreve built his first 'grotesque' Mississippi steamboat, the *Washington*, George Stephenson, along with several other Englishmen, patented a locomotive engine. At once the use of railroads spread to various collieries in the United Kingdom. In 1825, shortly after Shreve's towering *George Washington* had amazed the Mississippi Valley, the Stockton–Darlington railway in England began to use a locomotive, sending 'a signal-man on horseback in advance.' Soon that company was running a daily coach that carried six passengers inside and twenty outside.[9]

In that same year, Thomas Gray published a book pleading for an iron railway between London and other large cities. He set forth the railroad's 'vast superiority in every respect over all the present pitiful methods of conveyance.' One of the most persuasive arguments concerned the speedy delivery of fresh fish inland. His picture of rapid travel was startling. The horse stagecoach that ran from York to London could only promise in its advertisements to perform 'the whole journey in four days (if God permits).'

While iron railways and locomotives were warmly advocated by Gray and other enthusiasts, they were vigorously opposed by most Englishmen. Elderly gentlemen were positive that they could not cross the tracks without being run over. Young gentlemen thought the locomotive might disturb the foxes and pheasants. Farmers vowed that cows would not graze within sight or sound of the engines, and that such iron monsters, snorting across the country, might cause calves to be birthed prematurely. Ladies had their own whispered fears. Still, although England had nearly a hundred canals which had cost above thirty million pounds, railroads steadily increased.[10]

In the United States, because of the far-reaching river system, interest in railroads lagged. The Valley streams were a blessing that the Americans accepted casually, but at which other countries marveled. The *Edinburgh Review* had once stated: 'One of the great sources in America is, and will be, an astonishing command of inland navigation: the Mississippi, flowing from the north of the gulph of Mexico, through 17 degrees of latitude; the Ohio and the Alleghany almost connecting it with the northern lakes; the Wabash, the Illinois, the Missouri, the Achansas, the Red River, flowing from the confines of New Mexico. These rivers, all navigable, and most of them frequented by steamboats, constitute a facility of internal communication not, we believe, to be paralleled in the whole world.' [11]

The steamboats that plied these American rivers were also a subject of wonder abroad. A writer in the British *Gentleman's Magazine* had declared: 'One of these on the Mississippi passes two thousand miles in twenty-one days, and this, too, against the current, which is perpetually running down. The above boat . . . carries 460 tons, at a very shallow draft of water, and conveys from New Orleans whole ships' cargoes into the interior of the country as well as passengers.' (The English tidewater rivers did not perpetually run down.)

The eastern United States produced a few early champions of the railroad. In 1812, Colonel John Stevens, of New Jersey, one of the first American steamboat inventors, busied himself writing to influential men, pleading that they persuade Congress to appropriate a couple of thousand dollars for railroad experimentation. One prominent man to whom he wrote was Chancellor Robert Livingston. The Chancellor could give Stevens no encouragement: he was convinced that one train would run over another ahead of it, and that nothing could prevent this. Other men in power were equally skeptical. They feared that the dampening of the wooden rails by rain would swell them so that the car wheels could hardly squeeze along on them. All were staggered by Stevens's proposal to put a hundred tons in motion on any road at a velocity of four miles an hour.[12]

The construction of the Bunker Hill Monument, in 1826, produced the first railroad in the country. The line, running from a granite quarry to a Neponset wharf, was three miles long. This railroad operated by gravity and two horses, except over a short inclined plane where a stationary engine and endless chains were employed. In the following year, a long road, of nine miles, was built in Pennsylvania, from an anthracite coal mine to the Lehigh River. It was operated by gravity and mules — the loaded cars coasted downgrade, one of them carrying the mules to haul the empty train back. Mule power was continued on the road for seventeen years before a locomotive was installed.[13]

The first general railroad in America, the Baltimore and Ohio, opened in 1830, when a thirteen-mile stretch of it was completed to Ellicott's Mills. It operated by a horse-locomotive — a horse in the locomotive-car treading an endless belt to furnish power. While drawing a car filled with editors and reporters, the horse-locomotive ran into a cow, and rolled, with its passenger car, down an embankment. The jolted and disarranged press gave a sour account of it to an already skeptical public. Sails, too, were tried on this road, but it was necessary to have a gale abaft, so the train seldom appeared unless a north-wester was blowing. In the same year, a railroad running from Charleston, South Carolina, *toward* Augusta was opened. Here, also, horse-power and sails were used. The Charleston *Courier*, of March, 1830, gave this account:

'Sailing on Land. — A sail was set in a car on our rail-road yesterday in the presence of a large concourse of spectators. Fifteen gentlemen got on board and flew off at the rate of 12 to fourteen miles an hour. . . . When going at the rate of twelve miles an hour . . . the mast head went by the board with the sail and rigging attached, carrying with them several of the crew. The wreck was descried by several friendly shipmasters who kindly rendered assistance in rigging up a jury-mast and the car was again put under way.' [14]

So far, the public did not take railways seriously. A car whisked fitfully by the wind down a track was diverting, as a novelty. The steam locomotive, built later at the West Point foundry for the Charleston line, was only a little less amusing; its boiler stood upright like a bottle, the wheels were four and a half feet in diameter. It gave good service, though, and by 1833 the Charleston Railroad was the longest in the world under one management — one hundred and thirty-seven miles.[15]

Meanwhile, a railroad had been built from Albany to Schenectady. Its locomotive, the 'De Witt Clinton,' made a first run in 1831. The whole countryside gathered along the track to see the train pass. When the five giddily painted coaches were filled with passengers, and the conductor, enthroned on a small buggy-seat in the tender, sounded a tin horn, the train lunged ahead with such a jerk that gentlemen were bounded from their places, 'to the detriment of their high beaver hats against the roof.' Smoke blew back into the faces of the passengers; the August sun slanted under the roof canopies; there were little cries from the ladies as sparks peppered their flimsy dresses and straw hats. At the first water station the train halted as abruptly as it had started. The passengers pitched violently forward or jerked backward. Hats were recovered, dignity resumed, and the journey continued. All the while, there was a series of accidents among the spectators lined along the way; horses reared, wheels tangled, and women screamed. Before the train made its return trip, rails were borrowed from a convenient fence and used, in some fashion, to lessen the jerk and the bumping of the coaches. The trip was a tremendous success. There was quite a stir about it in the newspapers.[16]

It was not long before regular schedules were established on several railroads. In 1832, an advertisement in a Philadelphia newspaper read: 'Notice to the Public. — The engine, with a train of cars, will be run daily, commencing this day, when the weather is fair; when the weather is not fair, the horse will draw the cars. Passengers are requested to be punctual at the hour of starting.'[17]

But for the mid-Valley, this dirty, jolting, and ludicrous railroad travel held no allure. Why be shaken half to pieces, or choked with dust, in a locomotive train? On the deck of a palatial steamboat, skimming along a clean, shimmering river, one could lounge at ease, watch the birds rising ahead to fly against the sky, and hear the echoes of the hand-boat bugles from the wooded shores; there was always music from the cabin, games, cool drinks, beautifully appointed meals, and a comfortable stateroom. All places worth shipping to, or visiting, were along the rivers. Railroads were not needed here.

Thus Walker R. Carter and his associates on the lawn at Gallatin believed. Steamboats multiplied at the wharves. The St. Louis shore, once piled with pelts, was now often stacked with cotton bales — this port was coming to be the largest inland cotton market in the world. Merchandise of every kind found its way there. More warehouses were springing up, and two new boat-building concerns had been organized. St. Louis, the lately remote frontier post, had been made a port of foreign entry eleven years ago,[18] and was becoming a trade and travel center of a rapidly expanding nation.

Shreve lounged broadly in his chair as this confident talk of river trade drifted about him. He felt a keen pride in St. Louis's water commerce. The huddle of *pirogues*, keels, and flatboats at the sandbar below the French village had sprung miraculously into a mile-long line of steamers. Only twenty-five years ago, in 1817, the first steamboat had come to this port — the *Zebulon M. Pike*, built at Henderson, Kentucky, by a Mr. Prentiss. Half the population had come to the riverbank and stood in the burning August sun to wonder at the vessel. It was hardly larger than Shreve's early keelboat, and no faster. It made three and a quarter miles an hour upstream, and had spent six weeks on the way from Louisville. The smoke spouting from the flue had been impressive, but muscle-power had proved the *Zebulon M. Pike's* best dependence. 'In the encounter with a rapid current the crew reinforced steam with the impulse of their own strength.' Poles and running-boards had been used, just as in the familiar jab-and-push navigation of barges and keelboats.[19]

Two years later, on a March day of 1819, Shreve had brought the *Washington* up to St. Louis from New Orleans. Its speed and elegance were a revelation to this out-of-the-way port. Two years after that, he had taken the *Washington* up the Missouri to Council Bluffs, and had written emphatically in defense of that ill-famed river. The Missouri had, he contended from the first, a definite future of steam navigation.[20]

For a while, only an occasional steamboat had found its way to St. Louis, but after the dead trees were cleaned out of the Mississippi above the Ohio, steam commerce on this stretch of river began to leap forward. Now these Mississippi boats, fashioned upon Shreve's models, furnished the most convenient and luxurious transportation the world had ever seen.[21] Shreve, gazing beyond his lawn, over the Grand Prairie, could vision them twinkling at night past dark forested shores, or lined in a white mass at the large ports. The great era of western steamboating was well on its way.

Shreve had a substantial interest in St. Louis shipping, and, from time to time, bought lots in the warehouse district. But he considered himself now primarily a farmer. For months at a time he would farm absorbedly, always experimenting.

His plantation was a village in itself, with clusters of darky cabins and stores of supplies. The mansion was always filled. Gathered into it, besides Walker Carter and his family, were old, orphaned, or lonely kinsfolk. Shreve's great-granddaughter, Emma Carter Edwards, writes: 'Gallatin seems to have been a refuge for numerous relatives — a large household, evidently.' Here young Henry Blair, Mary's lively nephew, pulled his endless pranks; through these big cool rooms lovely little Callie Blair, who was to marry wealthy Mr. Ames, of Boston, played and laughed; in the stately parlor, slight, auburn-haired Amelia Blair was to marry tall, lean, blue-eyed Ben Dorsey, up from Kentucky. At Christmas, the house would be crowded with guests and ringing with the voices of children. The drive was lined with sleighs or carriages. There were times when it was near to being a hospital. Childhood epidemics swept it; and there was a shocked day when lively young Henry Blair, injured at skating, was laid across the dining-table while city doctors administered laudanum and amputated a twice-broken leg. Christenings, weddings, and funerals, the passing traveler, and a never-ceasing stream of old Louisville friends, up by steamboat, kept this gracious home a busy miniature world.[22]

The veranda at Gallatin was a social place on late summer afternoons. Ladies in hoop-skirted filmy dresses dallied over their embroidery; gentlemen sipped sangaree; darkies came and went with trays of bottles, glasses, and ice. There was the laughter of children from the lawn as they rode back and forth on a decrepit horse, old Rock, a present to Shreve from General Jackson. The hair was gone from the top of the horse's tail, and the oldest darkies vowed that a cannon ball had clipped it off at the battle of New Orleans. Shreve was devoted to Rock, and made him as much a part of the family as any of the aged and young who found a haven at Gallatin.[23]

The gentlemen were likely to draw to one side and talk of steamboating, or speculate on whether Texas, which had won its freedom from Mexico in 1837, would be admitted into the United States. The Democrats were enthusiastic about taking it into the Union; the Whigs, on the other hand, argued that such a move would increase the nation's tax burden, extend slave territory, and might set ablaze a war with Mexico. In one way or another, the word, Texas, was on every tongue.

To St. Louisians, there was much more to the Texas question than the possible acquisition of land, or weight thrown on the side of slavery — there was the status of the busy land trade route, the Santa Fe Trail. The trail passed over ground now disputed between Texas and Mexico. Forty years before this, a French merchant of Kaskaskia had ventured into a trade, across the wilderness, with the Spanish-Mexican provincial capital, Santa Fe. Several men had followed him in this, carrying their goods over the plains on the backs of Mexican mules. Accounts of immense profits reaped in the Santa Fe commerce lured still other intrepid merchants to launch out in it. This was a perilous business, for if the traders escaped the attacks of Indians and reached Santa Fe, they were likely to be imprisoned there by Spanish officials.

There had always been legends of mysterious wealth somewhere across the great plains. In 1540, rumors had wafted over Mexico that large stores of gold, silver, and precious stones were hoarded in a community called the Seven Cities of Cibola, in the country to the northwest. Perhaps, the Spanish-Mexicans fancied, these were the fabulous Seven Cities that adventurers had sought in the Atlantic long before Columbus happened upon the New World. The Seven Cities, instead of being on an island vaguely west of the Canaries or Azores, might lie on this continent, almost at hand! Most of the elusive points in the world had come to be given a haven in the vast unknown America and its western ocean. Maps and globes made in 1530 had depicted India as somewhat above the land of the Aztecs, with Thibet only a step farther north. The inhabitants of the Seven Cities of Cibola, up there on the plains, were said to be a highly cultivated people, distinguished by their very long fingernails. Their houses were several stories high, each successive story smaller than the one below it. No one could deny that this description savored of Cathay.

Francisco de Coronado, Governor of Nueva Galicia, in western Mexico, resolved to find this community where precious metals were said to be so abundant that there were whole streets of silversmiths. He raised a splendid company and set out. After a weary search and many hardships, he had reached the Seven Cities on a rather barren plateau. Instead of Chinese notables in silks and jewels, silversmiths and treasure stores, he found a small population of Zuni Indians, living in poverty. These Indians were light-colored and intelligent. They irrigated and fertilized their land, tended their fields and gardens, domesticated the wild turkey, cut and dressed stone, wove cotton and wool, fashioned artistic pottery, made a little turquoise jewelry, and had secret orders and excellent laws. The stories of their houses were stepped-back only on one side; none but their surgeons wore long fingernails. This was not Cathay. Coronado and the remnant of his company returned to Mexico in disillusion.[24]

Now, across the region where the Spanish had hunted the treasures of the Orient, French merchants of St. Louis and neighboring towns were finding a wealth of trade. After Mexico won its independence from Spain, in 1821, St. Louis merchants had begun to invest large sums of money in this commerce. They loaded their merchandise on wagons, each drawn by a troop of Mexican mules. Later, the Southern States took to raising large, strong mules — with eight or twelve of these to a wagon, enormous loads could be hauled.

At first the wagon caravans traveled directly west from the Missouri River, and over the plains to the Rockies, pausing at the colorful Mexican town of Taos, set between lofty ridges. Later, they followed along the west bank of the Arkansas; when that stream turned northwest, the wagons forded it, continued to Raton Pass, and south through wild, beautiful scenery to Santa Fe.[25]

Santa Fe was an unkempt, walled town, made up of low, square mud-brick houses. It swarmed with dogs. The Governor's Palace, a larger adobe house than the others, had a distinguishing colonnade along its front, and the only glazed windows in the capital. Although it was piously named for the Holy Faith of Saint Francis, Santa Fe was no model of deportment. Gaming was its principal interest. Town officials, military men, doctors, merchants, women, and even children, might be seen gambling at cards on any shady street corner.

Nevertheless, this was a prime place for trade. When a caravan arrived, the glad cry of 'Los Americanos!' went up on all sides. The populace left their games and crowded around the tired, grimy drivers and the amazingly loaded wagons. The excited, voluble welcome rose above the braying of mules and barking of dogs. The imports were in great demand at any price. Common cotton cloth brought two or three dollars a yard. Hospitality to the visitors took the form of a hastily arranged dance, or 'fandango.' The women turned out to the ball in their picturesque formal costumes, consisting of full bright-colored skirts, and scarfs that wound about their heads and torsos in a graceful hood and bodice.

The Mexican officials had a different kind of welcome for the traders. Each loaded wagon was charged a flat tariff of five hundred dollars. The Americans offset this charge by a simple ruse — before they reached Santa Fe the merchandise of three wagons was piled upon one, and the discarded wagons burned. Besides this import duty, the Mexicans fixed a heavy export tax on the gold and silver that was paid the aliens for their wares. The resourceful Americans had a ready answer for this, too. They constructed large false axle-trees on their wagons, and in these most of their gains were hidden before they reached the examining officers on their way out of the province.

Henry Shreve was keenly interested in the Santa Fe trade. It played profitably into the steamboat commerce. Boats from the Ohio and from New Orleans brought wares to load the caravan wagons; gold and silver from Mexico

flowed east and south. The Santa Fe trade needed to be
made safe, all St. Louis steamboat men insisted. Congress
should take over Texas, and protect the lower end of the
Trail. Texas, Texas — the name could be heard on every
side in steamboat talk. It had been like pinning a political
badge on steamboats when the large cabin, that Shreve
had been first to build on the second deck, was dubbed the
'Texas.'

In the spring of 1844, Henry Shreve, and all St. Louis,
forgot Texas and politics for a while. Through the winter,
unusually heavy snows had fallen in the northwest
country. When they began to thaw in April, every rivulet
was brimmed. By May, the Mississippi was overflowing.
Boats rode high on the levee. After a few days, the water
fell and the danger seemed past. Then a deluge of rain
set in over the whole mid-Valley. Creeks galloped to the
rivers. The Mississippi rose until it reached the buildings
on Front Street. Here the water paused, and slowly receded. The townsfolk relaxed their long strain.

All this time, the floods of the Missouri had been roaring
down through the plains. As they raged into the Mississippi, the most torrential rains ever seen in the Valley
drenched the whole Northwest for ten days. Mountains
loosed avalanches of snow. Floods swept down the foot-
hills and over the prairies, surging to the trunk stream.

The Great River spread until it was three to six miles
wide. It covered Front Street in St. Louis. Illinoistown,
opposite, was under water. People all along the Illinois
lowlands had fled to the bluffs. Houses, barns, cattle, and
fowl were carried away. Boats steamed in and out the
Illinois woodlands. The pupils of a convent in Kaskaskia

had taken refuge at Colonel Menard's home, located on the loftiest point of land in that region; a steamer, chartered to carry these refugees to St. Louis, 'received them at Colonel Menard's door, and passed along the road to St. Louis, on which there was from six to fifteen feet of water.' [26]

Gallatin Place was safe on the high Grand Prairie, but its fields were water-swept and gullied. Streams raced through its picturesque gorges. Shreve, after a look at his ruined planting, went into town to view the flood from the now islanded warehouses on Front Street. A waste of water stretched as far as he could see. Huge trees floundered in the channel current, caught against submerged Bloody Island or reared and stacked at points of the bluffs. The snag-boats and their new masters would have much to do.

The great flood of 1844 subsided, leaving devastation behind it. Trade and steamboating suffered. Then gradually, business men began to reach out, and presently Texas and politics were to the fore again. The whole country was agitated now over the proposed annexation of this territory. Hot debates resounded from street corners and boat decks. The aged Albert Gallatin, in his eighty-fourth year, disappointed, but thrilled, the Democratic Party by standing 'with superb courage before a hostile and turbulent crowd in New York to protest against the annexation of Texas as the prelude to a war of imperialistic aggression.' [27]

Despite loud opposition, the Democratic Congress voted to annex Texas. President Tyler, having turned his back on the Whigs who had elected him, signed the bill as a last flourish before he retired from office. St. Louis was overjoyed. It could almost feel itself expand.

Mexico had long since given warning that it would consider the annexation of Texas by the United States as an act of war, and now withdrew its Minister from Washington. The persecution of Americans venturing into Mexico became more flagrant. A clamor for war began to sound through the United States. Underneath the general indignation over Mexican insults lay a deeper motive — a hunger for more territory. The nation's land area was so vast that some of it was still unexplored, yet there was an insistent popular demand, not only for Texas, but for California, with its San Francisco harbor. From all quarters chimed the early colonial claims that the original grants included land from sea to sea. There was an overtone hum, too, about the country's 'manifest destiny.' The Union must look out upon both oceans. It owed Europe and Asia, as well as itself, a full east and west gaze.[28]

St. Louisians, because of the hazards of the Santa Fe Trail,[29] were particularly eager to have Mexico conquered. They wondered if their sad, soft-treading President, James K. Polk, would ever rouse to it. The whole government, for that matter, was tiptoeing around the Mexican issue because of a diplomatic dispute with England over the Oregon country.

The United States contended that its territory in the northwest reached to the lowest point of Russian America (Alaska), leaving Canada no Pacific coast. The British claimed the west coast from the southern point of Alaska to the top of Mexico's province of California, giving the United States no Pacific outlet. A good deal of tension had developed over these conflicting claims. Americans chanted a slogan, 'Fifty-four forty or fight.' Many had only a vague idea of what 'fifty-four forty' was about, but they were keen for a fight, with one foe or another.

As the Oregon matter neared a satisfactory compromise, the American indignation concentrated on Mexico. A 'protecting army,' that had been sent into Texas to occupy the strip disputed between that state and Mexico, was especially anxious for real conflict. All that was needed now was a fresh Mexican offense to touch off hostilities. Mexico, however, was annoyingly discreet. Then, one day a party of American dragoons discovered a few Mexicans on a hilltop, and charged them in 'self-defense.' A large Mexican force was below the crest of the hill, out of sight. The Americans were surrounded, some of them killed and others wounded. At last, the awaited *casus belli* had been provided.[30]

When a report of this encounter reached Washington, soft-treading President Polk sent a fiery war message to Congress. He requested means of 'prosecuting the war with vigor, thus hastening the restoration of peace.' News of the message electrified the country. War was at hand. War!

In May, Congress declared the land-hungry, trade-hungry war. A month later, while feverish preparations for the struggle were under way, a treaty was signed with Britain, giving the Oregon country, up to the forty-ninth — not fifty-fourth — parallel of latitude, to the United States. From this immense tract, the states of Washington, Oregon, and Idaho, and parts of Montana and Wyoming, were later to be carved.

The young men of St. Louis were elated when a call for three thousand volunteers, to form part of an 'Army of the West,' was published in the local newspapers. There would be three other armies, but the congenial task of capturing Santa Fe would be given to the Army of the West. The zealous recruits met over a blacksmith shop on Third Street. Here was organized Battery A of the Missouri Light Artillery, consisting principally of young elegants from the town's prominent families.[31]

One June day, a crowd gathered on the levee to see these fledgling soldiers, with their horses and baggage, off on a steamboat, bound up the Missouri for Fort Leavenworth. Not long after, the St. Louis Flying Artillery plodded in broken columns toward the west, each of its long brass guns laboriously drawn by four horses.

The crisp uniforms of the 'city's pets,' as these young blades had been dubbed, were soon bedraggled and grimy; streams had to be waded, and clouds of prairie dust moved with the columns. The sun blazed down, the nights were chill. The once soft-living city youths rode long, ate their poor fare, drank at creek sides, and slept on the ground, grew strong, brown, and lean, kept a high spirit of adventure, and fought like veterans.[32]

Although Henry Shreve had favored war for the protection of Americans in the Southwest, he had not taken much part in the town's preparations. Mary was not well. As she sat with her hands folded and eyes serene, she seemed to be fading out of life. The doctors, brought from the city, could do nothing. On February twenty-fifth, three months before the outbreak of war, Mary Shreve passed away.[33]

Shreve roamed the farm restlessly. At times he would take his eldest grandson, Henry Carter, on these rambles, point out the fields and orchards, garden and lawns, and say, 'You will have this when I am gone.' He wanted his namesake to follow him as the master of Gallatin. It was not, however, to turn out so.[34]

Now that Mary was gone, Gallatin Place showed the lack of her supervision. Rebecca Carter had taken charge, but the big house and its endless company, along with her own family responsibilities, proved a severe strain on her. Walker Carter argued that it was his wife's efforts in behalf of an Episcopal orphanage in the city that tired her; after her death, thirteen years later, he insisted that it was the orphanage that had killed her. He never dreamed that her bearing and rearing nine children might have had a bit to do with it.[35]

Shreve's friends suggested that he get someone to take charge of his home. By some chain of circumstances, Lydia Rodgers, daughter of Mr. John Rodgers, of Boston, was brought West to preside over the place. She was hardly thirty, and 'very distinguished looking.' To be sure, she was a Yankee, but she had excellent social connections, it was whispered in discreet asides at Gallatin. Under Lydia Rodgers's firm hand, the household affairs ran smoothly. All petty anxiety was taken off its master.

To Shreve, at first, Lydia Rodgers was no more than an automaton. Before the year was out, he had married her.[36]

The St. Louis port was booming now. Troops bound from the east or north for the Mexican front were outfitted here. Military supplies for the army were shipped from here. The Santa Fe Trail was kept dusty with mule-wagon caravans. To supply these, a two-mile line of steamboats crowded to the St. Louis levee. Everything added to the power and importance of steamboat traffic. The war was stringing out much longer than the Valley folk had expected. Wars are always to be fleet, dashing affairs, but settle down to long, patient struggles.

Henry Shreve watched the conflict restlessly. Robert E. Lee, who had been so discontented in his river work, was in his element at the battle front. Many young Mississippi steamboat men were now in the army. Shreve regretted that he must stay behind while his friends fought,[37] but he was sixty-two, his motions slow, his step lagging.

Still, his mind was vigorous and busy. He looked out over the rapidly changing Valley and measured its progress. Its shipping was now the most impressive in the world. Forty-four years before, an American vessel was seized at Liverpool because it had eighty bales of cotton on it; that large amount of cotton could not be produced in the United States, the English officials contended [38] — it was a matter for investigation. Last year more than two million bales of American cotton had been marketed. Thirty-seven years before, Shreve had brought the first load of Galena lead down the Mississippi — last year the Galena district exported $2,225,000 worth of lead.[39] The railroads were creeping west. Convenient adhesive postage stamps had made their appearance. The electric telegraph, invented by a disappointed artist, Samuel Morse, had become established in the East and was reaching for the middle country. It was Henry O'Reilly, an energetic editor of a New York State newspaper, champion of many a cause, who had arranged with the proprietors of the telegraph to bring a line west. O'Reilly was convinced that telegraph communication would prove invaluable to news publishing.[40]

In St. Louis, innovations were crowding upon each other. Three years ago Erastus Wells and Calvin Case had promoted a city horse-omnibus line. People were shy of using it, at first, 'not thinking it an exactly genteel way of traveling about the streets.' Later, it had grown popular and branched out.[41] Illuminating gas was replacing coal-oil lamps. The waltz had been 'imported by M. René Paul (with a consignment of drygoods) from Philadelphia.'[42] The town buzzed with fraternal organizations whose members, in costume, ornamented the frequent public parades. There was a new theater. The handsome Catholic cathedral boasted paintings by Rubens, Raphael, Guido, and Veronese — gifts from European royalty.[43] The city was built solidly out to Tenth Street, and sparsely for a half-dozen blocks beyond.

As the Mexican War dwindled to a close, with a complete victory for the United States, St. Louis troops set out on their way home up the Mississippi from New Orleans. The boats, timed to arrive on July fourth, docked in the morning while all the bells on the river and in the town pealed. Whistles blew and cannon boomed. The volunteer fire companies and other organizations, in splendid regalia, met the heroes at the landing. Playing bands led the way to the new Planters' Hotel. Later the soldiers and their hosts, with most of the populace following them, marched out beyond Tenth Street to Lucas Grove, for the welcoming speeches.[44]

This celebration of the freeing of the Santa Fe Trail from Mexican oppression was a great day for St. Louis. To Henry Shreve, driving in the long procession or filling a wide place on one of the benches at the Grove, it was a great day for the rivers. He could foresee a steadily increasing southwestern commerce feeding the steamboats at this rapidly growing port.

Before Shreve had ceased to exult over the freed south-western trade, he found new cause for satisfaction: the telegraph line from the East was heading for St. Louis. It reached Illinoistown in midwinter. There it encountered the problem of crossing the mile-and-a-half-wide Mississippi. Nevertheless, in two days the wire had been brought from a tall mast on the Illinois shore to a hundred-and-eighty-five-foot shot-tower on the Missouri side. Another mast on Bloody Island held up the sag. A St. Louis newspaper of December 23, 1847, proclaimed: 'The first streak of lightning passed through the wires yesterday.' [45] Henry Shreve, whose ingenuity had made this once isolated trading-post a center of continental trade, was chosen to send the first real message over the wire — a greeting to President Polk.[46]

Shreve and his friends wanted to show their appreciation to O'Reilly for having brought the telegraph to them, and the usual testimonial dinner was planned. An invitation was sent to the guest of honor on January 30, 1848. O'Reilly replied that circumstances compelled him to decline. These circumstances proved to be a serious quarrel with the Morse Company over lines projected still farther west. The vindictiveness of his opponents was to break the expansive Irishman's heart. Anyway, St. Louis had its telegraph and the celebration was held.[47]

Soon after the New Year, the Mexican War was finished and in March a treaty signed. Mexico's claim to Texas was relinquished; a tract, including Upper California and an area that would later be New Mexico, Nevada, Arizona, and parts of Colorado and Wyoming, was ceded to the United States for $18,750,000. The American hunger for territory had been appeased; the destiny of the Union to stretch from sea to sea was fulfilled.

While the country still wondered over this far-flung extension of its boundaries, a sensational piece of news spread over it: even before the Mexican treaty was signed, gold had been discovered in California's Sacramento Valley.

Gold! The word seemed to tingle through the land. Men left their plows, counters, or desks and set off to the West on a blind gamble. Shreve, an aging adventurer, watched this migration thoughtfully. He and the Great River would bide their time. Part of the adventure would sweep this way — everything came to the Mississippi.

In the East, men bound for the Sacramento sailed around the Horn, or stopped at Panama, crossed the Isthmus, and took ship at the other side. Cornelius Vanderbilt started a boat line to Nicaragua, and through the San Juan River to Lake Nicaragua. He built docks on the east and west coasts, twelve miles of macadam road and eight fine steamers. His route was two days faster than the Panama way; his boats were crowded.

As Shreve had foreseen, much of the great adventure came to the Mississippi. Gold-seekers floated down every stream to it, journeying up or down the River for a convenient start westward. In St. Louis there was a good deal of hasty wagon-building, and a demand for oxen, mules, and all caravan supplies. Troops sent West to protect the emigrants were outfitted here.[48] There was a wave of steamboat construction, especially for the Missouri River. The cleared Missouri had become very important, stretching, as it did, several hundred miles toward the Sacramento. Gold would find its way back across the plains to the Mississippi. Inland steamboating would handle the enriched Valley trade.

Almost any enterprise in St. Louis was now a mine of
potential wealth. The town was changing fast — too fast,
the older people thought. Men who had jolted their carts
complacently up and down the rough cuts in the stone bluff
had grumbled when the first street was paved, declaring
that it broke their wooden cart wheels — now they en-
dured a number of paved streets. It was no longer seemly
for the negro women to file, singing, with the town's
clothes in panniers on their heads or hips, out to Mill
Creek on washday, to gossip and rub, cover the bushes
with wet linen, and loll until it dried. It had grown common to have locks on doors. Laws of every kind, instead of
personal honor and decorum, prevailed.[49] Easterners, with
their practical, unjoyous ways, were coming in greater
numbers. Germans had sifted here to escape the revolu-
tion in their homeland, bringing their beautiful but incom-
prehensible music and their appalling industry. The
French deplored all this. The Valley they had once dominated was taking on alien ways. It had all begun, perhaps,
when Pierre Chouteau finally became a partner of John
Jacob Astor in fur-trading. After that, nothing had seemed
secure.

Henry Shreve liked to ponder the rapid changes. He was
eager for progress and growth. Steamboat tonnage in the
home waters of the United States amounted to 411,823;
that of all the British Empire was 168,078 tons.[50] Far the
greater part of this country's home tonnage plied in the
Mississippi Basin, and bore annually, along with hand-
boats, over $432,000,000 worth of freight. St. Louis
handled more and more of this commerce. The port had a
special destiny.[51]

In the autumn of 1848, after the close of the Mexican War, cholera scourged the Valley. Winter stamped it out of St. Louis, but fugitives from a spring epidemic in New Orleans started the plague here again. Before the authorities could rally to fight it, another disaster befell the city.

On May 17, 1849, at ten o'clock at night, Henry Shreve and his guests at Gallatin noticed a red glow on the eastern horizon. They watched it spread. A faint sound of whistles reached them. St. Louis must be afire. Shreve had horses brought. He and his friends set out hastily for town. Other horsemen joined them at each crossroad. They galloped on together toward a vermilion sky. As they neared the city they could hear the shouts of men and crackle of wood above the whistles and alarm bells. The warehouses on Front Street stood out black and intact against the fierce glow. The fire was beyond them. The whole river seemed ablaze. It meant only one thing — steamboats were burning.

The levee was crowded. Men pulled the fire apparatus around, or stood helpless. Some were cutting craft loose from their moorings to let them drift downstream. No steam was up to drive them to safety. Blazing steamboats wove crazily about. They bumped other vessels, sending streamers of fire across them; they pursued boats trying to escape, as though bent on setting all the craft along the river in flames. The sky, the water, and the Illinois woods were coppered.

The conflagration had started when the steamboat *White Cloud* caught fire, burned its hemp mooring cable, drifted about in the capricious current and collided with the steamers tied up ashore, igniting them. One after another was torn from its berth, or caught as it tried to escape, until now more than twenty steamboats were rocking about, in flames. Nothing could be done for them. The firemen turned their efforts to saving the other moored boats.

Suddenly the spectators were horrified to see flames leaping behind them. Live embers, driven by the wind, had fallen on the full warehouses. The crowd surged inland. The fire roared to the southwest, devouring whole blocks of buildings. Merchants, bankers, farmers, boatmen, and slaves worked desperately to check the onslaught, or to hurry goods from threatened areas. The fire-fighting equipment, of which the town had been so proud, was futile against this holocaust. A store of gunpowder was brought. Men ran ahead of the blaze to get it placed. A few minutes later, the first blast came. The ground rocked; flame leaped into the sky and smothered in a volume of smoke, leaving the red skeletons of buildings to gray and crumble.[52]

The fire died slowly from the river. The night was still now except for the terse orders of exhausted men and the cries of women searching for their dead. The first daylight showed a scene of utter desolation. There were blocks of charred and shattered buildings. Black, denuded boat hulls, half-sinking, groaned as they bumped and scraped together.

Shreve was chilled and tired as he looked over the devastated waterfront. He and Walker Carter had suffered their own losses in all this, but it was the sacrifice of that long line of craft to the orgy of fire that preyed on the old river man. He had known every one of those steamboats. Yesterday they had poised there proudly, their decks and cabins and white lacy woodwork rearing above the warehouses — only one other port in the world, New Orleans, could furnish such a sight. Now the wrecked and blackened hulls were like the corpses of friends. St. Louis and the Mississippi had taken a staggering blow.

Still stunned by its calamity, St. Louis turned from its destroyed shipping and business district to fight the spreading cholera. Doctors worked from house to house until they fell with fatigue. Terrified supplicants crowded the churches. Funerals filed constantly in the streets.[53] A superstition swept through the stricken town: the magnetic telegraph and its mysterious waves were responsible for the hideous severity of the plague![54] The tired doctors wondered if there might not be truth in this report. Before the city had checked the epidemic by rigid rules of sanitation and quarantine, one third of its populace had died.

Above all this tragedy, St. Louis commerce rose on new wings. Nothing was so indestructible as trade. It sprang afresh from the ashes of its own corpse. Boats had to be built to replace craft lost in the fire. Larger warehouses grew up along the levee. Substantial business buildings were beginning to cover the fire-swept blocks. Materials for all this came from Pittsburgh and Philadelphia, from New Orleans, the upriver limestone quarries, the Missouri iron mines.

The gold migration through this port increased steadily. California, named by the early Spanish explorers for a fictional island 'close to the terrestrial paradise,' drew all men's eyes. Adventurers, traders, and statesmen discussed better ways to reach there than by boat and wagon. A railroad to the Far West was needed.

This was no new contention. St. Louis business men had held several meetings to debate the subject. The whole nation debated it. The question of a Pacific railroad bobbed up as a political issue in every election. Asa Whitney, a New Yorker, had popularized the idea of a Pacific road by persistent letters to newspapers, and by Lyceum lectures. In his pleas to different sections of the country he varied the proposed route so deftly that every hamlet envisioned itself a future railroad metropolis. Whitney's main appeal was: 'A short route to the Orient!' [55]

The cry was taken up. At a meeting in Philadelphia, after Whitney had made a stirring speech, resolutions in favor of the road were offered. One of them began: 'Whereas the completion of a railroad from Lake Michigan to the Pacific would secure the carrying of the greater part of the commerce of the world to American enterprise, and open the markets of Japan and the vast Empire of China, of all India . . .' and so on. [56]

The Committee on Public Lands, in 1846, had proposed to the United States Senate that one tenth of the one thousand million acres of public land be donated toward the construction of a Pacific railroad. One of its most telling arguments hung on the ever-alluring riches of the Orient:

'The products of the American soil will be exchanged for the rich commodities of Asia; and when the millions of mouths have tasted American bread, the high destinies of the commerce will have been fixed. . . . The opening of this highway across the American continent would attract the attention of the world; it would establish a short route to the riches of India. . . . It would certainly not be unreasonable to suppose that this intercourse would have extensive influence . . . and upon the semi-barbarians who would be drawn by these facilities of intercourse from the other side of this line of communication, the most salutary effects would be produced.' [57]

Congress was doubtless impressed, but not enough. For now, three years later, the Pacific railroad was not even surveyed. Men still traveled westward by ox-wagon, boat, on horseback, and afoot. The Asiatics, for want of our enlightening influence, languished in their barbarism.

The agitation for a Pacific railroad went on. The chance of becoming a link between Europe and Asia set American imaginations soaring. It was to be five years more before a thinker of the Saint-Simonist cult in France, Vicomte Ferdinand de Lesseps, would manifest his social philosophy by advocating a canal from the Red Sea to the Mediterranean, giving Europe a short route to the Orient. The Saint-Simonists, in their plan for the regeneration of the world, believed implicitly that means of rapid communication between countries and races would do away with war for all time.[58]

Missouri's fiery, dueling Senator, Thomas H. Benton — he had killed Charles Lucas, a brilliant young St. Louis attorney, in a duel on Bloody Island years before — long opposed the building of a Pacific railroad. Now he sturdily recommended it, provided the road should start from St. Louis. In February of 1849, Benton introduced a bill in the Senate to launch the construction of a national road from the Mississippi to the Pacific Ocean, 'to be an iron railway where practicable, and a wagon road where a railway was not practicable.' Nothing came of this bill.[59]

Henry Shreve had become a staunch advocate of railroads. He believed, as many steamboat men did, that railroads would substantially serve the waterways by bringing the remote parts of the country in touch with the Mississippi. Men generally considered railroads as crude auxiliaries to the water-roads. The Valley river transportation was the most remarkable traffic in the world. Its steam tonnage was more than twenty times as great as all other United States steam tonnage. It was the most powerful and useful trade factor in existence. A railroad to the Pacific would be a sound adjunct to it, Shreve maintained.

Congress had been unable to agree on giving aid for the building of a Pacific railroad. Each member who favored such aid carried about with him the chart of a route favoring his district or state. Railroads on paper started from the Great Lakes, from New Orleans, and from many points between, and streaked to the west coast in the most direct line, with total disregard of engineering difficulties.[60]

Impatient at this impasse, Henry Shreve and a group of his friends, Pierre Chouteau, Jr., John O'Fallon, Edward Walsh, and others, took the matter into their own hands. They resolved to give the needed railroad a push-off by constructing the first lap of it themselves. They met and organized the Pacific Railroad Company.[61]

This company was incorporated in March of 1849, with a proposed capital stock of ten million dollars. The road would be built from St. Louis to the west border of Missouri, in the confident expectation that any Pacific road later fostered by the Government or by eastern capital would shrewdly include this link. Thus, St. Louis would not be missed in favor, say, of Chicago.

Other St. Louisians feared that their city, despite the lure of this considerable link, might be passed by. Lately, Stephen A. Douglas, who had come from Vermont to seek his fortune in the Valley, and was now a United States Senator from Illinois, had put in effective strokes to have the transcontinental road, if built, start from Chicago. St. Louis looked up from the apathy laid upon it by successive disasters, and called a municipal meeting. After much parley a set of resolutions was adopted. Ignoring the gold excitement in California, these began: 'Whereas, The idea of establishing a thoroughfare of travel and commerce between Europe and Asia, across the continent of America, has been cherished by the philanthropist and statesman since the days of Columbus . . .' and grew in splendid phrases to a plan of calling a convention at St. Louis to discuss a Pacific road. Influential men of various states would be invited to attend.

The invitations were sent out. Mr. John Darby, and other members of a committee, called on Thomas H. Benton and asked him to make a speech that would counteract the influence of Stephen A. Douglas in favor of his Chicago plan. The old fire-eating Senator accepted with avid snorts. He did not like Douglas in any case, he said: 'His legs are too short, sir. His coat, like a cow's tail, hangs too near the ground.' [62]

The convention assembled in the St. Louis Courthouse, on October 15, 1849. Stephen A. Douglas had been selected, with all the courtesy of gallant enmity, to preside over the meeting. He was conducted with grave dignity to the rostrum, the eyes of the whole assembly on his coat-tails, where Benton had fixed them. The suave but belligerent little statesman opened the session. It moved on fitfully to the awaited speech of Thomas Benton, whose remarks were likely to roast an antagonist and serve him up with pepper sauce.

This time, however, Benton did not waste breath on spicy personalities. His speech was expansive, magnificent, gathering fervor as it went. The Senator was laying a railroad, to stay laid, out of St. Louis, across the plain, and even mountain. As he neared his grand climax, he gazed beyond the gold fields of California and winged on to the traditional theme — a short route to the Orient. He cried, 'Let us complete the grand design of Columbus by putting Europe and Asia into communication!' As a final brandish, he suggested that a peak of the Rockies be hewn into a colossal statue of Columbus with arms outstretched, declaiming to the passing trains, 'There is the East, there is India!' [63]

In a surge of enthusiasm, the assembly appointed a committee to prepare an address to the people of the Union, soliciting their co-operation to induce Congress to act favorably in the matter of a Pacific road — out of St. Louis.

Henry Shreve and his friends did not wait on the whims of Congress. They went ahead with their Pacific railroad. (It was to reach the capital of the state six years later.) Other parts of the country looked jealously at the preparations for this stretch of road, and by another year, hopeful railroad links were springing up all about.

The agent of one of these dangling links, the New Orleans, Opelousas, and Great Western, predicted that the 'hundreds of millions of gold produced in California; the great increase in the whale trade in the north Pacific; an increased trade with Mexico and South America; the absolute certainty of finally crushing the Chinese walls and overthrowing Japanese non-intercourse,' would bring his road and its St. Louis *branch* a prodigious transportation business.

Henry Shreve's name does not appear in the rolls of the later meetings of the Pacific Railroad Company. He was not well. Although only sixty-five years old, he was weary. His life had been strenuous and full. Sitting in the comfortable living-room at Gallatin, with the hum and movement of his large household about him, he looked through the crackling wood fire into his memories. He could see the Valley in all its changes, its wealth enriching the lives of a growing people. Shallow-bottomed steamboats, with their multiple decks and white wood trimming, floated in an intricate pattern of movements on the clean free rivers. And now the railroad was about to bring the two oceans to the Mississippi!

Shreve did not feel like an old man, but within his lifetime he had seen the Union triple its territory, and the wilderness transformed into farms, neat villages, and busy ports. He had watched the aloof French, Spanish, and German groups blend into English-speaking Americans, with the distinctive American outlook — individualistic, freedom-loving, visionary, yet practical. It was good to have had a strong hand in all this change, Shreve reflected; and it was good to lay down his tasks and see others pick them up.

Mellowed and meditative, Shreve saw the Christmas season approach. The house filled with guests. There was the breezing-in of youngsters from the coasting hill, the noisy exit of a skating party, the merriment of darkies in the far kitchen, a shaft of sudden cold as an old negro pushed wide the side door to bring in a log for the fire. The wood crackled, sparks blinked against the soot-lined flue. A long row of stockings hung from a wooden mantel shelf. A pine tree was set up between the windows and festooned with strung cranberries and popcorn. Sleigh-loads of friends came from the city to drink eggnog. Young men stretched their snugly booted legs and talked politics, railroads, and steamboating. Topics might fly far afield, dispose of California gold or the Chinese wall, but they drew back inevitably to steamboats and the rivers.

Shreve listened when they talked about the rivers. The navigable streams were the arteries of the nation. In the first half of the century, they had peopled the middle Valley. The year of 1850 was drawing to a close. No one knew what greatness the rivers might bring in another half-century. Shreve mulled this over contentedly. He was like a grizzled lion, and often a drowsy one, as he sat with the murmur of talk drifting past him. Beyond the red embers of a log he could see the gray, driving rivers.

Not long after the New Year (January 9), Shreve was shaken by the death of his little daughter, Florence, younger of the two children by his second wife.[64] A gloom settled over Gallatin. Its master was less well. The winter chilled him. He was now definitely an ill man.

March brought a touch of spring. The sixth was a day of clear sky and bracing wind. Sunlight reached in the long windows and gilded the lint of the blanket in Shreve's armchair. On the rivers the morning sun had brightened the boatmen's *capots* as the oars dipped and lifted. It had slanted across the water and carved the bluffs out of the mist. . . . The sun was fading. The river and sky were gray. Evening was closing in. That was the tinkle of music from the *Washington's* salon, and the distant voices of passengers. Night was at hand — a silent, transparent night. The old river man, his children and grandchildren about him, had made his last port.

The *Missouri Republican*, of March 7, 1851, printed the news of his passing, and a tribute to his life and work: 'He was for nearly forty years closely identified with the commerce of the West . . . and contributed largely to the safety of Western commerce. To him belongs the honor of demonstrating the practicability of navigating the Mississippi with steamboats.' [65]

Word of Henry Shreve's death was flashed up and down stream to the large ports, and carried by steamboat, barge, and canoe to the most obscure landing. A few men remembered the determined youthful *patron*; many knew the older indomitable champion of the water-roads. He had stopped here with his keelboat; he had steamed the little *Enterprise* yonder. He had brought the *George Washington* to port there, its top higher than the bluffs — the town was deserted as merchants, farmers, negroes, and Indians gathered on the bank to stare at the strange craft. Days were recalled when the crash of attacked water forests resounded through the countryside. There had been a day when the sensational news came up the rivers that Shreve had worn the Livingston-Fulton monopoly down — the Mississippi outlet was freed.

After Shreve was gone, it grew upon his friends that his contribution to American progress had been lightly accepted by his country. His steamboat and snag-boat designs had brought him nothing. Promises made by the Government, at various times, to repay him for the use of his snag-boat invention were left unfulfilled. Congress appears to have leaned upon the plea of necessity — that as Shreve's device offered the 'only remedy for evils of many centuries' growth, so the government could not avoid the use thereof.' Shreve did not press claims, 'preferring to wait for even tardy justice from that government he so long and faithfully served.' [66]   His heirs, on advice, petitioned Congress for the payment they believed was due. The claim was allowed thirty years later; Congress had discussed the rights of Shreve and his heirs to such remuneration at intervals for forty-seven years. Fifty thousand dollars was the sum awarded [67] — just two thirds of what had been paid to the heirs of Robert Fulton and Chancellor Livingston for the use of Fulton's boats, the *New Orleans* and *Vesuvius*, in the War of 1812.[68]

Henry Shreve had not felt ill-paid for what he had done, as far as only himself was concerned. He had ranged the rivers he loved, serving them with a whole heart and iron will. His labors had speeded and shortened the trade routes to a wealth which the whole populous middle country now enjoyed while its orators prated of India and Cathay. It was said of Shreve, before his death: 'His career has been devoted to the mitigation of human toil, and the development of the natural resources of his country. . . . The scattered and unprotected few who sought in vain for purchasers of their surplus productions have swelled to millions busy sending the fruits of a teeming soil to the remote corners of the earth.' [69]

The old river man, who had found the broad mid-Valley a wilderness and left it an empire, was dead. The inland river steamboating, in which he had taken such pride, was climbing toward its zenith.

CHAPTER

Ten

HENRY SHREVE had passed from the rivers, but the Valley water transportation, which he had done so much to foster, continued to grow in volume. Shreve had believed implicitly that steamboat navigation would expand steadily as the productiveness of the Mississippi Basin increased. Multiplying wagon roads and short railway lines would facilitate the movement of produce to the waiting boats. Shreve had not foreseen — no one had — that inland river traffic would reach its height in a few years, and then swiftly decline. The golden age of western steamboating opened when the snag-boat *Heliopolis* cleared the dead trees from the Mississippi bed; its most prosperous and picturesque years were the last decade before the Civil War.

In the early days of Valley steamboating, only the Ohio and the Missouri had carried any great amount of freight to the Mississippi. Most of this was bound for New Orleans, to be exported from there to the Atlantic coast or to Europe. The removal of the Great Raft of Red River brought trade from a thousand miles upstream, along the Texas and Indian Territory border, and from the rapidly populating drained swamplands of Louisiana. The settlement of the Northwest began to pour grain, timber, cattle, and ore through the tributaries of the Mississippi, and down the Great River to the Gulf.

By 1848, the Ohio shipyards, where most of the western boats were built, could not keep up with their orders. 'Every available shipwright was employed, and some boat gangs worked at night by torch light at double wages.' [1] Boatyards at Pittsburgh, New Albany, Louisville, St. Louis, and other places were operating at full capacity. The Missouri River, where traffic had been augmented by the emigration to California, demanded more and more tonnage. The Upper Mississippi transportation had substantially increased: the forty-one steamboat arrivals at St. Paul in 1844 had multiplied by eight in 1851, and by twenty-five in 1857. [2] In the late eighteen-fifties, more than a thousand steamboats passed annually through the Louisville-Portland Canal, around the Falls of the Ohio.

The inland water vessels, which followed the pattern of Shreve's later boats, were the pride of the Valley, and a matter of wonder to east-coast Americans and Europeans. Charles Dickens, after he had journeyed down the Ohio to Cincinnati in 1840, wrote: 'These western vessels are foreign to all ideas we are accustomed to entertain of boats. They have no mast, cordage, tackle or other such boat-like gear; nor have they anything in their shape at all calculated to remind one of the boat's head, stern, sides or keel.'

An English engineer, David Stevenson, visited the Mississippi Valley in 1838, and gave this graphic report of the steamboats: 'The vessels on western waters ... have a most singular appearance, and are no less remarkable as to their machinery. ... The hull is covered with a deck at the level of about five feet above the water, and below this deck is the hold, in which the heavy part of the cargo is carried. The whole of the machinery rests upon the first deck; the engines being placed near the middle of the vessel, and the boilers under the two smoke chimneys. The fire doors open towards the bow, and the bright glare of the wood fire, along with the puffing of the steam from the escapement pipe, produce a most singular effect at night, and . . . announce the approach of the vessel when it is still at a great distance. . . . The large cabin contains the gentlemen's sleeping berths, and is also used as a dining room. This part of the western steamers is often fitted up in gorgeous style. From the gallery surrounding the chief cabin, two flights of steps lead to the hurricane deck, which in many steamers is at least thirty feet above the level of the water. . . . When two engines are used, the ends of the piston rods work in slides, and the connecting rods on both are attached to cranks on the paddle-wheel axle, placed at right angles to each other. . . . The cylinders are invariably placed horizontally.' [3]

The Baron de Gerstner, traveling through the United States several years later, paid tribute to the inland steamboats: 'The steamboats in the West . . . are throughout very flat, and go, when loaded, generally five feet deep; some, however, only thirty to thirty-six inches. . . . The elegant boats contain a large splendidly furnished and ornamented saloon, used as a dining room, and an adjoining saloon for the ladies. The saloons are surrounded by small apartments [staterooms], each of which contains two berths, and round the state rooms is an open gallery. . . . Such a vessel offers to a European an imposing and entirely novel aspect. All steamboats upon the western waters have high-pressure engines, the pressure of steam being 60 to 100 pounds per square inch. It is to be regretted that steam navigation was carried on in America five years before it was successfully tried in Europe. It would be still more regretted, if, at the present . . . we were still to hesitate in Europe to adopt the American plan of construction.'[4]

Steamboats in 1850 to 1860 still fitted these descriptions, but they had grown in size and general 'elegance.' There were some boats of six hundred to one thousand tons. Their owners vied with each other to provide the handsomest cabins, best meals, and most music. Mark Twain, in his *Life on the Mississippi*, says: 'The steamboats were finer than anything on shore. When a citizen stepped on board a big fine steamboat he entered a new and marvelous world . . . pilot house, hurricane deck, boiler deck guards, all garnished with white filigree work of fanciful patterns; inside a far receding snow white "cabin"; porcelain knob and oil picture on every stateroom door; curving patterns of filigree work, touched up with gilding, stretching overhead all down the converging vista; big chandeliers every little way, each an April shower of glittering glass drops; lovely rainbow-light falling everywhere from the colored glazing of the skylights.'

The competition in table fare and service was carried to absurd lengths. The menus were astounding. Besides the variety of meats and accompanying dishes served at a single sitting, as many as a dozen desserts were arranged in a semicircle about the plate: tall glasses of custards, bowls of puddings and ice creams, small platters of cakes and pies. The diner could eat from all of them.[5] Silver, porcelain, glass, and linen were a matter of vanity. 'The napkins at each plate were folded with a beauty and intricacy of design whose variation with each meal was wonderful to behold.' [6]

There was always music. Most of the cabin hands, who were usually free negroes, and the white deck-hands (stevedores and roustabouts) could play an instrument or sing. Musical ability went far toward getting a job on a Mississippi steamer. [7] When the waiters were busy serving the table, the firemen and rousters would twang and fiddle. As a boat pulled out from shore, all the men who could be spared gathered at the bow and sang. [8]

The bar of a steamboat was an important social factor. There political policies were created, condemned, or changed, sections of the country eloquently advertised, commercial ventures organized, and all weighty matters overhauled. The bar was, moreover, a rich enterprise. Although the lessee paid a princely sum for the right to operate it, his net earnings were enormous. 'Men who owned life leases of steamboat bars willed the same to their sons as their richest legacies.' [9]

Card-playing was a conspicuous feature of river steamboat travel. Gold pieces, brought from the broad money belts that men customarily wore around their waists, clinked as they were stacked on the card tables. Most of the play was for sport, but some of it was by way of business. Professional gamblers traveled up and down the river in pairs. Two partners would come aboard separately and manage a public introduction later; then they went through the mummery of losing large sums of money until they had advertised themselves as easy prey. Disarmed passengers put up high stakes in games against them. The seemingly naïve partners made laughable blunders, but they won. Their practiced fingers studied the cards, which they had marked by shaving off a line at the end or side, and shuffled them knowingly. The heavy gold coin belts of their opponents grew steadily lighter.[10]

Mississippi travel received international advertisement from great picture panoramas that were exhibited far and wide. These were unwinding rolls of canvas upon which had been painted views of the Mississippi and its countryside. In 1839, John Rawson Smith and John Risley presented a panorama of the Upper Mississippi Valley. This was shown throughout the United States and Europe. It was viewed in Oslo in 1852, where it aroused great interest. · In about 1849, John Banvard began to show a vast panorama of the Mississippi River from St. Louis southward. 'His canvas, with its many scenes, was three miles long.' When it was on exhibition in the East, special railway excursions were run to carry the crowds to it. In New York and Boston more than four hundred thousand persons saw it. In London Banvard's canvas was on view for twenty months. Admissions to it exceeded six hundred thousand. In 1849, Henry Lewis traveled about with a panorama depicting river scenes from St. Louis to Fort Snelling, near Minneapolis. His canvas was twelve feet high and thirty-six hundred feet long. By another year there were eight or ten panoramas of the Upper Mississippi alone.[11]

These exhibitions did much to popularize the so-called Fashionable Tour on the Mississippi. Easterners began to speak of the Upper Mississippi as a vacation route. Southerners flocked to New Orleans to take the Tour boats. Many came from Europe to travel up and down the Great River whose cliffs and rapids, cypress shores and canebrakes, had been so exotically set forth to them. Steamboat meals and service reached a new high mark. Orchestras expanded. Gentlemen with stylish side-whiskers, tall beaver hats, frock coats, broad pantaloons, and the popular 'varnished' shoes promenaded the decks or danced; ladies in wide, hooped skirts, tight basques with low shoulder seams and bell sleeves, small hats and high-heeled shoes sat in the prevailing languid manner, or tripped the new polka. The Minnesota *Pioneer's* editor said of the Mississippi tour: 'Why, it is an exhilarating luxury, compared with which, all the fashion and tinsel and parade of your Newports and Saratogas, are utterly insipid.' [12]

In this Golden Age of steamboating, another river institution, the Show Boat, began to operate in a magnificent way. Back in the flatboat era, floating dramshops or gambling dives sometimes added to their lure by having the boat-hands sing, wrestle, or do what acrobatics they could. With this beginning, and because everyone gravitated to the rivers with what money he had to spend, the show boat was inevitable. The floating theaters were usually barges without power, towed by a small steamer. The barge had a lower deck for the stage and the white audience, and an upper deck — 'nigger heaven.' It also contained bunks for the company of players. The towing steamer provided the mess hall and crew quarters.

In 1852 at Cincinnati, Captain Jack, a familiar figure along the rivers, completed his great *Floating Palace*, constructed especially for the Spalding and Rogers circus. The amphitheater could seat a thousand persons to view the usual circus performance of bareback riding, jumping through paper hoops, and so on. The *Floating Palace* gave exhibitions down the Ohio and Mississippi to New Orleans, then crossed the bay to Mobile. The following year, it came up to St. Louis and moored at the foot of Poplar Street, where it gave performances for three days. Its thousand seats would not accommodate the crowds; 'permissions' to stand outside and look in the windows were sold at a dollar apiece. For the next seven years the *Floating Palace* continued to show along the Ohio, Missouri, and Mississippi Rivers. After that, Captain Jack engaged the steamboat *Banjo*, and with a French Zouave troupe visited the towns along the Lower Mississippi, Red River, La Fourche, and the Atchafalaya.[13] Another show boat, *Romance Wonderland*, traveled up and down the rivers for thirty years, giving melodramas in which virtue finally triumphed over considerable and not unattractive sin.[14]

In its later years, the *Floating Palace* had adopted the steam organ that was invented in 1855 by J. C. Stoddard, of Worcester, Massachusetts. The Greek name, Calliope, made up of two words that meant 'sweet-voiced,' was given to this set of strident steam whistles. The instrument proved a successful advance agent. Many passenger boats adopted it. The piercing notes, reaching far ahead, echoed from the cliffs or spread over the lowlands. The calliope became inseparable from the glamour of the steamboats and beauty of the rivers.[15]

During all these years the river ports prospered. In 1853, there were 3307 steamboat arrivals at St. Louis — 529 more than at New Orleans.[16] The waterfront was lined with steamboats, two or three deep. As far back as 1845, St. Louis had felt its growing power and the increasing importance of its location. At a convention held that year to frame a new constitution for the State of Missouri, one draft included an offer of St. Louis to the nation as its capital. This draft was rejected, and with it died the offer.[17]

In 1854, St. Louis was the third city of the Union in enrolled steam tonnage. Only New York and New Orleans outstripped it, and the enrolled tonnage of those ports included ocean steamers. By 1856, St. Louis extended seven miles by the curve of the river, and about three miles inland.[18]

Another steamboat disaster occurred at St. Louis in that year. A bitter cold winter formed ice to the depth of two or three feet in that part of the Mississippi. There was a sudden rise of water on February twenty-seventh. The ice began to move. Some of the steamboats, wintering in that port, were shoved ashore; others were torn from their moorings and pushed gradually to the lower dike. Then the ice drifted faster; it broke up and commenced to gorge. Piles of it, twenty to thirty feet high, were forced up on the shore or against the lower dike, burying the steamboats. In a few hours forty steamers, some of them the finest on the river, had been partially or completely destroyed.[19]

Everything, it seemed, happened to steamboats. The disasters of fires, collisions, explosions, and ice jams brought the average life of a steamboat down to five years. It paid, nevertheless, to invest a hundred thousand to two hundred thousand dollars in a steamer because the principal, entirely wiped out within a short time, would bring double its amount in earnings. The *Altona*, 'the fastest boat that ever plowed the river,' built in 1857 to run between St. Louis and Alton, paid for herself in one year. And the *Lady Franklin* earned four times her cost in her two years of life.[20]

New Orleans had its best commerce in 1859. In that year it received from the rivers 2,187,560 tons of freight.[21]

But shippers there were not deceived by these figures — the freight was comparatively local in origin, most of it coming from no farther north than Red River. The importance of that city as an export base was on the wane — the growing railroad lines were forcing it 'to a position of insignificance as an exit for the Valley trade.' [22]

St. Louis was thriving on the new Upper River trade. The number of passengers carried on steamboats to and from that port in the year that ended in September, 1855, was reported as 1,045,269.[23] In 1859, 3658 steamboats arrived there.[24] The city had grown so large that its omnibus line was no longer adequate. A street horse-car system had been built; on July Fourth (1859) the first car was run over the line, Erastus Wells, president of the company, driving the horses. The trip was made amid cheers and difficulties. Small rocks from the roadbed were pushed up on the track by the horses' hoofs, derailing the car frequently.[25] The faults of the road were soon rectified. St. Louisians felt quite progressive and metropolitan. By the following year their city had a population of 188,587.[26] The steamboat arrivals numbered 3754.[27]

All the while, the railroads were weaving a mesh to strangle river traffic. The first division, thirty-nine miles long, of the Pacific Railroad which Henry Shreve had helped to found, was put under contract soon after the old river man's death. The initial spadeful of earth was removed on July 4, 1851, on the south side of Chouteau's Pond, and was the occasion of a great popular demonstration. A parade to the Pond started from Fourth Street at eight o'clock in the morning with military groups, bands, the Governor and his aides, the Mayor, aldermen, fire department, glee club, the United Ancient Order of Druids, three temperance societies, citizens in carriages and citizens on horseback, making up the procession. One of the orators for the occasion said of the prospective railway: 'But whither does it tend? When you have constructed the road to the frontier of Missouri, what power can stop it there? Beyond lie the extended plains ... and the old Eastern World. My mind recoils from the magnitude of the contemplation. ...' [28]

The winter of 1852 saw the Pacific Railroad finished to a small settlement called Sulphur Springs, five miles from the city. The first division, to Franklin (afterward called Pacific), Missouri, opened on July 19, 1853 — one can imagine the disappointment that must have prevailed because this opening could not have been held on July Fourth. Henry Shreve would have been delighted with the early effects of the Pacific Road. The railway began immediately to serve the steamboats. 'Without a farm along its line, and with its western terminus in a dense forest, this great railroad began to connect the Mississippi with the back country.... The "receipts per Pacific Railroad" were: lead, 1556 pigs; iron, 88,350 pounds pig, 530 blooms; wheat, 3418 bushels; hides, 5200 pounds; whiskey, 214 barrels; wood, 370 cords; wine, 9 casks, 7 barrels ... hubstuff, 25 cords; and hoop-poles 570,000.' [29]

This railroad was opened to Jefferson City, in the center of the state, on November 1, 1855. A train consisting of fourteen coaches, carrying prominent men from all over the country, started from St. Louis amid great fanfare, to make the first run over the whole road. The weather was stormy; a torrent of rain had fallen since the evening before. About two thirds of the way to its destination, the train began to cross the Gasconade River. The bridge gave way,

precipitating ten of the coaches nearly thirty feet.
Twenty-eight persons were killed and many were injured.
Ten years later, this road, which was to become the Missouri Pacific, was completed to Kansas City. It reached
the west coast in May of 1869.[30]

The first railroad to unite the Atlantic with the Mississippi, the Chicago and Rock Island, was laid to that river
in February of 1854. The celebration of the event was held
the following summer — a joint railroad and steamboat
excursion to the Falls of St. Anthony. 'So lavish were the
preparations that an eastern newspaper reported that the
affair "could not be rivaled by the mightiest among the
potentates of Europe."' [31]

After speeches and parades, two trains left Chicago on
June fifth. At Rock Island it was found that the five
steamboats that had been chartered would not hold the
crowd; two additional boats had to be provided. The
twelve hundred persons aboard the seven vessels were
served a feast, while bells rang and whistles blew. The
river breeze was refreshing; the moonlight showed the
stream and shores in all their night glamour. Strangers
were awed by the towering cliffs of Lake Pepin and delighted with the mist-hovered Falls of St. Anthony. The
steamboat trip was decidedly the most memorable part of
the railroad excursion. The New York *Tribune*, which had
a reporter at the celebration, urged travelers 'to follow the
wake of the just completed Railroad Excursion, ascend the
Upper Mississippi, the grandest river of the world, flowing a thousand miles between shores of incomparable
beauty.' [32]

The Baltimore and Ohio, by means of various short
links, made complete rail connection with the Mississippi

in 1856. It was decided to honor this achievement by running a series of trains from Baltimore to St. Louis, with stops along the way. Eminent men of the nation were invited to fill the coaches. The trains arrived at St. Louis, over a ferry, about midnight of June 24, 1856, and were greeted by a hundred guns and a torchlight procession.[33]

The steamboat men knew now that the railroads, which at first had promised to be no more than feeders of the river traffic, were powerful and still growing rivals of the waterways. The Galena lead that Henry Shreve had been first to take downriver for export from New Orleans was now carried by rail, canal, and lake to the East. Furs found their way directly east, too, rather than south by the rivers. Despite the increasing competition of the railways, river steam tonnage continued to advance all through the fifties. The intra-Valley trade between points north and south more than made up for all losses to the rails.

The great advantage that the locomotive trains had over the steamboats was speed. Not only the exports, but the passengers, were deserting the rivers. Delightful as water travel was, with its open-air promenades, clean breezes, music, dancing, and games, Americans preferred to go the faster way. The dirty, noisy trains were getting most of their patronage. Desperately the steamboat companies began to advertise speed rather than luxury. There appeared the 'Lightning Line' between Louisville and New Orleans, the 'Cincinnati and New Orleans Express Line,' and the water 'Railroad Line' from St. Louis to New Orleans.[34]

Steamboats could no longer afford to cut into their running time when they fueled. Henry Shreve's *Washington*, on its record trip of twenty-four days from New Orleans to

Louisville, had had to put in at shore twice a day while the crew sawed or chopped wood and carried it aboard. The wood-yards, established later by the settlers, had greatly shortened the fueling time. Now even faster ways of taking on wood, or sometimes coal, had to be found. The fuel was ready on a scow or flatboat which was hitched to the steamer, and loading was done while the boat drove ahead on its run.

This process was witnessed in 1860 by Charles Francis Adams, grandson of John Quincy Adams, while he was making a trip up the Mississippi. He gave this description of it: 'To me all seemed strange and unreal, almost weird — the broad river bottom, deep in shadow, with high bluffs rising dim in the starlight. Presently I saw them wood-up while in motion, and the bright lights and deep shadows were wonderfully picturesque. A large flat-boat, piled up with wood, was lashed alongside, and, as the steamer pushed steadily upstream, the logs were thrown on board. As the hands, dressed in their red flannel shirts, hurried backward and forward, shipping the wood, the lurid flickerings from the steamer's "beacon lights" cast a strong glare over their forms and faces.'[35]

When speed became highly essential in river navigation, steamboat racing took on a public importance. Races had early become a matter of daily routine on the rivers. Two boats sailing in the same direction, and not far apart, were in sharp competition for the trade along the route. Whichever arrived first at a landing carried off most of the waiting passengers and freight.[36] Making fast time, in such cases, was a necessity. Captains, crews, and passengers got a sporting thrill out of the port-to-port contest.

Besides these races to monopolize local business, a

steamboat owner occasionally set about establishing a speed record to popularize his boat; he would challenge a rival steamer, then spread the news of the coming race. Mark Twain wrote: '... a race between two notorious fleet steamers was an event of vast importance. ... Every encumbrance that added weight or exposed a resisting surface to the wind was removed.' When the boats got under way, the forced draft was put on, the furnaces roared, the flues threw out volumes of smoke. The outcome was front-page news over the whole Valley.[37] Among the noted races was that between the *Eclipse* and the *A. L. Shotwell*, from New Orleans to Louisville, in 1853. The *Eclipse* made the trip in four days, ten and a third hours; the *A. L. Shotwell*, in a few minutes less. The following year there was a race between the *Baltic* and the *Diana* from New Orleans to Louisville.

The most famous race in Mississippi annals took place in the declining days of steamboating: the storied and sung contest between the *Natchez* and the *Robert E. Lee*.

The *Natchez*, commanded by Captain Thomas P. Leathers, had, on one of its commercial trips, steamed from New Orleans to St. Louis in three days, twenty-one hours, and fifty-eight minutes. This brought a challenge from Captain John W. Cannon, of the *Robert E. Lee*. The challenge was accepted. Before the race, Captain Cannon removed all the rigging outfit and superstructure of the *Robert E. Lee*; he refused passengers and freight, and arranged to have coal waiting in floats along the way. Captain Leathers, of the *Natchez*, made no special preparations, and loaded his boat as usual. The two vessels left New Orleans a few minutes apart on June 30, 1870. 'The world was notified of the race by telegraph and cable,' and its progress was flashed over two continents. People from all over the country lined the riverbanks to see the boats, which were not far apart, roar past. At Cairo, Illinois, the *Natchez* ran aground in a fog. The *Robert E. Lee* sailed on, full tilt, to St. Louis, where it was received with great furor. After all, it had beaten the commercial trip of the *Natchez* hardly three hours and a half. Its time was three days, eighteen hours, and thirty minutes.[38]

The ordinary runs of Mississippi boats had grown faster than early steam enthusiasts had dreamed was possible. Henry Shreve had amazed his hearers at a Louisville banquet in 1817 when he predicted that steamboats would sometime make the trip to that port from New Orleans in ten days — he had lived to see the *Bostona* make the run in five days, eight hours (1849); and in the same year, the *Missouri* covered the distance from New Orleans to St. Louis in four days, nineteen hours.[39] Every art of builder and operator was employed toward giving the river vessels fleetness. In order to make good time, a steamboat had to be loaded so as to have just the right pitch. 'If a boat was known to make her best speed when drawing five and a half feet forward and five feet aft, she was carefully loaded to that figure.' [40]

In spite of all the efforts made by steamboat men to retain the popularity of river transportation, they were steadily losing to the railroads. River men who had welcomed the locomotive train now felt a deep bitterness against it. The bridges, that railway companies were beginning to build across the streams to replace the ferries, added to river-navigation woes. Boat-owners organized for a fight against these bridges.

The Chicago and Rock Island Railroad, in 1853, had

begun a wooden bridge across the Mississippi at Davenport, Iowa. It 'was built in the face of powerful opposition and a prohibitive ruling by Jefferson Davis, Secretary of War, for it crossed a government reservation.' Soon after this bridge was finished (in 1856), the steamboat *Effie Afton* swung against it; the galley stove tipped over and a fire broke out. The boat's owner sued the Railroad Bridge Company. The case came up in the Circuit Court in September of 1857, Abraham Lincoln acting as attorney for the Bridge Company. The jury failed to agree and was discharged. There were hints that the *Effie Afton* disaster had been staged to provide a suit. In May of 1858, James Ward, a steamboat owner of St. Louis, filed a bill in the United States District Court, Southern Division of Iowa, praying that 'the bridge be declared a nuisance and ordered removed.' Steamboat men continued to complain that the bridge obstructed navigation. Congress, in 1866, finally passed an act requiring that this bridge be replaced by another, half the cost to be paid by the United States.[41]

Other bridges were built, each one bringing a storm of complaints from the steamboat owners. The boat smoke-stacks could not go under them — some of these stacks were over a hundred feet tall.[42] It may have been that they were built tall to court trouble — bridge advocates openly said so. The controversy was long and acrimonious. In the end, very high bridges, or those with a draw span, had to be constructed.

Although railroads continued to advance from east to west, there were almost none running north and south in the middle Valley by 1860. The trains might carry the exports to the East, but the up-and-down intra-Valley trade went by the rivers. Now even this river traffic was imperiled. The country was moving rapidly toward a conflict which, although it appeared to be arising from the question of slavery, rested upon fundamental differences of occupational and trade interests between the agricultural South and the industrial East.[43] Shippers and statesmen of the mid-Valley feared that, if war came, the Mississippi navigation might be shut off.

When an ordinance of secession was adopted in Louisiana on January 26, 1861, the following resolution was offered: 'Resolved, That we, the people of the State of Louisiana, recognize the right of free navigation of the Mississippi River and its tributaries by all friendly States bordering thereon. And we also recognize the right of egress and ingress of the mouth of the Mississippi by all friendly States and powers. . . .'[44] The Governors of both Ohio and Indiana, in messages to their legislatures, expressed grave fears that the mouth of the Mississippi might be restricted. The Illinois State *Journal* declared: 'The great North-west will wage war . . . as long as she has a man or a dollar, but what she will enjoy the right of free and unobstructed navigation of her natural Southern outlet.'[45]

Whatever differences the North and South had, they agreed upon an unfettered Mississippi traffic. Afterward, war itself laid down restrictions. Southern cotton was a war necessity for the North, and was cut off. Sugar, molasses, rice, and tobacco were later placed under the embargo. At the same time, the Northern States held back foods and manufactured goods from the Confederacy. The policies of both sections of the country were to admit cargoes easily, but to send them sparingly. The Mississippi trade, already depleted by incursions of the railways, was nearly destroyed.

After the Civil War, inland river traffic picked up. But the heyday of Mississippi navigation was over. The railroads continued to branch and reach; they carried freight and passengers to each other, not to the rivers. Steamboating grew ever more confined to the short haul and pleasure excursions. Tugged barges largely replaced capacious cargo boats — in 1865, there were 1141 barge arrivals at St. Louis.[46] Few palatial passenger steamers were built.

Throughout these lean times, steamboat men nursed the conviction that, with better river conditions, they could yet compete successfully with the railroad companies. They grew more insistent upon improved channels. Little enough attention had been given to river clearance since Henry Shreve had quit belaboring the War Department for funds. President Polk had held that the Government could not constitutionally make appropriations for river improvement, and many followed him in this contention; at the same time he claimed that the Federal Government had exclusive jurisdiction over the rivers and 'the right to regulate commerce between the States.' John C. Calhoun, on the other hand, had designated the Mississippi an 'inland sea,' to the improvement of which the powers of the central Government might be applied.[47]

After Polk had been out of office awhile, the conviction grew among statesmen that the Government had the right and obligation to furnish funds for the betterment of rivers, harbors, and bays. The snag-boats were put to work. Their use came to be accepted as unquestionably essential. Beginning in 1888, $100,000 was appropriated annually during the next thirty-three years for timber-removing in the Lower Mississippi. Since the World War, the possibilities of Valley river navigation have come strongly to the fore, bringing 'into the limelight the novel snag boats, the most extraordinary vessels which Uncle Sam supports — either in or outside his navy.' In 1921, three large snag-boats were maintained on the Mississippi, one on the Ohio, and smaller ones on the Arkansas and Missouri, breaking off the huge new 'planters,' which were 'buried ten to forty feet deep.' [48]

Citizens and statesmen of the middle country have tried, from time to time, to revive a great water traffic on the Mississippi. The favorite slogan of mid-western shippers, 'Fourteen feet through the Valley,' would rise to a clamor. Conventions were held; speeches were made about the nation's neglect of the greatest navigable river system in the world; eloquence depicted myriads of large vessels steaming between the Gulf and the Lakes; appeals were sent to Congress. Nothing much came of all this.

Meanwhile, the Great River plunges on its way, unmindful of its lost prestige as a trade route. While it no longer teems with craft, hundreds of flat-bottomed, multiple-decked steamboats, such as Henry Shreve first brought to the Valley, sail it or mark time at the not too busy ports. Snag-boats patrol two thousand miles of it. Tours make their less frequent way down to New Orleans or up to the Falls of St. Anthony. The deep-toned boat whistles boom across the lowlands, rousing the landings to mild activity. The calliope echoes at sunset from the white limestone cliffs above Alton, bringing folk to the wharves for a moonlight ride to the mouth of the Illinois.

The colorful era of Mississippi River steamboating, which Henry Miller Shreve had been foremost in creating, drowses in a long twilight, waiting for another man of iron to set it toward a new day.

THE END

Notes

CHAPTER I

1. Rev. Timothy Flint, *Geography and History of the Mississippi Valley*, Cincinnati, 1832.
Librarians in the Science Room, New York Public Library.

2. Henry E. Chambers, *A History of Louisiana*, Chicago and New York, 1905; James K. Hosmer, *A Short History of the Mississippi Valley*, Boston, 1901; Theodore Roosevelt, *Winning of the West*, New York, 1894–96.

3. C. H. Heffelfinger, 'John Colter, the Man Who Turned Back,' *Washington Historical Quarterly*, vol. 26; Harlow Lindley, 'Western Travel, 1800–1820,' *Mississippi Valley Historical Review*, vol. 6.

4. Elliot Coues, editor, *Expeditions of Zebulon Montgomery Pike, 1805, 1806 and 1807*. Published, Philadelphia, 1810; republished, New York, 1895.

5. Luther Prentice Allen, *A Genealogy of the Shreve Family*, Greenfield, Illinois, 1901.

6. 'Personal Narrative of Lieu. John Shreve,' *Magazine of American History*, vol. 3.

7. Judge Samuel Treat, 'Political Portraits with Pen and Pencil: Henry Miller Shreve,' *United States Magazine and Democratic Review*, vol. 22 (1848). (The second installment of this biography is under the title, *Popular Portraits with Pen and Pencil*.)

8. 'Journal of Col. Israel Shreve, 1788,' *Magazine of American History*, vol. 2. 'Letters of Israel Shreve,' in same volume.

9. Louis Houck, *A History of Missouri*, Chicago, 1908.

10. Israel Shreve's letter to his brother in New Jersey, in *Magazine of American History*, vol. 2.

11. Note by the Editor of the *Magazine of Pennsylvania*, vol. 52.

12. Luther Prentice Allen, *Genealogy of the Shreve Family*.

13. 'Letters of Israel Shreve,' *Magazine of American History*, vol. 2.

14. Rev. Timothy Flint, *Recollections of the Last Ten Years*, Boston, 1826; reprinted, New York, 1932; *Geography and History of the Mississippi Valley*, Cincinnati, 1832; Samuel Treat, *Political Portraits with Pen and Pencil*.

15. Mentioned as a barge in some accounts.

16. Frederick Brent Read, *Up the Heights to Fame and Fortune: Henry M. Shreve*, Cincinnati, 1873. Also, as described by the late I. Shreve Carter of St. Louis, grandson of Henry Shreve.

17. Thaddeus Mason Harris, *Journal of a Tour into the Territory Northwest of the Alleghanies*, Boston, 1805. Reprinted in Reuben Gold Thwaites, *Early Western Travels*, Cleveland, 1904–07.

18. Fortescue Cumings, *Sketches of a Tour to the Western Country, 1807–09*, reprinted in Reuben Gold Thwaites, *Early Western Travels*; Emerson Gould, *Fifty Years on the Mississippi*, St. Louis, 1889.

19. Samuel Treat, *Political Portraits*.

20. Fortescue Cumings, *Sketches of a Tour*; Thaddeus Mason Harris, *Journal of a Tour*.

Description of ports on the Ohio, by Cumings and Harris, and also: Christian Schultz, *Travels on an Inland Voyage*, New York, 1810; Thomas Ashe, *Travels in America*, London, 1806–07; Lyman P. Powell, *Historic Towns of Western States*, New York, 1900.

Description of terrain, birds, etc.: Rev. Timothy Flint, *Geography and History of the Mississippi Valley*, Cincinnati, 1832.

21. Snags: Christian Schultz, *Travels on an Inland Voyage*.

22. Blennerhassett and his island: Thomas Ashe, *Travels in America*; Christian Schultz, *Travels on an Inland Voyage*; Fortescue Cumings, *Sketches of a Tour*; Adolphus M. Hart, *A History of the Valley of the Mississippi*, New York, 1853.

23. Fortescue Cumings, *Sketches of a Tour*.

24. George Thornton Fleming, *A History of Pittsburgh and Environs*, New York, 1922.

25. Description of rivers: Christian Schultz, *Travels on an Inland Voyage*; Fortescue Cumings, *Sketches of a Tour*; Timothy Flint, *Geography and History of the Mississippi Valley*; F. Michaux, *Travels to the West of the Alleghanies*, London, 1805; James Hall, *Statistics of the West*, Cincinnati, 1838.

26. Description of the Mississippi current: Timothy Flint, *Recollections of the Last Ten Years*; James T. Lloyd, *A Steamboat Directory*, Cincinnati, 1856; Timothy Flint, *Geography and History of the Mississippi Valley*; James Hall, *Statistics of the West*.

27. John Darby, *Personal Recollections*, St. Louis, 1880.

28. Edward G. Mason, 'Kaskaskia and Its Parish Records,' *Magazine of American History*, March, 1881; Stuart Brown, *Old Kaskaskia Days and Ways*, Historical Library of Illinois, Publication No. 10; Firmin Rozier, *A History of the Mississippi Valley*, St. Louis, 1890.

29. Judge Samuel Treat, *Political Portraits*.

30. John Thomas Scharf, *A History of St. Louis City and County*, Philadelphia, 1883; Philip Skrainka, M.D., *St. Louis, Its History and Ideals*, St. Louis, 1910; Thomas Edwin Spencer, *The Story of Old St Louis*, St. Louis, 1914; Lyman P. Powell, *Historic Towns of Western States*, New York, 1900; Edward Villere Papin, *The Village Under the Hill, A Sketch of Early St. Louis*, Missouri Historical Society Publications, vol. 5, 1927; Isaac H. Lionberger, *Annals of St. Louis*, Missouri Historical Society, 1929; Marshal Smelser, 'Housing in Creole St. Louis,' *Louisiana Historical Quarterly*, vol. 21.

31. Christian Schultz, *Travels on an Inland Voyage*.

32. Firmin Rozier, *A History of the Mississippi Valley*.

33. Samuel Treat, *Political Portraits*.

CHAPTER II

1. Samuel Treat, *Political Portraits*.

2. *Ibid.*

3. *Ibid.*

4. John D. G. Shea, *Discovery and Exploration of the Mississippi Valley*, New York, 1852. Also legends extant along the Upper Mississippi.

5. Samuel Treat, *Political Portraits*.

6. Description of rapids and reefs: Henry Shreve's later letters.

7. Samuel Treat, *Political Portraits*.

8. Frederick Brent Read, *Up the Heights to Fame and Fortune*; J. Fair Hardin, 'The First Great River Captain,' *Louisiana Historical Quarterly*, vol. 10, 1927. Family tradition.

9. Henry E. Chambers, *A History of Louisiana*, American Historical Society, Chicago and New York, 1925.

10. Samuel Treat, *Political Portraits*.

11. *Ibid.*

12. Description of the Upper River: Elliot Coues, editor, *Expeditions of Zebulon Montgomery Pike*, 1810; Major Stephen H. Long, U.S.A., *Voyage in a Six-Oared Skiff to the Falls of St. Anthony*, Minnesota Historical Collection, vol. 2; Timothy Flint, *Geography and History of the Mississippi Valley*; James Hall, *Statistics of the West*.

13. Samuel Treat, *Political Portraits*.

14. John Thomas Scharf, *History of St. Louis*.

15. The Pacific Fur Company and John Jacob Astor: James Parton, *Famous Americans of Recent Times: John Jacob Astor*, Boston, 1867, 1884 and 1897; Alexander Ross, *Adventures on the Columbia River*, Cleveland, 1904; *Dictionary of American Biography*.

16. Changes in St. Louis: Isaac H. Lionberger, *Annals of St. Louis*; Logan U. Reavis, *St. Louis, the Future Great City of the World*, St. Louis, 1870; Logan U. Reavis, *St. Louis, the Commercial Metropolis of the Mississippi Valley*, St. Louis, 1874.

17. Timothy Flint, *Geography and History of the Mississippi Valley.*

18. Max Savelle, 'The Founding of New Madrid,' *Mississippi Valley Historical Review*, vol. 19; Fortescue Cumings, *Sketches of a Tour*; Louis Houck, *A History of Missouri*, Chicago, 1908.

19. Henry Shreve's letters.

20. Natchez: Christian Schultz, *Travels on an Inland Voyage.*

21. *Ibid.*

22. Timothy Flint, *Geography and History of the Mississippi Valley*; Mark Twain, *Life on the Mississippi*, Boston, 1883.

23. Timothy Flint, *Geography and History of the Mississippi Valley.*

24. François-Xavier Martin, *Louisiana*, New Orleans, 1829; John R. Spear and A. H. Clark, *History of the Mississippi Valley*, New York, 1903.

25. Baton Rouge: Fortescue Cumings, *Sketches of a Tour.*

26. Henry E. Chambers, *A History of Louisiana.*

27. John R. Spear and A. H. Clark, *History of the Mississippi Valley.*

28. Georges Oudard, *The Amazing Life of John Law.* From the French of G. E. C. Massé, New York, 1928.

29. New Orleans: Alcée Fortier, *A History of Louisiana*, Paris, 1904; Albert Phelps, *Louisiana, A Record of Expansion*, Boston, 1905; Christian Schultz, *Travels on an Inland Voyage*; Lyman P. Powell, *Historic Towns of Western States*; Thomas Ashe, *Travels in America.*

30. Samuel Treat, *Political Portraits.*

31. *Ibid.*

CHAPTER III

1. Emily Wilder Leavitt, *The Blair Family of New England*, Boston, 1900.

2. Luther Prentice Allen, *Genealogy of the Shreve Family.*

3. Samuel Treat, *Political Portraits.*

4. John H. Latrobe, *A Lost Chapter in Steamboat History*, Baltimore, 1871.

5. Thomas Boyd, *Poor John Fitch*, New York, 1935; George Henry Preble, *A Chronological History of Steam Navigation*, Philadelphia, 1883 and 1895; *Dictionary of American Biography:* John Fitch.

6. Early steamboat inventors: George Henry Preble, *A Chronological*

History of Steam Navigation; Fred Erving Dayton, *Steamboat Days*, New York, 1925; Emerson Gould, *Fifty Years on the Mississippi*, St. Louis, 1889; Thomas W. Knox, *Robert Fulton*, New York, 1886; Robert H. Thurston, *Robert Fulton*, New York, 1891.

7. Audubon: Firmin Rozier, *History of the Mississippi Valley*.

8. The comet of 1811: *Ibid.*; Professor Winthrop, *Two Lectures on Comets*; Supplement, Boston, 1811.

9. The *New Orleans* was a stern-wheeler, sky-blue: George H. Preble, *A Chronological History of Steam Navigation*.

It was a side-wheeler: George Byron Merrick and William R. Tibbals, *The Genesis of Steam Navigation*, Proceedings of 1911, State Historical Society of Missouri.

The *New Orleans* had a propelling wheel at the stern: *Lloyd's Steamboat Directory*.

The wheels of the *New Orleans* were uncovered: J. Stoddard Johnston, *A Memorial History of Louisville*, Chicago, 1896.

The *New Orleans* was 116 feet long: Emerson Gould, *Fifty Years on the Mississippi*. It was 138 feet long: Fred Erving Dayton, *Steamboat Days*.

The *New Orleans* had a draft fit only for floods: George B. Merrick and William R. Tibbals, *The Genesis of Steam Navigation*. It drew only two feet of water: Ohio Archaeological and Historical Publications, vol. 22.

This boat was of 350 tons burden: Robert Baird, *A View of the Valley of the Mississippi*, Philadelphia, 1832. It was of 400 tons burden: Emerson Gould, *Fifty Years on the Mississippi*.

The *New Orleans* sailed from Pittsburgh on October 27, 1811: Ohio Archaeological and Historical Publications, vol. 22. On October 1, it reached Louisville from Pittsburgh: George Henry Preble, *A Chronological History of Steam Navigation*. The Pittsburgh *Gazette* of Friday, October 25, 1811, reported: 'The Steam Boat sailed from this place on Sunday last.' This would have made its sailing date October 20. The *New Orleans* left Pittsburgh on October 20: John H. Latrobe, *The First Steamboat on Western Waters*, Baltimore, 1871.

10. Christian Schultz, *Travels on an Inland Voyage*; Timothy Flint, *Geography and History of the Mississippi Valley*.

11. The *Shreve Genealogy* mentions this child as Harriet, but descendants of Henry Shreve give the name as Mary.

12. Firmin Rozier, *A History of the Mississippi Valley*; John Thomas Scharf, *History of St. Louis*; Timothy Flint, *Recollections of the Last Ten Years*.

13. The *Louisiana Gazette* of January 13, 1812, reported: 'The New Orleans from Pittsburgh arrived here Friday last.'

14. Samuel Treat, *Political Portraits*: 'That downward trip convinced him [Fulton] that the New Orleans could never return to Pittsburgh, and she was consequently used as a trading packet between New Orleans and Natchez.'

15. Samuel Treat, *Political Portraits*.

16. James Hall, *The West, Its Commerce and Navigation*, Cincinnati, 1848; Lewis Collins, *History of Kentucky*, Covington, Ky., 1874; John Thomas Scharf, *History of St. Louis*.

17. Emerson Gould, *Fifty Years on the Mississippi*; John H. Morrison, *History of American Steam Navigation*, New York, 1903; Fred Erving Dayton, *Steamboat Days*, New York, 1925.

18. Samuel Treat, *Political Portraits*; J. Stoddard Johnston, *Memorial History of Louisville*, Chicago, 1896.

19. Samuel Treat, *Political Portraits*.

20. H. Dora Stecker, *Constructing a Navigation System in the West*, Ohio Archaeological and Historical Publications, vol. 22; Samuel Treat, *Political Portraits*; John H. Latrobe, *A Lost Chapter in Steamboat History*.

21. John H. Latrobe, *A Lost Chapter in Steamboat History*.

22. Samuel Treat, *Political Portraits*.

23. Charles Gayarré, *A History of Louisiana*, New Orleans, 1903; Alcée Fortier, *A History of Louisiana*, Paris, 1904.

24. Samuel Treat, *Political Portraits*.

25. *Ibid.*

CHAPTER IV

1. Samuel Treat, *Political Portraits*; Luther Prentice Allen, *Genealogy of the Shreve Family*.

2. The *Enterprise* was 45 tons: John Thomas Scharf, *History of St. Louis*; James Hall, *The West, Its Commerce and Navigation*; Lewis Collins, *History of Kentucky*; Samuel Treat, *Political Portraits*. It was 75 tons: James T. Lloyd, *Steamboat Directory*; George Henry Preble, *A Chronological History of Steam Navigation*.

The *Enterprise* was the first boat to discard the use of sails: Emerson Gould, *Fifty Years on the Mississippi*. It was fitted with masts and sails: John H. Morrison, *History of American Steam Navigation*.

3. Read McAdams, 'New Orleans and the War of 1812,' *Louisiana Historical Quarterly*, vols. 16 and 17; Alcée Fortier, *History of Louisiana*.

4. J. Fair Hardin, 'The First Great River Captain,' *Louisiana Historical Quarterly*, vol. 10, no. 1; Caroline Pfaff, 'Henry Miller Shreve,' *Louisiana Historical Quarterly*, vol. 10, no. 2; Samuel Treat, *Political Portraits*.

5. John Thomas Scharf, *History of St. Louis*; James Hall, *The West, Its Commerce and Navigation.*

6. Samuel Treat, *Political Portraits.*

7. *Ibid.*

8. *Ibid.*

9. Read McAdams, 'New Orleans and the War of 1812.'

10. *Ibid.*

11. James Parton, *Life of Andrew Jackson*, New York, 1912.

12. *Ibid.*

13. *Ibid.*

14. Gaspar Cusachs, 'Lafitte, the Louisiana Pirate and Patriot,' *Louisiana Historical Quarterly*, vol. 2; Mitchell V. Charnley, *Jean Lafitte, Gentleman Smuggler*, New York, 1934.

15. Henry E. Chambers, *History of Louisiana*; Ira Flory, Jr., 'Edward Livingston's Place in Louisiana Law,' *Louisiana Historical Quarterly*, vol. 19; Edwin L. Sabin, *Wild Men of the West.*

16. Samuel Treat, *Political Portraits.*

17. *Ibid.*

18. Henry Shreve commanded a battery at the battle of New Orleans: Letter from Samuel H. Shreve of New York, 1895, to Barclay White of Mount Holly, New Jersey.

19. James Hall, *The West, Its Commerce and Navigation*; Samuel Treat, *Political Portraits.*

20. The *Vesuvius* lifted off the Batture and given government tasks: John Thomas Scharf, *History of St. Louis.*

21. Emerson Gould, *Fifty Years on the Mississippi*; Samuel Treat, *Political Portraits.*

22. Charles Gayarré, *History of Louisiana*, New Orleans, 1903.

23. Alcée Fortier, *History of Louisiana*; Charles Gayarré, *History of Louisiana.*

24. Samuel Treat, *Political Portraits.*

25. *Ibid.*

26. *Ibid.*

27. The *Enterprise* sailed over flooded fields: James T. Lloyd, *Steamboat Directory*; Samuel Treat, *Political Portraits.*

28. A dinner given for Henry Shreve at Louisville after he arrived from New Orleans with the *Enterprise* is mentioned in *History of Kentucky* by Lewis Collins, and in other accounts, but is in much doubt and has not been included here.

29. Emerson Gould, *Fifty Years on the Mississippi.*

30. Henry Shreve's second child, Rebecca, was born October 3, 1813:

Family records in possession of Emma Carter Edwards, great-granddaughter of Henry Shreve.

31. Conversation of the late I. Shreve Carter, St. Louis, grandson of Henry Shreve.

CHAPTER V

1. Caroline Pfaff, 'Henry Miller Shreve,' *Louisiana Historical Quarterly*, vol. 10; Garnett Laidlaw Eskew, *Pageant of the Packets*, New York, 1929.

2. Samuel Treat, *Political Portraits*.

The *Washington* was of 400 tons burden: Lewis Collins, *History of Kentucky*; James Hall, *The West, Its Commerce and Navigation*; Emerson Gould, *Fifty Years on the Mississippi*. It was of 345 tons burden: the *Gazette*, Cincinnati, September 23, 1816. It had a single wheel at the stern: *Gazette*, Cincinnati. Pictures show it as a side-wheeler. These are drawings, possibly from hearsay.

3. The *Washington* was much ridiculed while being built: Samuel Treat, *Political Portraits*.

4. Owners: *Niles' Weekly Register*, Saturday, July 20, 1816.

5. Timothy Flint, *Geography and History of the Mississippi Valley*.

6. Description of the *Washington*: Samuel Treat, *Political Portraits*; James T. Lloyd, *Steamboat Directory*; George Henry Preble, *A Chronological History of Steam Navigation*; *Niles' Weekly Register*; John H. Morrison, *History of American Steam Navigation*.

7. Samuel Treat, *Political Portraits*.

8. The *Enterprise* case: J. Fair Hardin, of the Shreveport Bar Association. 'An Outline of Shreveport and Caddo Parish History,' in *Louisiana Historical Quarterly*, vol. 18; Samuel Treat, *Political Portraits*; H. Dora Stecker, *Constructing a Navigation System in the West*; Caroline Pfaff, *Henry Miller Shreve*; Emerson Gould, *Fifty Years on the Mississippi*.

9. Emerson Gould, *Fifty Years on the Mississippi*.

10. Aaron Ogden's controversy with Robert Fulton: United States Archives, 1811, no. 302.

11. *Old South Leaflets*, vol. 5, no. 108, Boston, 1902.

12. John H. Latrobe, *Lost Chapter in Steamboat History*.

13. *Journal of Benjamin Latrobe*, New York, 1905.

14. The *Washington* explosion: James T. Lloyd, *Steamboat Directory*; Louisville *Courier*, March 21, 1832; from Caroline Pfaff, *Henry Miller Shreve*.

15. Ethel C. Leahy, *Who's Who on the Ohio River*.

16. James Hall, *Notes on the Western States*.

17. Samuel Treat, *Political Portraits*.

18. Wharf Register at New Orleans.

19. Samuel Treat, *Political Portraits*.

20. *Ibid.*

21. *Ibid.*

22. Family Records; Luther Prentice Allen, *Genealogy of the Shreve Family*: Caroline Pfaff, *Henry Miller Shreve*.

23. John H. Morrison, *History of American Steam Navigation*.

24. Dora Stecker, *Constructing a Navigation System in the West*.

25. Samuel Treat, *Political Portraits*.

26. *Ibid.*; James T. Lloyd, *Steamboat Directory*; George Henry Preble, *A Chronological History of Steam Navigation*.

27. Letter of the *Aetna's* captain, De Hart, written January 28, 1842: 'ended passage at Falls with one wheel in 60 days.' On its second trip, in 30 days, arrived badly damaged. From Frederick Brent Read, *Up the Heights to Fame and Fortune*.

28. J. Fair Hardin, 'An Outline of Shreveport and Caddo Parish History,' *Louisiana Historical Quarterly*, vol. 18.

29. Samuel Treat, *Political Portraits*; H. M. M'Murtrie, *Sketches of Louisville*; Emerson Gould, *Fifty Years on the Mississippi*.

30. Samuel Treat, *Political Portraits*.

31. This is not the Edward Livingston of New Orleans, but is a New York heir of Chancellor Livingston.

32. J. Fair Hardin, 'An Outline of Shreveport and Caddo Parish History.' Mr. Hardin reproduced here for the first time (in *Louisiana Historical Quarterly*, vol. 18) records of case no. 1003, Heirs of Fulton and Livingston against Henry Shreve, discovered in the ancient files of the United States District Court, in the attic of the Federal Building at New Orleans.

33. Samuel Treat, *Political Portraits*.

34. *Ibid.*

35. J. Fair Hardin, 'An Outline of Shreveport and Caddo Parish History,' *Louisiana Historical Quarterly*, vol. 18.

36. *Ibid.*

37. Louisville *Journal*, April 19, 1817; from Ethel C. Leahy, *Who's Who on the Ohio*.

38. *Ibid.*

39. The *Washington* made the trip in twenty-four days: Louisville *Journal*, April 19, 1817. It made the trip in twenty-one days: Louisville *Courier*, published in 1832. It made the trip in twenty-five days: Samuel

Treat, *Political Portraits*; George Henry Preble, *A Chronological History of Steam Navigation*.

40. J. Fair Hardin, 'An Outline of Shreveport and Caddo Parish History,' *Louisiana Historical Quarterly*, vol. 18.

41. Ben Casseday, *History of Louisville*, Louisville, 1852; Samuel Treat, *Political Portraits*.

42. Samuel Treat, *Political Portraits*.

43. *Ibid.*

44. James Hall, *The West, Its Commerce and Navigation*.

45. Ethel C. Leahy, *Who's Who on the Ohio*.

46. *Dictionary of American Biography*.

47. Other boats of Shreve's: The *Ohio*, 443 tons, owned by Shreve and Blair; the *Napoleon*, 332 tons, owned by Shreve, Miller and Breckenridge; the *Post Boy*, 200 tons. From L. A. Williams, *History of the Ohio Falls Cities and Their Counties*; James Hall, *The West, Its Commerce and Navigation*; Samuel Treat, *Political Portraits*.

48. This case in the State Supreme Court is mentioned in *Political Portraits*, by Samuel Treat, who was a contemporary of Henry Shreve's in St. Louis; in *Up the Heights to Fame and Fortune*, by Frederick Brent Read; and in other accounts. However, no record of a decision in such a case in the State Supreme Court has come to light, according to J. Fair Hardin, in the *First Great River Captain*, and Henry P. Dart, late Editor of the *Louisiana Historical Quarterly*.

49. John H. Morrison, *A History of American Steam Navigation*.

50. *Audubon's Journal*. Edited by Howard Corning, Boston, 1929.

51. James T. Lloyd, *Steamboat Directory*; Samuel Treat, *Political Portraits*.

52. Samuel Treat, *Political Portraits*.

53. W. Bullock, *Sketch of a Journey Through the Western States of North America* (1827). Reprinted in Reuben Gold Thwaites, *Early Western Travels*.

CHAPTER VI

1. Samuel Treat, *Political Portraits*.

2. *Ibid.*

3. *Ibid.*

4. *Ibid.*

5. Letters of Henry Shreve.

6. Letters.

7. Samuel Treat, *Political Portraits*; and Letters of Henry Shreve.
8. *Ibid.*
9. *Ibid.*
10. *Ibid.*
11. *Ibid.*
12. Samuel Treat, *Political Portraits*.
13. Letters of Henry Shreve.
14. Letters.
15. Letters.
16. Letters.
17. Letters.
18. Letters.
19. Letters.
20. Letters.
21. Letters.
22. Letters.
23. Letters.
24. Letters.
25. Letters.
26. Letters.
27. Frederick Brent Read, *Up the Heights to Fame and Fortune.*
28. Letters.

CHAPTER VII

1. General Randolph Marcy and G. B. McClellan, *Exploration of the Red River of Louisiana*, Washington, D.C., 1853.
2. Maude Hearn O'Pry, *Chronicles of Shreveport*, New Orleans, 1928.
3. General Randolph Marcy and G. B. McClellan, *Exploration of the Red River of Louisiana*.
4. Samuel Treat, *Political Portraits*.
5. *Ibid.*
6. Letters of Henry Shreve.
7. Letters.
8. Letters.
9. Timothy Flint, *Geography and History of the Mississippi Valley*.
10. A. A. Parker, *A Trip to the West and Texas*, Boston, 1836.
11. Description of Natchitoches: Christian Schultz, *Travels on an Inland Voyage*.
12. The moon was one day past its second quarter: *British Nautical Calendar*.

13. Letters of Henry Shreve.

14. Letters.

15. Letters.

16. Letters.

17. Letters.

18. James Craik, *History of Christ Church, Louisville*, 1862.

19. Letter from Emma Carter Edwards; Luther Prentice Allen, **Genealogy of the Shreve Family**.

20. Lyman P. Powell, *Historic Towns of Western States*.

21. Letters of Henry Shreve.

22. Letters.

23. Letters.

24. Letters.

25. William Glover, 'History of the Caddo Indians,' *Louisiana Historical Quarterly*, vol. 18; J. Fair Hardin, 'An Outline of Shreveport and Caddo Parish History,' *Louisiana Historical Quarterly*, vol. 18; Maude Hearn O'Pry, *Chronicles of Shreveport*; Spear and Clark, *History of the Mississippi Valley*.

26. William Glover, *History of the Caddo Indians*.

27. *Ibid.*

28. Letters of Henry Shreve.

29. Letters.

30. Letters.

31. Mark Twain, *Life on the Mississippi*, Boston, 1883.

32. Letters of Henry Shreve.

33. Stella M. Drumm, *Robert E. Lee and the Improvement of the Mississippi River*, Missouri Historical Society Collections, vol. 6 (1928); Douglas Southall Freeman, *Robert E. Lee: A Biography*, New York, 1934.

34. Letters of Henry Shreve.

CHAPTER VIII

1. J. Fair Hardin, 'An Outline of Shreveport and Caddo Parish History,' *Louisiana Historical Quarterly*, vol. 18.

2. *Ibid.*

3. Letters of Henry Shreve.

4. Letters.

5. Letter of A. H. Bowman, Lieutenant of Engineers of the War Department, written from Memphis, April 16, 1837.

6. Letters of Henry Shreve.

7. Samuel Treat, *Political Portraits*.

8. Letters of Henry Shreve.

9. Letters.

10. Letters.

11. Letters.

12. Letters.

13. Letters.

14. Letters.

15. Letters.

16. Letters.

17. Samuel Treat, *Political Portraits*.

18. J. Fair Hardin, 'An Outline of Shreveport and Caddo Parish History,' *Louisiana Historical Quarterly*, vol. 18.

19. Henry E. Chambers, *A History of Louisiana*.

20. Read McAdams, *New Orleans and the War of 1812*.

21. Marshall S. Snow, *History of the Development of Missouri and St. Louis*, St. Louis, 1908.

22. Albert Bettinger, *The Future of Navigation on Our Western Rivers*, Ohio Archaeological and Historical Publications, vol. 22.

CHAPTER IX

1. Land records supplied by Kenneth Tisdel of the St. Louis Municipal Library.

2. Steamboat whistles appeared in about 1841: Thomas W. Knox, *Robert Fulton*.

3. Land Records, St. Louis Municipal Library.

4. Letter from Emma Carter Edwards.

5. *Dictionary of American Biography*.

6. Samuel Treat, *Political Portraits*.

7. Nicholas Wood, *A Practical Treatise on Railroads*, London, 1838.

8. *Ibid.*

9. Thomas Gray, *Observations on a General Iron Rail Way*, London, 1825.

10. *Ibid.*

11. *Ibid.*

12. John Stevens, *Documents Tending to Prove the Superior Advantages of Railways and Steam-Carriages over Canal Navigation*, New York, 1812.

13. William H. Brown, *History of the First Locomotives in America*, New York, 1874.

14. *Ibid.*

15. *Ibid.*

16. *Ibid.*

17. *Ibid.*

18. Isaac H. Lionberger, *Annals of St. Louis*, St. Louis, 1929.

19. John Thomas Scharf, *History of St. Louis, City and County.*

20. Letters of Henry Shreve.

21. Isaac H. Lionberger, *Annals of St. Louis.*

22. Letters from Emma Carter Edwards; and from Amelia Dorsey, great-niece of Mary Blair Shreve.

23. Letter from Colonel and Mrs. Nelson G. Edwards (Emma Carter Edwards), Kirkwood, Missouri.

24. Frederick W. Hodge, *Spanish Explorers in the Southern United States*, New York, 1907.

25. Colonel Henry Inman, *The Old Santa Fe Trail*, New York, 1897.

26. John Thomas Scharf, *History of St. Louis.*

27. *Dictionary of American Biography.*

28. Justin H. Smith, *The War with Mexico*, New York, 1919.

29. *Ibid.*

30. William Jay, *A Review of the Mexican War*, Philadelphia, 1849.

31. Thomas Edwin Spencer, *The Story of Old St. Louis.*

32. *Ibid.*

33. Family records furnished by Emma Carter Edwards.

34. Letter from Emma Carter Edwards.

35. Letter from Emma Carter Edwards.

36. Letter from Emma Carter Edwards.

37. Samuel Treat, *Political Portraits.*

38. Americanized *Encyclopaedia Britannica.*

39. James Hall, *The West, Its Commerce and Navigation.*

40. *Dictionary of American Biography.*

41. Marshall S. Snow, *History of the Development of Missouri and St. Louis.*

42. John Thomas Scharf, *History of St. Louis.*

43. Logan U. Reavis, *St. Louis, the Future Great City of the World.*

44. Thomas Edwin Spencer, *The Story of Old St. Louis.*

45. Alvin Fay Harlow, *Old Wires and New Waves*, New York, 1936.

46. Samuel Treat, *Political Portraits.*

47. John Thomas Scharf, *History of St. Louis.*

48. Marshall Snow, *The Development of Missouri and St. Louis.*

49. Edward Villere Papin, *The Village Under the Hill.*

50. Fred Erving Dayton, *Steamboat Days.*

51. Samuel Treat, *Political Portraits.*

52. The St. Louis Fire: John Thomas Scharf, *History of St. Louis;*

Isaac H. Lionberger, *Annals of St. Louis*; Logan U. Reavis, *St. Louis, the Future Great City*; Thomas Edwin Spencer, *The Story of Old St. Louis*.

53. Thomas Edwin Spencer, *The Story of Old St. Louis*.

54. Alvin F. Harlow, *Old Wires and New Waves*.

55. Katherine Coman, *Economic Beginnings of the Far West*, New York, 1912.

56. Eugene V. Smalley, *The History of the Northern Pacific Railroad*, New York, 1883.

57. Sidney Breese, *Early History of Illinois*, Chicago, 1884.

58. *Encyclopaedia Britannica*: Suez Canal; Ferdinand de Lesseps.

59. John Thomas Scharf, *History of St. Louis*.

60. Robert R. Russel, 'The Pacific Railroad a National Issue in Politics Prior to the Civil War,' *Mississippi Valley Historical Review*, vol. 12.

61. Dorothy Jennings, *The Pacific Railroad Company*, Missouri Historical Society Collections, vol. 6. (Includes Charter.)

62. John Darby, *Personal Recollections*.

63. Rupert Sargent Holland, *Historic Railroads*, Philadelphia, 1927.

64. Luther Prentice Allen, *Genealogy of the Shreve Family*.

65. The full account in the *Republican* states that Henry Shreve died at the home of his son-in-law, and this is repeated in most accounts. His son-in-law lived at the Shreve home.

66. Samuel Treat, *Political Portraits*.

67. News item in *Magazine of American History*, vol. 6.

68. Fulton heirs were paid $76,000 for government use of the *Vesuvius* in the War of 1812: Emerson Gould, *Fifty Years on the Mississippi*. The steamboat *New Orleans* also served in that war.

69. Samuel Treat, *Political Portraits*.

CHAPTER X

1. George Byron Merrick, *Old Times on the Upper Mississippi*, Cleveland, 1909.

2. Frank Haigh Dixon, *A Traffic History of the Mississippi System*, National Waterways Commission, Document no. 11 (1909).

3. John H. Morrison, *A History of American Steam Navigation*.

4. *Ibid.*

5. George Byron Merrick, *Old Times on the Upper Mississippi*.

6. Henry E. Chambers, *History of Louisiana*.

7. George Byron Merrick, *Old Times on the Upper Mississippi*.

8. Isaac H. Lionberger, *Annals of St. Louis*.

9. George Byron Merrick, *Old Times on the Upper Mississippi.*

10. *Ibid.*

11. Theodore C. Blegen, 'The Fashionable Tour,' in *Minnesota History*, a quarterly magazine, vol. 20.

12. *Ibid.*

13. John Thomas Scharf, *History of St. Louis*; Walter B. Stevens, *St. Louis, the Fourth City*, Chicago and St. Louis, 1911.

14. Fred Erving Dayton, *Steamboat Days.*

15. Emerson Gould, *Fifty Years on the Mississippi*; Fred Erving Dayton, *Steamboat Days.*

16. John Thomas Scharf, *History of St. Louis.*

17. Walter B. Stevens, *St. Louis, the Fourth City.*

18. James T. Lloyd, *Steamboat Directory.*

19. George Byron Merrick, *Old Times on the Upper Mississippi.*

20. *Ibid.*

21. Frank Haigh Dixon, *A Traffic History of the Mississippi System.*

22. E. Merton Coulter, 'Effects of Secession upon the Commerce of the Mississippi Valley,' *Mississippi Valley Historical Review*, vol. III, no. 3 (December, 1916).

23. *Ibid.*

24. John Thomas Scharf, *History of St. Louis.*

25. Marshall S. Snow, *History of the Development of Missouri.*

26. *Ibid.*

27. John Thomas Scharf, *History of St. Louis.*

28. *Ibid.*

29. *Ibid.*

30. *Ibid.*

31. William John Petersen, 'The Rock Island Railroad Excursion of 1854,' *Minnesota History*, a quarterly magazine, vol. 15.

32. *Ibid.*

33. Seymour Dunbar, *A History of Travel in America*, Cincinnati, 1915.

34. Emerson Gould, *Fifty Years on the Mississippi.*

35. Theodore C. Blegen, 'The Fashionable Tour,' in *Minnesota History*, a quarterly magazine, vol. 20.

36. George Byron Merrick, *Old Times on the Upper Mississippi.*

37. *Ibid.*

38. Robert Malcolm Keir, *Pageant of America*, London, 1927.

39. Mark Twain, *Life on the Mississippi.*

40. *Ibid.*

41. Fred Erving Dayton, *Steamboat Days.*

42. *Ibid.*

43. Letter of Major Rufus Shirley of Tennessee to William C. Shirley of Illinois.

44. Alcée Fortier, *History of Louisiana*.

45. E. Merton Coulter, 'Effects of Secession upon the Commerce of the Mississippi Valley,' *Mississippi Valley Historical Review*, vol. III, no. 3 (December, 1916).

46. John Thomas Scharf, *History of St. Louis*.

47. Emerson Gould, *Fifty Years on the Mississippi*.

48. George E. Dacy, 'Pulling the Mississippi's Teeth,' *Scientific American*, vol. 125, no. 4 (July 23, 1921).

Bibliography

Allen, Luther Prentice. A Genealogy of the Shreve Family. Greenfield, Illinois, 1901.

Ashe, Thomas. Travels in America. London, 1810.

Baird, Robert. A View of the Mississippi Valley. Philadelphia, 1832.

Bettinger, Honorable Albert. The Future of Navigation on Our Western Rivers. *Ohio Archaeological and Historical Publications*, vol. 22.

Billon, Frederic L. Annals of St. Louis. St. Louis, 1886.

Blegen, Theodore C. The Fashionable Tour on the Upper Mississippi. *Minnesota History, a Quarterly Magazine*, vol. 20.

Boyd, Thomas. Poor John Fitch. New York, 1935.

Brackenridge, Henry M. Views of Louisiana. Baltimore, 1817.

Bradbury, John. Travels in the Interior of America in the Years 1809, 1810, and 1811. London, 1812.

Breese, Sidney. The Early History of Illinois. Chicago, 1884.

Brown, Stuart. Old Kaskaskia Days and Ways. Historical Library of Illinois, Publication 10, 1905.

Brown, William H. The History of the First Locomotives in America. New York, 1874.

Buck, Solon Justus. Illinois in 1818. Springfield, Illinois, 1917.

Bullock, W. Sketch of a Journey Through the Western States of North America, 1827. Reprinted in *Early Western Travels*, by Reuben Gold Thwaites, Cleveland, Ohio, 1904–07.

Burgess, John William. The Middle Period. New York, 1897.

Carey, Matthew. Essays on Railways. Philadelphia, 1830.

Carter, Clarence Edwin. Great Britain and the Illinois Country. *American Historical Association Prize Essays*, vol. 2, 1908.

Casseday, Ben. A History of Louisville. Louisville, Kentucky, 1852.

Chambers, Henry E. A History of Louisiana. American Historical Society, Chicago and New York, 1925.

Charnley, Mitchell V. Jean Lafitte, Gentleman Smuggler. New York, 1934.

Colden, Cadwallader D. The Life of Robert Fulton. New York, 1817.

Colden, Cadwallader D. A Vindication of the Steam-Boat Right Granted by the State of New York. New York, 1819.

Collins, Lewis. A History of Kentucky. Covington, Kentucky, 1874.

Cotterill, R. S. Southern Railroads and Western Trade. *Mississippi Valley Historical Review*, vol. 3, Cedar Rapids, Iowa.

Coues, Elliot, editor. The Expeditions of Zebulon Montgomery Pike, 1805, 1806, and 1807. Philadelphia, 1810. Reprinted, New York, 1895.

Coulter, E. Merton. Effects of Secession Upon the Commerce of the Mississippi Valley. *Mississippi Valley Historical Review*, vol. 3, no. 3.

Craik, James. History of Christ Church, Louisville. Louisville, Kentucky, 1862.

Cumings, Fortescue. Sketches of a Tour to the Western Country, 1807–09. Reprinted in *Early Western Travels*, by Reuben Gold Thwaites, vol. 4, Cleveland, Ohio, 1904–07.

Cusachs, Honorable Gaspar. Lafitte, the Louisiana Pirate and Patriot. *Louisiana Historical Quarterly*, vol. 2.

Dacy, George H. Pulling the Mississippi's Teeth. *Scientific American*, vol. 125, no. 4.

Darby, John F. Personal Recollections. St. Louis, 1880.

Dayton, Fred Erving. Steamboat Days. New York, 1925.

De Bow's Review, vol. XIX (n. s. vol. II).

Dictionary of American Biography: John Jacob Astor, Albert Gallatin, Thomas Gibbons, George Morgan, Aaron Ogden, Cornelius Vanderbilt, Asa Whitney.

Dixon, Frank Haigh. A Traffic History of the Mississippi River System. National Waterways Commission, Document 11, December, 1909.

Drumm, Stella. Robert E. Lee and the Improvement of the Mississippi River. *Missouri Historical Society Collections*, vol. 6, 1928.

Duer, William Alexander. Letter to Cadwallader D. Colden, Esq. Albany, 1817.

Dunbar, Seymour. A History of Travel in America. Cincinnati, 1915.

Edwards, Richard, and M. Hopewell. The Great West and Her Commercial Metropolis. St. Louis, 1860.

Eskew, Garnett Laidlaw. The Pageant of the Packets. New York, 1927.

Flagg, Edmund. The Far West. New York, 1838.

Fleming, George Thornton. A History of Pittsburgh and Environs, vols. 1 and 2. New York, 1922.

Flint, Reverend Timothy. Geography and History of the Mississippi Valley (1807–08). Cincinnati, 1832.

Flint, Reverend Timothy. Recollections of the Last Ten Years. Boston, 1826; reprinted, New York, 1932.

Flory, Ira, Jr. Edward Livingston's Place in Louisiana Law. *Louisiana Historical Quarterly*, vol. 19.

Fortier, Alcée. A History of Louisiana, vols. 3 and 4. Paris, 1904.

Freeman, Douglas Southall. Robert E. Lee: A Biography. New York, 1934.

Freeman, Louis R. Waterways of Westward Wandering. New York, 1927.

Gayarré, Charles. A History of Louisiana. New Orleans, 1903.

Glover, William. A History of the Caddo Indians. *Louisiana Historical Quarterly*, vol. 18.

Gould, Emerson. Fifty Years on the Mississippi. St. Louis, 1889.

Gray, Thomas. Observations on a General Iron Railway. London, 1825.

Gummere, Amelia Mott. Friends of Burlington. *Magazine of Pennsylvania*, 1844.

Hall, James. Notes on the Western States. Philadelphia, 1838.

Hall, James. Statistics of the West. Cincinnati, 1836.

Hall, James. The West, Its Commerce and Navigation. Cincinnati, 1848.

Hardin, J. Fair. The First Great River Captain: Henry Miller Shreve. *Louisiana Historical Quarterly*, vol. 10.

Hardin, J. Fair. An Outline of Shreveport and Caddo Parish History. *Louisiana Historical Quarterly*, vol. 18.

Harris, Thaddeus Mason. Journal of a Tour into the Territory Northwest of the Alleghanies. Boston, 1805. Reprinted in *Early Western Travels*, by Reuben Gold Thwaites, Cleveland, Ohio, 1904–07.

Hart, Adolphus M. A History of the Mississippi Valley. New York, 1853.

Hart, Adolphus M. Life in the Far West. New York, 186–.

Heffelfinger, C. H. John Colter, the Man Who Turned Back. *Washington Historical Quarterly*, vol. 26.

Hodge, Frederick Webb. A Handbook of American Indians. Government Printing Office, Washington, D.C., 1907–10.

Hodge, Frederick Webb. Spanish Explorers in the Southern United States: Original Narratives. New York, 1907 and 1925.

Holland, Rupert Sargent. Historic Railroads. Philadelphia, 1927.

Hosmer, James K. A Short History of the Mississippi Valley. Boston, 1901.

Houck, Louis. A History of Missouri. Chicago, 1908.

Hulbert, Archer Butler. The Ohio River, a Path of Empire. *Natural Waterways Journal*, October, 1929.

Illinois, Centennial History of. Springfield Centennial Commission, 1918.

Inman, Colonel Henry. The Old Santa Fe Trail. New York, 1897.

Jay, William. A Review of the Mexican War. Philadelphia, 1849.

Jenness, Diamond. The American Aborigines. University of Toronto, 1933.

Jennings, Dorothy. The Pacific Railroad Company. *Missouri Historical Society Collections*, vols. 4 and 5, 1926 and 1927.

Johnston, J. Stoddard. A Memorial History of Louisville. Chicago, 1896.

Kaempffert, Waldemar. Popular History of American Invention. New York, 1924.

Keir, Robert Malcolm. Pageant of America, vol. 4. London, 1927.

Knox, Thomas W. Robert Fulton. New York, 1886.

Latrobe, Benjamin, The Journal of. New York, 1905.

Latrobe, John H. The First Steamboat Voyage on Western Waters. Maryland Historical Society, Baltimore, 1871.

Latrobe, John H. A Lost Chapter in the History of Steam Navigation. Baltimore, 1871.

Leahy, Ethel C. Who's Who on the Ohio River. Cincinnati, 1931.

Leavitt, Emily Wilder. The Blair Family of New England. Boston, 1900.

Lindley, Harlow. Western Travel, 1800–1820. *Mississippi Valley Historical Review*, vol. 6.

Lionberger, Isaac H. Annals of St. Louis. Missouri Historical Society, 1929.

Lloyd, James T. A Steamboat Directory. Cincinnati, 1856.

Long, Major Stephen H., U.S.A. Voyage in a Six-Oared Skiff to the Falls of St. Anthony in 1817. Minnesota Historical Society Collections, vol. 2.

Marcy, General Randolph, and G. B. McClellan. Exploration of the Red River of Louisiana. Senate of 32d Congress, 1853.

Martin, François-Xavier. Louisiana. New Orleans, 1829.

Mason, Edward G. Kaskaskia and Its Parish Records. *Magazine of American History*, March, 1881.

Mather, Irwin F. The Making of Illinois. Chicago, 1917.

McAdams, Read. New Orleans and the War of 1812. *Louisiana Historical Quarterly*, vol. 10.

McClellan, Elisabeth. Historic Dress in America. 2 vols. Philadelphia, 1904 and 1910. Reprinted, 1917.

M'Murtrie, H. M. Sketches of Louisville. Louisville, Kentucky, 1819.

Merrick, George Byron. Old Times on the Upper Mississippi. Cleveland, 1909.

Merrick, George Byron, and William R. Tibbals. The Genesis of Steam Navigation. State Historical Society of Missouri, *Proceedings* of 1911.

Michaux, F. A. Travels to the West of the Alleghanies. London, 1805.

Miller, Andrew. New States and Territories. Washington, D.C., 1819.

Monette, John W. Progress of Navigation and Commerce on the Mississippi. *Mississippi Valley Historical Review*, vol. 7.

Morrison, John H. A History of American Steam Navigation. New York, 1903.

Niles' Weekly Register, Baltimore, July 20, 1816.

Nuttall, Thomas, F.L.S. Travels into Arkansas Territory, 1819. Philadelphia, 1821.

Ogden, George W. Letters from the West (from 1821). New Bedford, Massachusetts, 1823.

Old South Leaflets, vol. 5, no. 108, Boston.

O'Pry, Maude Hearn. Chronicles of Shreveport. New Orleans, 1928.

Oudard, Georges. The Amazing Life of John Law. From the French of G. E. C. Massé. New York, 1928.

Papin, Edward Villère. The Village Under the Hill, a Sketch of Early St. Louis. *Missouri Historical Society Publications*, vol. 5, 1927.

Parker, A. A. A Trip to the West and Texas, 1834. Boston, 1836.

Parton, James. Famous Americans of Recent Times: John Jacob Astor. Boston, 1867, 1884, and 1897.

Parton, James. Life of Andrew Jackson. New York, 1912.

Petersen, William John. The Rock Island Excursion of 1854. *Minnesota History, a Quarterly Magazine*, vol. 15, St. Paul, Minnesota.

Pfaff, Caroline. Henry Miller Shreve. *Louisiana Historical Quarterly*, vol. 10.

Phelps, Albert. Louisiana, a Record of Expansion. Boston, 1905.

Pike, Zebulon Montgomery, The Expeditions of, 1805, 1806, and 1807. Philadelphia, 1810; edited by Elliot Coues and reprinted, New York, 1895.

Powell, Lyman P. Historic Towns of the Western States. New York, 1900.

Preble, George Henry. A Chronological History of Steam Navigation. Philadelphia, 1883 and 1895.

Railways Compared with Canals and Common Roads. Scotsman, Edinburgh, 1812.

Read, Frederick Brent. Up the Heights to Fame and Fortune: Henry Miller Shreve. Cincinnati, 1873.

Reavis, Logan U. St. Louis, the Future Great City of the World. St. Louis, 1870, 1873–76.

Reavis, Logan U. St. Louis, the Commercial Metropolis of the Mississippi Valley. St. Louis, 1874.

Roosevelt, Theodore. Winning of the West. New York, 1894–96.

Ross, Alexander. Adventures of the First Settlers on the Oregon and Columbia Rivers. Cleveland, 1904.

Rozier, Firmin. History of the Mississippi Valley. St. Louis, 1890.

Russell, Robert R. The Pacific Railway Issue in Politics Prior to the Civil War. *Mississippi Valley Historical Review*, vol. 12.

Russell, Israel. Rivers of North America. New York, 1907.

Sabin, Edwin. Wild Men of the West. New York, 1939.

Scharf, John Thomas. The History of St. Louis City and County. Philadelphia, 1883.

Schultz, Christian. Travels on an Inland Voyage. New York, 1810.

Scroggs, William O. Rural Life in the Lower Mississippi Valley in 1803. *Mississippi Valley Historical Association Proceedings*, vol. 8, Grand Rapids, Iowa, 1916.

Shea, John D. G. Discovery and Exploration of the Mississippi Valley: Original Narrative of Père Marquette. New York, 1852.

Shea, John D. G. Early Voyages Up and Down the Mississippi. Albany, 1861.

Shepard, Elihu. The Early History of St. Louis and Missouri. St. Louis, 1870.

Shreve, Colonel Israel, The Journal of. *Magazine of American History*, vol. 2.

Shreve, Colonel Israel, Letters of. *Magazine of American History*, vols. 2 and 28.

Shreve, Henry Miller, Letters of.

Shreve, Lieu. John, The Personal Narrative of. *Magazine of American History*, vol. 3.

Skillman, W. D. The Western Metropolis, or St. Louis in 1846. St. Louis, 1846.

Skrainka, Philip, M.D. St. Louis, Its History and Ideals. St. Louis, 1910.

Smalley, Eugene V. History of the Northern Pacific Railroad. New York, 1883.

Smelser, Marshal. Housing in Creole St. Louis. *Louisiana Historical Quarterly*, vol. 21.

Smith, John Kendall. A History of New Orleans. *Louisiana Historical Quarterly*, vol. 16.

Smith, Justin H. War with Mexico. New York, 1919.

Snow, Marshall S. History of the Development of Missouri and St. Louis. St. Louis, 1908.

Spear, John R., and A. H. Clark. A History of the Mississippi Valley. New York, 1903.

Spencer, Thomas Edwin. The Story of Old St. Louis. St. Louis, 1914.

State Papers of 1811. National Archives, no. 302.

State Papers of 1816. National Archives, no. 401.

Stecker, H. Dora. Constructing a Navigation System in the West *Ohio Archaeological and Historical Publications*, vol. 22.

Stevens, John. Documents Tending to Prove the Superior Advantages of Railways. New York, 1812.

St. Louis County, Missouri, Land Records of.

Taylor, Jacob, and M. O. Crooks. A Sketch Book of St. Louis. St. Louis, 1858.

Thurston, Robert H. Robert Fulton, His Life and Its Results. New York, 1891.

Treat, Judge Samuel. Political Portraits with Pen and Pencil: Henry Miller Shreve. *The United States Magazine and Democratic Review*, vol. 22, 1848.

Tredgold, Thomas. A Practical Treatise on Railroads and Carriages. London, 1825.

Twain, Mark. Life on the Mississippi. New York, 1899–1910.

A Vindication by Cadwallader D. Colden of the Steam-Boat Right Granted by the State of New York. New York, 1819.

Washington, George, Extract from Diary of. *Magazine of Pennsylvania*. vol. 18, p. 400.

Williams, L. A. History of the Ohio Falls Cities and Their Counties. Cleveland, 1882.

Winsor, Justin. A Narrative and Critical History of North America. Boston, 1889.

Winsor, Justin. The Westward Movement. Boston, 1897.

Winthrop, Professor. Two Lectures on Comets: Supplement. Boston, 1811.

Wood, Nicholas. A Practical Treatise on Railroads. London, 1838.

Index